Modern Writers

The 'Modern Writers' series

This new series of short guides to contemporary international writers
includes the following titles:

Christopher Moody

Solzhenitsyn

Oliver & Boyd

186475.

Oliver & Boyd

Croythorn House
23 Ravelston Terrace
Edinburgh EH4 3TJ

0   05   002902   9   Hardback
0   05   002903   7   Paperback

First published 1973

Second Revised Edition 1976

Printed in Hong Kong by
Dai Nippon Printing Co. (Hong Kong) Ltd.

Contents

Special Note

In deference to Solzhenitsyn's own wishes, as expressed through his legal representative in Switzerland, permission to quote from some of his works which are in copyright in the West has been refused by the publishers concerned. The treatment of the following works in this book is therefore unsupported by direct quotation: the novels *Cancer Ward* and *August 1914*, the plays *The Love-Girl and the Innocent* and *A Candle in the Wind*, the stories *The Easter Procession* and *The Right Hand* and the *Prose Poems*. The interested reader may however wish to refer to the readily available editions of these works listed in the *Bibliography*.

Where the above restrictions do not apply, and passages have been quoted, page references are given in the text to the following editions:

One Day in the Life of Ivan Denisovich Tr. Ralph Parker (with modifications) Gollancz 1963

The First Circle Tr. Michael Guybon, Collins (Harvill Press) 1968

The Gulag Archipelago Tr. Thomas P. Whitney, Harper & Row 1974

In the case of the stories *Matryona's Home, An Incident at Krechetovka Station, For the Good of the Cause* and *Zakhar Kalita* the translations are my own and the page references to the Russian text in *Alexander Solzhenitsyn. Sobranie sochinenii*, tom 1, Frankfurt am Main 1969.

For permission to quote from the above-mentioned English translations of *One Day* and *The First Circle* thanks are due to Victor Gollancz Limited, and the Harvill Press Limited, respectively. Acknowledgements are also due to Penguin Books for extracts from *Solzhenitsyn: A Documentary Record* by Leopold Labedz, and the translation of Solzhenitsyn's Lenten letter is reprinted by courtesy of *The Sunday Telegraph* of London and

SOLZHENITSYN

Michael Bordeaux. *The Gulag Archipelago* is quoted with the permission of Harper & Row as is the *Letter to the Soviet Leaders*.

Finally, I should like to express my gratitude to Marguerite Jooste for her assistance with the French sources I have drawn upon; to Tony Seward of Oliver and Boyd for his assistance in overcoming the difficulties encountered in preparing the book for publication; and to my wife Elize for her unfailing love and loyalty.

1 Biography

Alexander Solzhenitsyn was forty-four when, in 1962, he made his sudden début as a writer with a short novel entitled *One Day in the Life of Ivan Denisovich*, (hereafter referred to as *One Day*). The Soviet and foreign press were unanimous in proclaiming it a masterpiece and a milestone in Russian literature and Soviet life. During the next eight years more stories, plays and two major novels were published. When, at the end of 1970, Solzhenitsyn was awarded the Nobel Prize for literature, it was hailed in the West and by many Russians, as a fitting recognition of a man who had become his country's finest living writer and a worthy successor to such giants of the past as Tolstoy and Dostoevsky. The Soviet authorities, however, reacted differently. The leaders of the Union of Soviet Writers deplored the award, while *Pravda* described Solzhenitsyn as 'an inner emigré, hostile to the life of the Soviet people'. A year earlier, he had been expelled from the Union of Writers and was under virtual house arrest outside Moscow.

Solzhenitsyn's ambiguous position was due to the controversial nature of his work and his own behaviour. Soviet critics noted the remarkable artistic qualities of *One Day* and of *Matryona's Home*, which appeared shortly after, but it was the subject matter of his stories which guaranteed their immediate success with Soviet readers. *One Day* was the first detailed description of Stalin's labour camps to appear in the Soviet Union, while *Matryona's Home* and *For the Good of the Cause* portrayed injustices in the Soviet village and provincial town. The long novels, *Cancer Ward* and *The First Circle*, unpublished in the Soviet Union, but circulating in thousands of manuscript copies, could be interpreted as a political indictment of the entire Stalinist system, many features of which still persisted.

Solzhenitsyn has never attempted to deny the political purpose behind his writing: on the contrary, he has frequently made a point of acknowledging it. He believes that 'by intuition and by his singular vision of the world, a writer is able to discover far earlier than other people aspects of social life and can often see them from an unexpected angle. This is the essence of talent . . . It is incumbent upon the writer to inform society of all that he is able to perceive and especially all that is unhealthy and cause for anxiety.'[1]

No writer is better qualified to comment on the Soviet experience during the last forty years than Solzhenitsyn. His life has coincided almost exactly with the Soviet era. As a child during the period of Lenin's New Economic Policy in the 1920s and as a student during the purges of the 1930s he witnessed the emergence and consolidation of Stalin's terrorist dictatorship over his country. Then it was his turn to share the lot of millions of Stalin's victims. As a front-line officer throughout the war he was in a position to understand something of the cynicism which led to the disaster. And he saw the absurd injustices which were perpetrated on so many of those who had fought when the war ended. Then followed his own eight years in prison and labour camps and three more in exile in the desert wastes of Kazakhstan.

In *Cancer Ward* Kostoglotov's fellow exile, the orderly Elizaveta Anatolyevna, cries in despair: When will people be able to read about what people such as they have endured? Only in a hundred years' time? When he finally returned to freedom in 1957, Solzhenitsyn was convinced that justice and the moral health of the country could not wait a hundred years. He wrote *One Day* because, as he remarked, he 'wanted to expose the false image of the labour camps.'[2] And he wrote more stories and his novels in order to expose every aspect and vestige of Stalin's influence on Soviet society. In 1969 he told a meeting of writers in Ryazan, quoting Biryukov's *Biography of Tolstoy*: 'The disease that we are

1. Pavel Licko. *Kulturny Zhivot* (Bratislava), 31 March 1967, pp. 1–10. A translation of Licko's interview with Solzhenitsyn and most of the documents connected with Solzhenitsyn's literary career can be found in *Solzhenitsyn: a Documentary Record*, edited by Leopold Labedz (London), 1970. These are the translations which have been quoted in this book.

2. Labedz, *ibid.*, p. 7.

suffering from is the murdering of people ... If we could recall the past and look it straight in the face—the violence we are now committing would be revealed,' and he went on himself, 'No!, it will not be possible indefinitely to keep silence about Stalin's crimes or go against the truth. There were millions of people who suffered from the crimes and they demand exposure. It would be a good idea, too, to reflect: What moral effect will the silence on these crimes have on the younger generation—it will mean the corruption of still more millions.'[3] Solzhenitsyn even used the few words he sent to the Nobel Prize banquet to underline his point: 'I cannot fail to mention a remarkable coincidence, that the day of the Nobel Prize awards coincides with Human Rights Day ... So let us at this banqueting table not forget that today political prisoners are maintaining a hunger-strike in order to assert their reduced or completely trampled rights.'[4]

From 1967 onwards Solzhenitsyn complemented this literary work with a series of outspoken letters and meetings with officials of the Union of Writers, in which he threw out a direct challenge to the Communist Party. In 1970 he became a member of the Committee for the Defence of Human Rights set up in Moscow by Academician A. D. Sakharov.[5] In everything he does he exhibits a passionate commitment to the cause of social justice in Soviet society. He is acutely conscious of the civic role which Russian writers have always accepted and has said: 'I am confident that I will fulfil my task as a writer under all circumstances ... No one can bar the way to truth and to advance its cause I am ready to accept even death.'[6] For many Russians Solzhenitsyn came to stand as a symbol of their campaign for democratic freedom and the humanisation of Soviet political life.

The emphasis which Solzhenitsyn himself puts on the political aspect of his work, coupled with the sensation which surrounds the publication of his books abroad, inevitably distracts attention from their enduring literary qualities. But long before the Nobel Prize committee referred to the 'ethical force with which he has pursued the indispensable traditions of Russian literature', serious

3. *Ibid.*, p. 156.
4. *Possev* (Munich), no. 1, 1971.
5. *Russkaya mysl'* (Paris), 12 November 1971.
6. Labedz, *op. cit.*, p. 69.

critics drew attention to the intense moral concern behind his urgent social and political message. His work is more than an external portrait of Soviet society under Stalin and under Stalin's heirs. At a deeper level it is an inquiry into the moral implications of the Soviet system and materialism in general. Many of the Russian writers with whom Solzhenitsyn is so often compared owed their success with their contemporaries as much to their political thinking as to the qualities of their art. Later, when the topical appeal of their ideas had been superseded there remained those insights into the human spirit for which they are revered today. At the core of Solzhenitsyn's books are the fundamental concerns which occupied his great predecessors—the problems of freedom and justice, truth and conscience, good and evil.

Soviet writers are notoriously, or perhaps admirably, reticent about their personal lives. Even such a prominent figure as Sholokhov has allowed only scanty biographical details to be made public. With Solzhenitsyn the problem is doubly difficult, for not only is he by natural inclination unusually retiring, but nothing of substance has been written about him or his work in the Soviet Union. He is reluctant to give interviews and even on the few occasions he has spoken to the press (always Western) in the Soviet Union and since his exile in 1974 it has been to protest against his own and others' treatment at the hands of the K. G. B. He has said little of substance about himself and his work. The only road from a writer to the reader, he believes, is through his books. In a sense his literary work is the autobiography of his later years. All save his novel, *August 1914*, stem from his personal experience in prison and exile, and several of his characters, such as Kostoglotov in *Cancer Ward* and Nerzhin in *The First Circle*, are based to some extent upon himself.

Alexander Isaevich Solzhenitsyn was born on 11 December 1918 at Kislovodsk, a spa town in the North Caucasus, in relatively poor circumstances. His father, a student at Moscow University, enlisted in the army as a volunteer without completing his course. He served as an artillery officer until the summer of 1918, when he was killed, six months before Solzhenitsyn was born. His mother was a shorthand typist and in 1924 she moved to Rostov-on-Don where Solzhenitsyn spent the rest of his childhood and youth. When he left school in 1936, he already harboured an ambition to become a writer but, being unable to realise his desire for a literary education in Rostov, lacking the means to go to Moscow and not wishing to leave his mother, he entered Rostov University to read mathematics and physics. 'I never intended to devote the rest of my life to mathematics. Literature was the greatest attraction, but I realised that mathematics would at least provide me with bread and butter.'[7] Solzhenitsyn showed considerable aptitude both for mathematics and physics, and on graduating in 1941 he received his Diploma, with merit. Meanwhile he had not neglected his literary inclinations. While at Rostov University he won a Stalin scholarship for postgraduate studies and used it to enrol for a correspondence course at the Institute of Philosophy, Literature and History in Moscow. This he also successfully completed in 1941. As a student he wrote a great deal in several genres and sent his first stories to the writers Boris Lavrenev and Konstantin Fedin with a view to their being published in the journal *Znamya*. They were rejected, ironically by the same man, Fedin, who was instrumental in preventing the publication of *Cancer Ward* thirty years later. These early stories were taken from Solzhenitsyn when he was arrested in 1945 and are probably still preserved in the Lubyanka files.

In 1937 Solzhenitsyn wrote a long descriptive essay about the Samsonov disaster, an episode in the First World War. He never abandoned the hope of one day writing a major work about the war and was finally able to use some of his material in the novel *August 1914*, written at the end of the 1960s.

For a time he thought of becoming an actor. The stage director Zavadsky, who established a drama school in Rostov, reported that he had talent, but the idea had to be given up when it was discovered that he suffered from chronic laryngitis.

Solzhenitsyn married Natalia Alekseevna Reshetovskaya, a chemistry student, in 1940 and on graduation the following year was given a post as physics teacher at the First Secondary School in the town of Morozovka in the Rostov region. But his first experience as a teacher was short, for the war had begun and on 18 October 1941, he was called up as a private soldier. At first, like Nerzhin in *The First Circle*, he served as a driver of horse-drawn vehicles, although he knew nothing about horses, but he was soon

7. Labedz, *op. cit.*, p. 4.

transferred to an artillery school where he did a one-year course, passing out with a commission in 1942. He was sent on a fortnight's journey to the Gorky region and 'all I saw and experienced there is reflected in *An Incident at Krechetovka Station*.'[8] He then went to the Leningrad front as the commander of an artillery position-finding company and served at the front without a break until February 1945, taking part in the battle of Kursk and marching through White Russia and Poland to East Prussia. He ended up as a captain with two decorations: the Order of the Patriotic War Class II and the Order of the Red Star.

In February 1945, during the battle for Königsberg in East Prussia, Solzhenitsyn was summoned by his brigade commander, Colonel Travkin. He was ordered to hand over his revolver and was stripped of his badges of rank and decorations. Still unaware of what was happening, he was taken away, but before he went General Travkin shook his hand. 'That handshake was one of the most heroic acts I had seen during the whole course of the war.'[9] Solzhenitsyn was arrested because he had been unwise enough to criticise Stalin in private correspondence with a friend, N. D. Vitkevich, although they had referred to him only by a pseudonym, *Pakhan*, which means 'A Ringleader of Thieves.'

'I knew that it was forbidden to write of military matters in letters from the front, but I thought it was permitted to think and reflect on events. For a long time I had been sending a friend letters clearly criticising Stalin though without mentioning his name. I thought he had betrayed Leninism and was responsible for the defects in the first phase of the war, that he was a weak theoretician and that his language was primitive. In my youthful recklessness I put all these thoughts down on paper.'[10] The letters were intercepted. Further stories and reflections in which he had criticised the weakness of Soviet writers were found in his map-case and were used for the fabrication of charges against him. He was accused of anti-Soviet propaganda and wishing to establish some anti-Soviet organization.[11]

Solzhenitsyn was taken to the Lubyanka prison in Moscow, where he was beaten and interrogated, an experience on which he

8. *Ibid.*, p. 5.   10. *Ibid.*
9. *Ibid.*   11. Surprisingly, Travkin suffered no reprisals for this gesture.

was able to draw when describing the fate of Innokenty Volodin in *The First Circle*. On 7 July 1945 he was sentenced in his absence by a three-man tribunal of the N.K.G.B.[12] under Article 58 of the criminal code of the Russian Republic. He was given eight years hard labour, the normal sentence for most 'crimes' under Article 58 at that time.

The geneticist Timofeev-Resovsky recalls meeting him in Butyrki prison where for some time they were confined in the same cell. Solzhenitsyn has left a description of it in his story *The Smile of the Buddha*, an episode in *The First Circle*. Timofeev-Resovsky organised a scientific technical society in the cell, which held seventy-five prisoners.[13] In *Cancer Ward* Solzhenitsyn describes how Kostoglotov found himself in a crowded Butyrki prison cell where every evening there were lectures given by professors, doctors of philosophy and people who were experts in some subject, whether it was atomic physics, Western architecture, genetics, poetry or bee-keeping. It was Solzhenitsyn himself who gave the lecture on recent developments in atomic physics, speaking of recent developments in atomic energy.

Solzhenitsyn spent the first months of his sentence in so-called correctional camps near Moscow, labouring on building projects in the city. Among these was a block of flats on Leninsky prospect for M.G.B. officials, where he laid the parquet flooring. He describes it in *The First Circle*. In 1946, he was sent to an M.G.B. group research institute on the outskirts of Moscow. It was on his own experience here that *The First Circle* is based. He spent four years in the research institute before being transferred, like his hero Gleb Nerzhin, to serve the last three years of his term in one of the newly established camps for political prisoners at Dzezkazgan in the province of Karaganda in Central Kazakhstan. There he developed the idea of writing *One Day*. Like his hero Ivan Denisovich, he worked as a brick-layer and foundryman. B. V. Burkovsky, who appears as Captain Buinovsky in *One Day*, recalled Solzhenitsyn, with whom he lived for three years, 'as a good comrade, an honest fellow. He was taciturn,

12. *N.K.G.B.* The Soviet security police between 1943 and 1946. Later it has been known as 'M.G.B.', 1946–53, and 'K.G.B.', 1953 to the present.

13. Z. A. Medvedev, *The Medvedev Papers* (London), 1971, p. 96, and A. I. Solzhenitsyn, *The Gulag Archipelago*, pp. 597–600.

never got involved in loud discussions.'[14] While in the labour camp, Solzhenitsyn developed cancer and, like Kostoglotov, the character who takes over from Nerzhin as the chief embodiment of Solzhenitsyn's own experience, he was operated on, but not cured.

In March 1953, Solzhenitsyn was released, having served his full sentence, plus one month which he was obliged to spend in a transit camp. By another ironical coincidence the first news he heard as he finally stepped out of the camp was that Stalin, the person ultimately responsible for the ordeal he had just passed through, had died. But like many others who had completed their terms, Solzhenitsyn's return to freedom was only partial. As a purely administrative measure, without any reasons being given, he was sentenced to perpetual exile in the village of Kok Teren (Green Poplar) in the Dzhambul Region of Kazakhstan on the edge of the desert. When asked to sign the document confirming the order, he agreed. He gives an impression of the sort of life he led in exile in *Cancer Ward*. Being the only qualified mathematics teacher in the village, he had no difficulty in getting a job. The director of the Regional Educational Board in Kok Teren recalls that one day in April 1953 there appeared before him 'a tall man with a pale face and deep set eyes, straight hair combed back and nervous hands fumbling with a worn old fur hat. He was wearing discoloured riding breeches and patched boots. None of this was in accord with the man's disarming simplicity and charm.'[15] This was Solzhenitsyn. In school, where he taught mathematics, physics and astronomy, he made a remarkably good impression on both teachers and pupils. He possessed the attributes of an ideal teacher. He was perfectly acquainted with his subject and 'knew how to create an atmosphere extraordinarily favourable to creative work'. One teacher recalls how 'he would enter the classroom like a gust of wind and straight away begin with the lesson'. At the beginning of his exile he lodged with a family in a house plastered with mud. Later he bought a house of his own where he spent the next two years. While in exile his cancer became acute and he was close to death when he managed to get to the Tashkent cancer clinic, the setting for *Cancer Ward*. He has stated that his description of Rusanov's arrival at the clinic was

14. *Izvestia* (Moscow), 15 January 1964.
15. *Leninskaya Smena* (Kazakhstan), 10 January 1965.

to some extent autobiographical, while the circumstances surrounding his discharge were probably similar to Kostaglotov's
and also to those in his short story *The Right Hand*.

As an exile Solzhenitsyn began to write down the stories and
the play *The Love-girl and the Innocent* which he had composed and
carried in his head while in the camp. He was also rejoined by
his wife. Like Nadya in *The First Circle*, she had been victimised
while he was in prison and at his insistence they had divorced.
Reshetovskaya had remarried and had two children, but when
Solzhenitsyn was released she returned to him.

In February 1956, his case was reviewed by the Military
Section of the Supreme Court. It was proclaimed that there had
been no substance in the original charges and that all action in
connection with his sentence should cease.[16] So he was released
from exile and allowed to return to European Russia. At first,
like the narrator of *Matryona's Home*, he settled in the country in
the Vladimir district. Later he moved to the town of Ryazan
a hundred miles south-east of Moscow.

Little has been made public about Solzhenitsyn's way of life or
character other than can be deduced from his literary and polemical writings. Since devoting himself to the full-time career of a
writer he has preferred to live in seclusion. In the early 1960s he
turned down the suggestion of friends that he might move to
Moscow, fearing that city life would undermine his concentration.
He subsequently changed his mind, but by then he had lost
official favour and was refused a residence permit. In 1965 he
contemplated moving to Obninsk, the scientific centre to the
south-west of Moscow. His wife, a highly qualified chemist, had
been teaching at the Ryazan Polytechnical Institute. She applied
for a post which was advertised at Obninsk and at first seemed
likely to be appointed, but opposition was expressed by the local
Party organization who feared, no doubt, that Solzhenitsyn's
presence might cause political complications. Unconstitutional
obstacles were placed in Reshetovskaya's way and eventually her
application was turned down.[17]

At first Solzhenitsyn had difficulty in finding accommodation in
Ryazan and was obliged to build himself somewhere to live, over

16. Labedz, *op. cit.*, p. 1.
17. Medvedev, *op. cit.*, pp. 36–42.

a garage. Later he took a shabby little wooden house without modern conveniences. The local authorities, apparently displeased with his story *For the Good of the Cause*, set in Ryazan, refused to allow improvements to be made. By 1967, he had managed to obtain a new ground-floor flat. In Ryazan also he worked as a mathematics teacher and there too he made an excellent impression. One of his pupils has described his teaching as 'stunning'.[18] As time went on he asked that his teaching load be gradually reduced to enable him to devote himself more to his then spare-time occupation of writing. This accounts for the fact that when at the end of 1962 he gave up teaching, he was earning only about 50 roubles (£20) per month. This and his wife's salary were sufficient for their modest needs. There were no children by the marriage.

Apart from writing, Solzhenitsyn liked to spend his leisure making expeditions into the surrounding countryside on a bicycle. He describes the object of one such journey in *Zakhar Kalita*. He also travelled by boat along the river Oka. Even while still in exile he had taken up photography and it is recorded that with his school colleagues he would regularly follow the local hunts, but armed only with his camera.[19]

Although apparently cured of cancer, Solzhenitsyn's health is not robust. But his mode of life is active and industrious. He appears as a tall man with a russet beard; he drinks sparingly and his only extravagance in the Soviet Union was a small car which he bought with the royalties he earned for *One Day* and which, appropriately, he called Denis Ivanovich.[20] His room in Ryazan was lined with books, many of them in foreign languages. He speaks German fluently and can read English.[21] The poets Pasternak and Tsvetaeva and the novelist and playwright Bulgakov are among his favourite Russian writers.

In addition to his flat in Ryazan, Solzhenitsyn bought a *dacha* in an area about forty miles from Moscow where he spent most of his summers in the 1960s. A visitor has described it:

18. *Literaturnaya Rossia*, 25 January 1963.
19. *Ibid.*
20. Nicolas Bethel, *New York Times*, 12 April 1970.
21. *Leninskaya Smena*, 10 January 1965.

There are two downstairs rooms and his study is in the upstairs room which has a small balcony. The roof is covered with corrugated asbestos, painted pink. There is a built-in garage for his green Moskvich car, trestles for sawing firewood, a wide bench which he made himself and a small wooden toilet. The porch is all covered with Russian vine.

A small stream runs beside the house and a beautiful view opens on the forest and field with, nearby, an abandoned church like those he has described so sympathetically in his short stories.[22]

By 1970 his marriage had broken down. His wife continued to live in Ryazan with her mother, while he accepted the hospitality of the 'cellist Mstislav Rostropovich, in the village of Zhukovka, near Moscow. He was living in Rostropovich's dacha at the time of his Nobel Prize award and wrote the first part of *August 1914* there.

He had been trying to obtain a divorce from his wife for more than two years, but it was reported that she was unwilling to agree. Meanwhile he had entered into a liaison with a 32-year-old mathematics teacher, also named Natalya, who in December, 1970 gave birth to his son. The boy was baptised.[23]

From 1965, Solzhenitsyn became an object of particular attention from the police and has protested about surveillance and interception of his mail. He was not permitted to renew his teaching profession, which he gave up in December 1962, following his success as a writer. Despite these hardships and the fact that he received little money in royalties from his books, his means were enough for the life of a dedicated writer which he had chosen for himself.

He completed *One Day* in 1958, but did not send it to Tvardovsky, the editor of *Novy Mir*, until 1961, when the intensification of Khrushchev's destalinisation policy led him to hope that it might be printed. The decision to publish such a controversial work could not be taken by Tvardovsky alone. By-passing *Glavlit*, the Soviet censorship board, he sent it direct to Khrushchev.

22. Labedz. *op. cit.,* p. 126.
23. *New York Times,* 19 June 1971.

Khrushchev decided to make use of the story to promote his policies and had twenty copies printed and sent to the members of the Praesidium (now Politburo) of the Central Committee of the Party. Khrushchev himself stated that it was he who authorised publication in the face of unnamed opposition. One hundred thousand copies of _Novy Mir_ were put on sale on 21 November 1962, and were sold out within hours. _One Day_ was a sensation and a second printing of 20,000 copies was immediately snapped up.

Soviet readers were left in no doubt as to what the publication of _One Day_ was intended to signify. As Tvardovsky wrote in the introduction, 'the pledge of a full and irrevocable break with everything which has darkened the past lies in a truthful and courageous understanding of all its consequences', and he quoted Khrushchev's words: 'We must do this so that such things can never happen again.' The press took up the theme. 'In the name of truth and justice', ran _Pravda_'s headline,[24] and the _Trud_ review appeared beneath the title 'Let the full truth be told'.[25] That _One Day_ enjoyed the official sponsorship of the Party was confirmed on 17 December when Leonid Ilyichev, Khrushchev's chief ideological lieutenant, informed a meeting of writers: 'Our Party endorses the healthy, life affirming critical trend in the art of socialist realism. Artistically powerful works that truthfully and boldly expose the arbitrariness that prevailed in the period of the cult of personality have been published recently with the approval of the Party's Central Committee. It is enough to mention Alexander Solzhenitsyn's story _One Day_.'[26] At the same meeting, Khrushchev is reported to have personally introduced Solzhenitsyn to all present.

The euphoria which surrounded the appearance of _One Day_ was short lived. November 1962 proved to be the crest of a wave of liberalisation which was about to break. Khrushchev's prestige, which had subdued the forces of conservatism in the Party ranks, almost immediately began to collapse as a result of political failures. Throughout the rest of the winter of 1962/3, he was under pressure which at one point had him fighting for his poli-

24. _Pravda_ (Moscow), 23 October 1962.
25. _Trud_ (Moscow), 12 December 1962.
26. _Pravda_, 22 December 1962.

tical life. Although he recovered in Spring 1963, he was never again so free to pursue personal policies. Solzhenitsyn's brief official patronage came to an end.

His next two stories, *Matryona's Home* and *An Incident at Krechetovka Station*, published in January 1963, did not enjoy the advantage of Party sanction. Nor did the play *The Love-girl and the Innocent*, at first accepted by the Sovremennik Theatre, but never produced. As early as 11 January reservations began to be voiced in the press and these grew steadily into a full-scale campaign against the historical message of Solzhenitsyn's work. It is true that in March, Khrushchev was still saying that *One Day* 'reflects Soviet reality during those years truthfully from Party positions',[27] but the critics were saying precisely the opposite and in the same month the chief conservative organ, the journal *Oktyabr*, added its weight to the opposition. The main charges levelled against Solzhenitsyn's stories concerned their narrow focus, his omission of any historical generalisation, and the patriarchal, unSoviet qualities of his peasant characters, Ivan Denisovich and Matryona.

Tvardovsky, editor of *Novy Mir*, vigorously countered these objections. He reminded the critics that *One Day* was supported by the Party leadership:

> In my opinion, *One Day* is one of those literary phenomena after whose appearance it is impossible to talk about any literary problem or literary fact without measuring it against this phenomenon.
>
> I will never forget how N. S. Khrushchev responded to this tale by Solzhenitsyn—to its hero, who retains the dignity and beauty of the man of labour under inhuman conditions, to the truthfulness of the account, to the author's Party approach to bitter and stern reality. At the first meeting Nikita Sergeyevich mentioned Solzhenitsyn in the course of his speech and introduced him to all of those present in the Palace of Meetings on the Lenin Hills.[28]

27. *Ibid.*, 10 March 1963.
28. *Ibid.*, 12 May 1963. Quoted by Priscilla Johnson in *Khrushchev and the Arts* (Massachusetts), 1965, p. 212.

Beneath the rhetoric, it was clear that the issue at stake was the fundamental Soviet dilemma of the 1960s, the moral need to face the past and the political fear of doing so. For besides presenting a truthful picture of the Stalin era, Solzhenitsyn was also raising sensitive questions about the present. The irrevocable break with the past was not being made and his stories were a threat to those who were unable or unwilling to make it. In this atmosphere, *For the Good of the Cause*, published in July 1963, was taken by the conservative critics as a direct challenge, which Tvardovsky surely intended it to be. Unlike the earlier stories set in the past and away from the centre of Soviet life, *For the Good of the Cause* referred to the present and the Party itself. The story became the subject of a sharp dispute between *Literaturnaya Gazeta* and *Novy Mir* lasting until the end of the year. The articles centred exclusively on the social and political accuracy of Solzhenitsyn's work. There was no attempt to consider the literary achievement.

With the attacks on Solzhenitsyn becoming steadily more bitter, the conflict took on a new urgency in December 1963, when the Committee to decide the award of the Lenin Prize for Literature was set up, and *Novy Mir* put forward *One Day*. The journal published a long article in its defence by the young critic Vladimir Lakshin.[29] The very title of Lakshin's article, 'Friends and Foes of Ivan Denisovich', showed the extent to which Solzhenitsyn's story seemed to symbolise the deep divisions among the intelligentsia and different sections of the Party. There was even a saying current in Moscow at the time which ran, 'tell me your attitude to *One Day*, and I'll tell you who you are'. Lakshin's courageous article, the only serious analysis of *One Day* to appear in the Soviet Union, was also one of the last to speak favourably of Solzhenitsyn. The veteran poet Samuel Marshak praised *One Day* in *Pravda*,[30] but others such as Ehrenburg, Chukovsky and Kaverin had to be content with private letters advocating that Solzhenitsyn be given the Prize. Their efforts proved to be of no avail. Too many reservations had by now been expressed in the press and conservative attitudes had apparently gained too much ground in high places for discussion of the questions raised by Solzhenitsyn to be given encouragement. *Pravda*'s final and authoritative comment

29. *Novy Mir* (Moscow), January 1964. Trans. Johnson, *op. cit.*, pp. 275–88.
30. *Pravda*, 30 January 1964.

was that 'A. Solzhenitsyn's story deserves favourable appraisal but it cannot be included among those outstanding works that are worthy of the Lenin Prize'.[31]

With the award of the Lenin Prize to a third-rate novelist, Oles Gonchar, in April 1964, Solzhenitsyn's career as a Soviet writer effectively came to an end. A short story, *Zakhar Kalita* which appeared in *Novy Mir* in 1966, passed almost unnoticed and was his last work to be published in the Soviet Union. Tvardovsky, however, who had supported Solzhenitsyn throughout, continued to persevere on his behalf. At first he accepted *The First Circle*, which was completed in 1964, and announced plans to publish it, although he must have been aware that his chances of being allowed to do so were now negligible. Meanwhile, Solzhenitsyn was busy writing the first part of *Cancer Ward* and this too, was provisionally accepted by *Novy Mir* in 1966.

Although it was less controversial than *The First Circle*, Tvardovsky was again unable to publish *Cancer Ward* without the recommendation of higher authority. With Khrushchev gone, he referred the manuscript to the Union of Writers. A special meeting of the prose section of the Union was convened on 17 November 1966, with Solzhenitsyn present. The participants, fifty-two in all, had each been given a copy of *Cancer Ward*, which they were obliged to read in a closed room. The discussion was frank and with certain reservations over detail, the character of Rusanov for instance, the meeting approved of the novel and agreed to recommend that it be published. Solzhenitsyn expressed his thanks for the friendly criticism.[32] As a result of the meeting, *Novy Mir* went ahead and set up the first eight chapters for publication. Delay followed delay, however, and a further turn in Solzhenitsyn's fortunes, coinciding with the novel's appearance in the West, finally demolished all hope of its being printed in the Soviet Union.

A new stage in the decline in Solzhenitsyn's official standing had in fact begun in 1965. He had taken the manuscript of *The First Circle* back for revision and in September three copies together with other papers, including a play *The Feast of the Victors*, were confiscated from a friend's flat by the K.G.B.

31. *Ibid.*, 11 April 1964.
32. Labedz, *op. cit.*, pp. 45–63.

Shortly after, the novel began to circulate in typescript among *samizdat* (self-publishing) readers. At the same time, apparently with official approval and with the object of discrediting Solzhenitsyn personally, a campaign of rumour and innuendo replaced the criticism in the press. His past was again called in question and the confiscated play was quoted against him. His public readings of his works, which had been very popular, were cancelled.

In May 1967, frustrated by his failure to publish his recent work and the lack of opportunity to defend himself publicly, Solzhenitsyn took the unprecedented step of circulating a long open letter to all the delegates to the Fourth Congress of the Union of Writers. The letter contained a sustained attack on the censorship:

> Our writers are not supposed to have the right, are not endowed with the right, to express their cautionary judgements about the moral life of man and society, or to explain in their own way the social problems and historical experiences that have been so deeply felt in our country. Works that might express the mature thinking of the people, that might have a timely and salutary influence in the realm of the spirit or on the development of a social conscience, are proscribed or distorted by the censorship on the basis of considerations that are petty, egotistical, and—from the national point of view—shortsighted. Outstanding manuscripts by young authors, as yet entirely unknown, are nowadays rejected by editors solely on the ground that they 'will not pass'. Many members of the (Writers') Union, and even many of the delegates of this Congress, know how they themselves have bowed to the pressure of the censorship and made concessions in the structure and concept of their books—changing chapters, pages, paragraphs or sentences, giving them innocuous titles— just for the sake of seeing them finally in print, even if it meant distorting them irremediably. It is an understood quality of literature that gifted works suffer (most) disastrously from all these distortions, while untalented works are not affected by them. Indeed, it

is the best of our literature that is published in
mutilated form.[33]

Solzhenitsyn also complained about the Union's failure to defend
his interests and about the slanderous stories being repeated con-
cerning him. The letter met with a ready response among many
of his fellow writers, who privately sympathised with much that he
had said. Letters, including one signed by eighty-one of the country's
most distinguished literary figures, asking that Solzhenitsyn's
demands be discussed at the Congress, were received by the
Secretariat.[34] Not unexpectedly, the Union leadership failed to
respond or to make any public mention of the controversy.

For Solzhenitsyn himself, his letter signified an important
change in his relations with the Party authorities. From being a
troublesome writer whom it was possible to ignore by the simple
expedient of refusing to publish his books, he was transformed
into a fearlessly outspoken critic of official policy in the arts.
Taking care to campaign for no more than justice and his legal
rights, Solzhenitsyn knew that his actions nevertheless invited
reprisals. His next confrontation with the Union of Writers
revealed the change in the official attitude towards him. In
September 1967, a meeting of the Union Secretariat under the
chairmanship of K. A. Fedin, took place to discuss Solzhenitsyn.[35]
This time opinion was almost unanimously hostile. *Cancer Ward*,
which Solzhenitsyn was still trying to get published, was generally
condemned. The poet Surkov described it as 'more dangerous
than Svetlana's memoirs' and Solzhenitsyn's works as a whole as
'more dangerous than those of Pasternak'. There was even a call
that he be expelled from the Union. In his turn, Solzhenitsyn
complained bitterly at the illegal treatment to which he was
being subjected. He was particularly irritated by his critics'
persistent references to *The Feast of the Victors*, which depicts the
behaviour of the Soviet forces at the end of the war. The play, he
repeatedly pointed out, was an early effort, which he himself now
rejected. He had made no attempt to have it published. On the
contrary, it was only because the K.G.B., having confiscated it,

33. *Ibid.*, pp. 64–5.
34. *Ibid.*, pp. 69–70.
35. *Ibid.*, pp. 82–100.

had themselves circulated it, that anyone knew of its existence. The meeting ended in deadlock, with the Union demanding that Solzhenitsyn should denounce the use of his books abroad for anti-Soviet propaganda and Solzhenitsyn insisting that his own complaints be considered first.

During the next few months, there was much behind-the-scenes activity surrounding Solzhenitsyn. Letters passed between him and the Union, and others from his supporters were circulated in manuscript almost as soon as they were written. Further meetings were held, but neither Solzhenitsyn nor the authorities would compromise. Eventually, on 26 June 1968, the Soviet people, who had remained oblivious to what was going on, were given some information in an unsigned article in *Literaturnaya gazeta*. Referring to several of the issues at stake, the article was so one-sided a version of what had been happening as to constitute a deliberate attempt to denigrate Solzhenitsyn publicly and associate his name with anti-Soviet forces abroad. It seemed that the K.G.B. was preparing a case against Solzhenitsyn, which was about to culminate in his arrest and trial after the manner of the Sinyavsky and Daniel affair three years earlier. But for some reason, this did not happen. Solzhenitsyn continued to divide his time between Ryazan and his dacha, under close surveillance but free to write and see his friends. It was not until late in 1969 that the decision was finally taken to expel Solzhenitsyn from the Union of Writers and thus deprive him of his status as a Soviet writer.

The act of expulsion was entrusted to the Ryazan branch of the Union of Writers, of which Solzhenitsyn was nominally a member. The proceedings took a now familiar turn with the officials accusing Solzhenitsyn of writing anti-Soviet books, although admitting that they had not read them, and the author complaining of victimization. According to his own transcript of the meeting, he was able to justify himself on every count.[36] But the verdict had clearly been handed down in advance from Moscow and Solzhenitsyn ended his statement: 'Well then, take the vote, you've got a majority. But remember that the history of literature will continue to take an interest in this meeting of ours today.'

36. *Ibid.*, pp. 148–58.

Solzhenitsyn's expulsion from the Union of Writers was made public on 12 November 1969. His conduct was described as 'anti-social in character and fundamentally at variance with the principles and tasks formulated in the Charter of the Union of Writers'.[37] The press ceased to refer to him as a writer, substituting the pejorative term *literator*. On the same day, Solzhenitsyn addressed his most virulent open letter so far to the Union of Writers. 'Is it not shameful,' he asked, 'that you trample your statutes underfoot in this manner? . . . It is no longer the timid, frosty period when you expelled Pasternak, whining abuse at him. Was this not shame enough for you?' And he went on: 'Blind leading the blind. You do not even notice that you are wandering in the opposite direction from the one you yourself announced . . . Were we not promised fifty years ago that never again would there be any secret diplomacy, secret talks, secret and incomprehensible appointments and transfers, that the masses would be informed of all matters and discuss them openly? . . . Hatred, a hatred no better than racial hatred, has become your sterile atmosphere.'[38] No Soviet public figure has ever challenged the actions of the Party in such terms. Solzhenitsyn's intemperate outburst was given wide publicity in the West and it was perhaps surprising that the official response amounted to no more than further denunciation in the press. On 26 November *Literaturnaya gazeta* asserted that Solzhenitsyn's letter, which it quoted selectively together with other letters and materials which had been sent abroad, finally proved that he had sold out to the enemies of the Soviet Union and that he stood opposed to the Soviet people and their literature. Once again, Solzhenitsyn's treatment provoked protest from his fellow writers. Letters were received by the Union of Writers from such figures as Tendryakov, Okudzhava, Evtushenko and at least seventy others.

Almost a year was allowed to pass with little further being heard from or about Solzhenitsyn. But in September 1970, his name began to feature prominently in the West in the public discussion of candidates for the Nobel Prize for literature. On 8 October it was announced that he had been awarded the Prize and again he became a focus of attention and adulation.

37. *Literaturnaya Gazeta* (Moscow), 12 November 1969.
38. Labedz, *op. cit.*, pp. 159–61.

Mindful, no doubt, of the pressure brought to bear upon Pasternak to oblige him to reject his Nobel Prize, he immediately made public his acceptance and said that 'as far as it depends on me, I intend to receive the Prize in person on the traditional day.'[39] Unfortunately for Solzhenitsyn, it did not ultimately depend on him. The Soviet press responded to the award with unaccustomed speed. On 9 October *Izvestia* printed a statement by the Union of Writers which deplored the award and described it as a politically hostile act.

As 10 December, the day for the conferment of the Nobel Prizes, approached, it became clear that Solzhenitsyn would not be able to attend and he confirmed this in an open letter to the Swedish Academy on 27 November. He informed the Swedes that he was reluctant to leave the Soviet Union for fear that he would not be permitted to return.

At that time, Solzhenitsyn was living as the guest of Mstislav Rostropovich. Irritated by the persecution of Solzhenitsyn, Rostropovich came out in his support with a polemical letter to the Soviet press, worthy of Solzhenitsyn himself.[40] As with Solzhenitsyn's correspondence, the press did not publish the letter, but Rostropovich also attracted reprisals for his boldness.

The Nobel Prize Day came and went with only a token address from Solzhenitsyn. Nor were any plans made for the medallion to be given to him in Moscow. But the matter was not allowed to rest by the Soviet authorities. The 17 December issue of *Pravda* carried the strongest attack on him yet to appear in the press, when a long article associated him for the first time publicly with political dissidents, notably Andrei Amalrik, who had just been sentenced to three years hard labour. The article described *Cancer Ward* and *The First Circle* as 'lampoons on the Soviet Union which blacken the achievements of our fatherland and the dignity of the Soviet people'. Such language in the Soviet Union is usually only the prelude to some form of direct action, and there were many, both within the Soviet Union and abroad, who feared that the events connected with the Nobel award would finally provide the pretext for Solzhenitsyn's arrest. But again, nothing happened. Whatever additional pressures were brought to bear

39. *The Times* (London), 1 December 1970.
40. *Possev*, no. 12, 1970, pp. 2–3.

upon Solzhenitsyn did not deter him from continuing to write or from sending his work abroad.

The novel on which he was working in Rostropovich's *dacha* represented a break with the themes which had hitherto been central to his fiction. In an epilogue written in 1971, he informed his readers that the development of the idea, first reflected in an essay written in 1937 on the Samsonov disaster, had remained his principal literary ambition, from which he had only been deflected by the circumstances of his life. He was now embarking on a cycle of historical novels depicting the First World War, and presumably the Revolution, from an angle which had hitherto been ignored by Russian writers. It was this long-standing ambition, rather than any intention of placating the Soviet authorities, which persuaded him to take up a relatively 'safe' subject uncoloured by delicate political considerations.

He offered to send his new novel, *August 1914*, to seven editors, but Leonid Brezhnev's remark at the Twenty-Fourth Party Congress in April 1971, that 'writers like Solzhenitsyn deserve only public scorn', inhibited them from even replying. Tvardovsky, who had all along refused to turn against Solzhenitsyn, had been relieved of his editorship of *Novy Mir* in 1970. In any case, Solzhenitsyn's attempt to publish his novel in the Soviet Union can have been no more than a gesture, for he had now adopted such a degree of intransigence towards the Soviet censorship that he was unwilling to accede even to such a minor change in his text as printing the word 'God' without a capital letter.

All Solzhenitsyn's previous unpublished manuscripts reached the West through *samizdat* copies being smuggled out or their being deliberately handed over by the K.G.B. agents. *August 1914* was sent abroad on Solzhenitsyn's own initiative. To safeguard the copyright and ensure dignified negotiations over the translations, he took the unusual step, for a Soviet writer, of appointing a Swiss lawyer to handle his affairs.

Efforts to find a way of handing over the Nobel Prize medallion and citation continued for sixteen months after the announcement of the award. Eventually it was arranged that a ceremony should be held in a Moscow flat on 9 April 1972 and that the secretary of the Swedish Academy should visit Moscow to make the presentation. But again the Soviet authorities intervened.

Solzhenitsyn himself was probably the cause of their doing so. On 30 March he suddenly decided to give his first interview to Western reporters and invited two Americans to meet him. The reason for his decision was clearly that the campaign of slander against him was becoming intolerable. Solzhenitsyn described how stories were being disseminated about the country suggesting that he had surrendered to the Germans in the war, was a collaborator and had Jewish blood. He and his friends were terrorised by the police. 'A kind of forbidden contaminated zone has been created around my family and there were people in Ryazan who were dismissed from their jobs for having visited me . . .'[41] His second 'wife' had also been dismissed from her job. They have 'decided to suffocate me. The plan is to either drive me out of society or out of the country, throw me in a ditch or drive me to Siberia or have me dissolve in an alien fog . . . It never occurs to them that a writer who thinks differently from the majority of society represents an asset to that society and not a disgrace or a reject.'

The publication of the interview in the West immediately provoked a rejoinder in the Soviet press. On 7 April a long article, previously published in Poland, was reprinted in the Soviet Union.[42] It contained a sustained polemic against *August 1914* and was doubtless the first which most Soviet readers had heard of the novel. The article accused Solzhenitsyn of denigrating Russians and Slavs in general and of glorifying the battle of Tannenberg in 'exactly the way the fascist leader Hitler spoke of it'. The novel's view of the Russian political movements of the time was also unacceptable. In a footnote the editors of *Literaturnaya Rossia* added: 'In our days when the frontiers of Europe which were formed as a result of the Second World War have been recognised by all states, Solzhenitsyn is again raising this question.' The theme of linking Solzhenitsyn's novel with his supposedly anti-Soviet feelings was taken up in an article published five days later.[43] It was insinuated that Solzhenitsyn is a Tsarist sympathiser and is pro-German. The newspaper also published letters attacking *August 1914* (which they could not

41. *New York Times*, 3 April 1972.
42. *Trud* and *Literaturnaya Rossia*, 7 April 1972.
43. *Literaturnaya Gazeta*, 12 April 1972.

have read) from non-Russian Soviet citizens, possibly in order to point to Solzhenitsyn's undoubted Slavophile sympathies. This newspaper attack carried a more sinister note—suggesting that Solzhenitsyn was abusing Soviet humanism and Soviet laws. Not for the first time in his difficult career as a writer, it seemed that the Soviet authorities were preparing to take direct 'legal' action against him, but again they refrained from doing so.

In August 1972 the lecture which Solzhenitsyn composed for the Nobel Prize ceremony was released in Stockholm in the annual publication of the Nobel Foundation. Solzhenitsyn used the lecture to affirm his traditionally Russian view of the nature of art and the role of the artist:

> For decades Russian literature has been outward
> rather than inward looking. It has never confined itself
> to frivolities, and I have no hesitation in continuing
> this tradition to the best of my ability. In Russian
> literature there has long been the inborn idea that a
> writer can do much for his people, and that this
> is his duty.

Art itself, Solzhenitsyn proclaimed, is mysterious, nevertheless it represents an absolute value, 'a truly artistic work is completely, irrefutably convincing and bends to its will even the heart which resists it.' Far from being dead in a materialist world, it has a more vital function to perform than ever before. In previous ages the varied scales of values evolved by different peoples posed no problem because they continued to live and act in isolation from each other. Modern communications, however, have brought these varying value systems into conflict and 'such mutual misunderstanding threatens the world with a swift and stormy end.' The twentieth century, with its rival ideologies, violence, and selfishness, is, in Solzhenitsyn's view, like the devils in Dostoevsky's *The Possessed,* on a path leading to self destruction, which a 'spirit of Munich' and a corrupted U.N. are paralysing man's power to resist. There are 'no firm generally approved concepts of goodness and justice . . . all such concepts are fluid and liable to change.'

But who, Solzhenitsyn asks, will bring the various scales of values together? Who will give the human race one united system of evaluation, for evil deeds and good deeds, for the unendurable and the endurable? Who will ever be able to make stubborn, narrow-minded human beings understand other people's distant joys and sorrows? 'Fortunately,' he answers, 'there is a way by which it can be done. It can be done, by art, by literature.' Literature can transmit the experience of one people to another, and of one generation to another:

> My friends! If we are worth anything at all, let us try to help. In our own countries, torn apart by different parties, movements, castes, and groups, who was there in the beginning, who was not a divisive force but a united one? Surely it is this that is essentially the writer's position: to give expression to the national language, which is a nation's main binding force, to give expression to the land on which his fellow-countrymen live, and in a few happy instances to express also the nation's soul.
>
> In this hour of alarm I think that world literature is capable of helping the human race to understand itself properly, in spite of what is being instilled into us by prejudiced people and groups.

Solzhenitsyn is ready for an obvious rejoinder:

> They will say, 'What can literature do against the merciless onslaught of open violence?' But let us not forget that violence does not live by itself and cannot live by itself. It can only exist with the help of *the lie*. Between these two there is a most intimate, natural, and fundamental connection. Violence can only be concealed by the lie, and the lie can only be maintained by violence. Any man who has once proclaimed violence as his *method* is inevitably forced to take the lie as his *principle*.

The central message of Solzhenitsyn's lecture and one of the main themes of all his writing is for all men to renounce the lie, to refuse to participate. And writers can do more, they can defeat it; a lie can stand up and resist many things in this world, but it cannot resist art:

> This is why I think, my friends, that in this hour of trial we are capable of helping the world. We have no weapons of death, but let this not be our excuse. Let us not give in to a life of ease and security. Let us go forward into battle!

Solzhenitsyn's attitude is an old-fashioned romantic one of the artist armed with a pen mightier than the sword going forth to slay the dragon of evil and falsehood. It is a call for the brotherhood of artists everywhere. Inevitably the lecture caused a stir abroad and some who had admired the writer's ardent championing of social justice at home were disappointed to discover that his traditional moral values led him to adopt a conservative stance on world issues. The lecture avoided any specific reference to the Soviet Union and provoked no official response from the Soviet leadership. For another year Solzhenitsyn's name was absent from the headlines.

Early in 1973 Solzhenitsyn's wife, Reshetovskaya, decided to withdraw her opposition to a divorce which she had been persuaded into maintaining by the K.G.B., and Solzhenitsyn was able to marry Natalya Svetlova. He was not, however, given permission to take up residence in Moscow in her flat off Gorky Street. With the lease on the summer accommodation he had rented just outside Moscow due to expire in the autumn, Solzhenitsyn was confronted by the prospect of being homeless. On 23 August he made public a letter he had addressed to the Minister of the Interior demanding his rights to live where he chose and in the same week he again agreed to answer questions from correspondents. Official pressures on him, he said, were worsening all the time. 'I receive letters with threats . . . to make short work of me and my family. . . .' and 'the many technical mistakes have convinced me these letters have been sent by the K.G.B.' But he warned the K.G.B. that should it decide to act against him 'my death will not make happy those people who count on it to stop my literary activity.' Immediately after his death or deprivation of liberty, he said, 'My literary last will and testament will irrevocably come into force . . . and then the main part of my works will start to be published, works I have refrained from publishing all these years.' [44] This was Solzhenitsyn's first public reference, albeit indirect, to *The Gulag Archipelago*. Solzhenitsyn devoted much of his long statement to details of the illegal persecution of dissenting Soviet citizens. He drew unfavourable comparisons between Soviet social practice and Western, but nevertheless expressed disappointment that his Nobel lecture had brought little increase in the level of foreign support for the cause of civil liberty in the Soviet Union. The force of world opinion, he insisted, could be very effective.

Less than a month later Solzhenitsyn returned to the same theme in another long statement, the main pretext for which was his nomination of Andrey Sakharov for the Nobel Peace Prize. Solzhenitsyn went on to attack the lopsided moral outlook prevalent in the West, which largely ignores the violence being committed daily in the Soviet Union and other communist countries and reserves its indignation for South Africa, French nuclear tests, and the Watergate affair in the U.S.A. All these are minor compared with the crimes in the Soviet Union and 'there seems little doubt,' he added, 'that what is going on in the Soviet Union is but a foreboding of the future of man.'

Although it did not become known until some months later, in September 1973, Solzhenitsyn made his last attempt while living in the Soviet Union to influence its leaders. In a sixty-page letter he gave explicit expression to his ideas for the restructuring of his country's moral foundations along the lines suggested in his novels.

But September 1973 also witnessed the beginning of the train of events which was to culminate in Solzhenitsyn's expulsion from the Soviet Union. The existence, if not the character, of *The Gulag Archipelago* had been known in the West since 1969 and Solzhenitsyn had allowed close friends to see it. But he had concealed it from the K.G.B., intending to release it only in the spring of 1975. In September, however, the K.G.B. learned that a former assistant of Solzhenitsyn, Elizaveta Voronyanskaya, had hidden a copy

44. *The Times* (London), 29 August 1973.

in Leningrad. After five days of interrogation she revealed the place of concealment and hanged herself. Solzhenitsyn had refrained from publishing *The Gulag Archipelago* for fear that persons mentioned in it and still living would suffer reprisal. But now no reason for withholding it remained and he authorized the publication of the first two of the seven parts in Paris in December 1973. Other parts were to follow. An effort was made by the K.G.B. to dissuade Solzhenitsyn from publication only three weeks after they had seized the manuscript. Through the mediation of his first wife, it was proposed that in return for a guarantee that he would not publish *The Gulag Archipelago* for twenty years he might publish *Cancer Ward* in the Soviet Union immediately. Solzhenitsyn gave them to understand that he might delay while having no intention of doing so.

The Gulag Archipelago is a vast compilation (some 1,800 pages) describing every aspect of the Soviet terror from 1918 onwards. Solzhenitsyn worked on it simultaneously with his novels, completing it in 1968. Minutely detailed and fiercely polemic, *The Gulag Archipelago* represented a challenge to the Soviet leaders of an altogether different order from anything Solzhenitsyn had previously published. They could not ignore it, more especially since foreign radio stations began immediately to transmit it to the Soviet Union. A vicious press campaign against Solzhenitsyn began in January 1974. A long article in *Pravda,* entitled 'The Path of Betrayal,' called *The Gulag Archipelago* 'a vicious fabrication' by 'a profoundly immoral man.' The author of this composition was 'literally choking with pathological hatred for the country where he was born and grew up, the socialist system, for the Soviet people.' [45]

Solzhenitsyn was quick to reply to his critics. '*Pravda* lies,' he wrote in a statement issued on 18 January, '*Pravda* asserts that in our country (there was) uncompromising criticism of the period up to 1956. So, let them show their uncompromising criticism. I have given them the fullest factual material. . . . The line of our propaganda organs is the line of savage fear of disclosure. It demonstrates how grimly they cling to

45. *Pravda,* 17 January 1974.

the bloody past and shows they want to drag it with them like an unopened bag into the future. . . . And now to the lies of *Literaturnaya Gazeta:* that in my book Soviet people are fiends and that the essence of the Russian soul is such that a Russian is prepared to sell out his father and mother for a ration of bread. Name the pages, liars.' [46]

Two days later Solzhenitsyn replied to foreign journalists who asked how his compatriots could show their support. 'Definitely not by any physical acts, but by rejecting the lie and by refusing to participate personally in the lie. . . . In our country the lie has become not just a moral category, but a pillar of state.' He added that he and his family were ready for any consequences of *The Gulag Archipelago* and his actions: 'I have fulfilled my duty to those who perished and this gives me relief and peace of mind.' [47]

On 8 February 1974 Solzhenitsyn received a summons to the state prosecutor's office, which he ignored. He refused a second on 11 February. On 12 February seven K.G.B. officers came to his wife's flat where he was staying and informed Solzhenitsyn that he was under arrest. Solzhenitsyn picked up the overnight bag he had been keeping ready, donned the sheepskin coat which he had worn in exile in the early 1950s, and went with them to Lefortovo Prison. There he was stripped and interrogated and informed that he was to be charged, as the press campaign had insinuated, with treason under Article 64 of the criminal code. Anticipating arrest, Solzhenitsyn had already prepared a statement in which he declared any court appointed to try him incompetent, that he would answer no questions and if forcibly incarcerated would not work even for one half hour for his oppressors. At 1:00 P.M. the next day Solzhenitsyn was told that by a decree of the Supreme Soviet he was to be deprived of his Soviet citizenship and deported. Within hours he was in West Germany.

Assured that as soon as convenient his family would be permitted to join him, Solzhenitsyn, amidst a blaze of often excessive publicity, considered where to live. He soon left the

46. *The Times* (London), 19 January 1974.
47. *Ibid.,* 22 January 1974.

home of Heinrich Böll, which had been his first sanctuary, and travelled to Norway, but returned to Germany and on to Switzerland. There in Zurich he rented a house and declared that for the forseeable future that would be his home. His wife, his own three children, and the eleven-year-old daughter of his wife's first marriage duly joined him in March.

Settling in to the life of an exile, Solzhenitsyn has made it clear that despite severance from his homeland and the constant attention of publicists and scholars as well as the large sums of money accruing in royalties he does not intend to change his way of life. The third and fourth parts of *The Gulag Archipelago* appeared in Paris in May 1974 and the final three parts are scheduled for publication within months. The sequel to *August 1914* is complete and the third part of his historical novel is well advanced. At the centre of Solzhenitsyn's life remains his literary work. But he has not abandoned the cause of civil liberty in the Soviet Union. Letters have continued to appear over his signature in support of persecuted writers and he has set up a fund from his royalties for the purpose of assisting the families of political prisoners in the Soviet Union.[48]

At the time of his arrest in 1945 Solzhenitsyn's political beliefs were still in line with the Marxist-Leninist teachings he had received in his youth. As he related in *The Gulag Archipelago,* it was only under the influence of the different points of view he met in prison and the camps that his faith began to break down. When he left the research institute, Marfino, in 1950 his cast of mind was close perhaps to the philosophical sceptic Nerzhin in *The First Circle.* By the end of the 1950s when he commenced his novels his attitude to ideology could possibly be summed up by what he wrote in *The Gulag Archipelago* of 1937; that perhaps it 'was needed in order to show how little their whole ideology was worth —their ideology of which they boasted so enthusiastically, turning Russia upside down, destroying its foundations, trampling everything it held sacred underfoot.' (p. 129)

Throughout *The First Circle* the image of Stalin is con-

48. Interview with Walter Cronkite. *Russkaya Mysl* (Paris), 11 July 1974.

trasted, always unfavourably, with that of Lenin. The Leninist Rubin is the most sympathetically drawn of the professional communists, and at the Makarygin's party the Jugoslav Dushan Radovic views their privileged mode of living objectively: 'We need a drastic cure for all this. We need to purge ourselves of this bourgeois corruption! Pyotr...All I want is to get back to Lenin.' (p. 371) Even in *Cancer Ward* Kostoglotov harks back to the 1920s as a time of real Marxism. But the main political discussion in *Cancer Ward*, written presumably in 1966–67, between Kostoglotov and the old Bolshevik Shulubin concludes with the rejection of political prescriptions altogether and their replacement with ethics as the sole guide to human conduct both personal and social. It should not of course be assumed that these and other opinions of Lenin expressed in the novels embrace Solzhenitsyn's entire philosophy. The novels were written to be published in the Soviet Union and the depiction of Stalinism as an unfortunate deviation from Lenin was in line with the policies initiated by Khrushchev and prevailing in the early 1960s.

Solzhenitsyn's object in his novels and in *The Gulag Archipelago* is to record the history of Russia and to explore the harrowing experiences it has inflicted on Russians during the last sixty years. They are not intended as a political programme for the future. This Solzhenitsyn took it upon himself to offer in his *Letter to the Soviet Leaders,* September 1973. As Abraham Brumberg has rightly observed Solzhenitsyn 'is not a political thinker, but a chronicler; not a political analyst but a critic—if you will a poet.' [49] His letter is a critique of Soviet policy both at home and abroad, a warning of the difficulties which lie ahead and an exposition of 'the only feasible and peaceful way in which you can save our country and our people.'

The message of the letter is easily summarised. The greatest imminent danger for Russia is a devastating war with China, but together with the rest of the world she also faces the prospect of a lethally polluted environment and the exhaustion of her resources through overexploitation. Mean-

49. Abraham Brumberg, *The New Leader*, 27 May 1974, p. 11.

while among the painful problems already present Solzhenitsyn lists unsuccessful agriculture, corrupt and idle bureaucracy, vast and wasteful military expense, polluted cities, a misguided educational system, the destructive effects of vodka, and the shameful exploitation of women. The cause of every one of these evils Solzhenitsyn ascribes to Marxism-Leninism, that 'murky whirlwind of progressive ideology' from the West and to the system of lies required to keep the mistaken and anyway dead ideology intact.

The solution Solzhenitsyn proposes is simple and radical. He advocates the abandonment of the world military role the Soviet Union is attempting to pursue, including the support of revolutionary movements everywhere and even the forced retention within the socialist camp of Eastern Europe. Russia must turn inward, discontinue the building of heavy industry, vast cities, and the export of raw materials and concentrate on opening up the Russian North-East, Siberia, not on the basis of uninterrupted progress but with a zero-growth economy. 'But there is a road block on the road to our salvation—the sole Progressive World View.' Solzhenitsyn advocates that Marxism-Leninism be eradicated root and branch as the official ideology and its replacement by a revitalized *Soviet* system. He doubts very much whether Russia is prepared for democracy. He advises rather a continuation of the authoritarian regime, but based upon truth, freedom of conscience, and 'sincere love for your whole people.' 'I myself,' he says, 'see Christianity today as the only living spiritual force capable of undertaking the spiritual healing of Russia.' But he asks no special privileges for it—just that it be treated fairly and not be suppressed.

There is nothing in Solzhenitsyn's Letter which is inconsistent with his previous writings. Nor are most of his ideas new. His information on the coming environmental disaster he readily admits is derived from Western sources. Many in both East and West will agree with what Solzhenitsyn has to say about the present conditions in Russia. The Letter, however, revealed some fundamental disagreements in the ranks of the Soviet dissidents. In a long critique as soberly rational as the Letter is emotional,

Andrey Sakharov, while concurring with many of Solzhenitsyn's points, found serious flaws in his reasoning. He questioned Solzhenitsyn's belief in the strength of ideology. Characteristic, rather, is 'ideological indifference and a pragmatic use of ideology as a convenient facade . . . retention of power and the fundamental features of the system are the chief criteria of the country's present leadership in difficult decisions.' And Sakharov insisted that Russia's problems could never be solved by abandoning scientific and technological quests and renouncing ties with the rest of the world. Sakharov reiterated, moreover, his conviction of the need for democratic conditions. 'I am convinced,' he concluded, 'that the nationalistic and isolationist direction of Solzhenitsyn's thinking, the religious patriarchial romanticism characteristic of him, leads him into very substantial errors and makes his proposals utopian and potentially dangerous.' [50]

In their disagreements Solzhenitsyn and Sakharov are in a sense reopening the Slavophile/Westerner debate which divided Russian intellectuals a century ago. It was the Westerners who triumphed then, for Western ideology and a desire to emulate Western progress predominated before 1917 and have done so since. Now Solzhenitsyn seems to be demanding a reversion not merely to prerevolutionary values but to prepetrine Russia. In several of his stories and novels he has indicated his preference for timeless rural Russia. In his *Lenten Letter* in 1972 he wrote of the 'radiant ethical atmosphere of Christianity' supplied by the Orthodox Church. Prepetrine Russia was authoritarian but it 'possessed a strong moral foundation, embryonic and rudimentary though it was—not the ideology of universal violence but Christian orthodoxy, the ancient, seven-centuries-old orthodoxy of Sergei Radonezhsky and Nil Sorsky, before it was battered by the Patriarch Nikon and bureaucratised by Peter the Great.'

It can be argued that Solzhenitsyn's view of Russian history before as well as after Peter the Great is excessively romantic. As Abraham Brumberg has pointed out, the Orthodox Church has always been bigoted and obscurantist and wherever possible a firm ally of the state, however harsh, rather than its

50. *The Times* (London), 16 April 1974.

adversary, not least in its support for the Soviet regime against Solzhenitsyn himself. The practical value of some of Solzhenitsyn's other ideas is also questionable. His assessment of the decadent West or his belief that the 'third world' will heed the warnings in good time and not take the Western path at all, for instance. Sakharov pointed out that any attempt to develop Siberia with simple technology and manual labour in such difficult conditions is predestined to fail. In *The Gulag Archipelago* part three Solzhenitsyn himself decried the use of such techniques on the White Sea Canal. There remains the extreme unlikelihood of the Soviet leaders being moved by a letter couched in such terms, cogent and sincere though it is. Solzhenitsyn's letter is a profoundly Russian work, extreme, passionate, at times mystical, and frequently at odds with itself. In assessing its importance 'one must take into account not only the author's lack of realism but his humanity and uncompromising dedication to moral values.' [51]

Solzhenitsyn's future in the West is uncertain. As he remarked in his Letter, 'It's where you're born that you can be most useful,' and Solzhenitsyn's thrust as both publicist and artist, has, from the outset been toward his fellow countrymen. Divorced from his cause at home, his moral authority there must be weakened. And cut off from the wellsprings of the Russian language and spirit his own artistic impulse may be in jeopardy. Certainly there are few precedents of an established Russian writer, once in exile adding to his literary reputation. But Solzhenitsyn is a man of courage and dedication. His *magnum opus* which began with *August 1914* is still far from complete and the literary possibilities of his own experience are undoubtedly far from exhausted. Amidst adulation and abuse, Solzhenitsyn remains faithful to what he regards as his sacred mission. In an open letter written in 1968 he said: 'I promise never to betray the truth. My sole aim is to prove myself worthy of the hopes of the Russian reading public. I promise them never to let them down.' [52]

51. Brumberg, *op. cit.*, p. 11.
52. Labedz, *op. cit.*, p. 148.

2 One Day in the Life of Ivan Denisovich and Matryona's Home

Alexander Solzhenitsyn has been described by different critics as both an old-fashioned writer and a genuine innovator. Paradoxically, both of these views are correct. In the early 1930s, when his fame in the Soviet Union was at its height, the official aesthetic of socialist realism, with its emphasis on optimism and education, was beginning to give way to a more candid and exploratory approach to Soviet life. Writers were being admitted to those dark areas of social and political evil which they had hitherto been obliged to by-pass. They were acquiring the freedom to question the assumptions which they had been expected to affirm. They were gaining the right to express private thoughts and exercise their consciences on moral and ethical problems, independently of official ideology. In other words, Soviet literature was quietly repossessing the traditions of critical realism bequeathed to it by its nineteenth-century forebears.

Writers like Tolstoy, Turgenev and Goncharov were expected, and largely accepted the obligation, to provide moral guidance and an authoritative commentary on the vital problems of their age. For Soviet writers the great task, presented to them by Khrushchev and eagerly taken up, was to come to grips with the Stalin years, with all their injustice, inhumanity and dishonesty. Yuri Bondarev's novel *Silence* and Victor Nekrasov's *Kira Georgievna* were revealing examples of the new trend. But writers attempting to correct the record of the past soon found themselves faced with the need to re-evaluate the present. Two stories, A. Yashin's *Vologda Wedding* and *Around and About* by Fyodor Abramov, which appeared in the winter of 1962–3, presented a depressing picture of contemporary life in the rural areas and described the complete failure of the collective farm system in both economic and human terms. They contrasted sharply with the image of the Russian countryside typical of the standard Soviet agricultural novel of the 1940s and 1950s. Solzhenitsyn's stories were, by common consent of those who liked them and those who did not, the most important contributions to this new literature of 'exposure'.

The difference between most of the new writers and the Stalin Prize novelists of the 1940s and 1950s was not as great as some Western critics imagined it to be. For one thing, they were still 'social command' writers, responding to, and ultimately controlled by, current Party dictates. They differed mainly in the degree of truthfulness with which they approached their subjects. And it was not only the critical stance and moral seriousness of the nineteenth-century novelists which inspired them. They also followed their manner of writing. They were still realists. The basic principles which governed the new wave of Soviet writing were still those of socialist realism, demanding a direct and rational treatment of surface reality. Cut off for nearly forty years from their own modernist movement and virtually unaffected by Western experimental developments, few Soviet writers knew anything different. They had been brought up on their own national classics and remained heavily in debt to them. As Mathewson has observed: 'I would consider Chekhov as the historical point of departure of the new writing.'[1]

Solzhenitsyn's artistic range is not as restricted as that of most of his contemporaries. Indeed, it is an indication of the breadth of his literary education that critics have been able to detect in his work the influence of nearly all the major nineteenth-century prose styles and writers. But he, too, has responded only to the realist traditions. Solzhenitsyn owes nothing at the Symbolists or later modernist trends. As he told the 1967 meeting of the Union of Writers, 'In the West they say the (Russian) novel is dead . . . but . . . we should publish novels—such novels as would make them blink as if from a brilliant light and then the "New Novel" would die down and then the "neo-avant-gardists" would disappear.'[2] There is little *arrierè-plan* of meanings in his work, no distorted chronology, and sparing use of such figurative devices

1. *Studies in the Soviet Union*, Vol. 3, no. 2 (Munich), 1963, p. 18.
2. Labedz, *op. cit.*, p. 99.

as metaphor and simile. Although he is said to be well read in foreign literatures, no critic has found this reflected in his own writing. On the contrary, Solzhenitsyn is intensely, even aggressively Russian in his outlook, and in some of his stories it is possible to detect Slavophile overtones. He frequently exhibits an almost mystical reverence for old Russian customs; his ideas reveal the inspiration of such nineteenth-century Russian thinkers as Solovyov and Dostoevsky; and in the language of his books as well as in his own speech, he deliberately eschews the numerous foreign borrowings which have, he considers, disfigured the Russian language during the last two and a half centuries. He has said: 'I have always felt that to write about the fate of Russia was the most fascinating and important task to be performed.'[3] And elsewhere: 'For my entire life I have had the soil of my homeland beneath my feet. Only its pain do I hear, only about it do I write.'[4] He seems to care little for the outside world except in so far as it can help him realise his aims at home.

Solzhenitsyn may be regarded as an old-fashioned writer in the sense that nearly all contemporary Soviet writers are old-fashioned. He has made no contribution to the advancement of the novel or the short story as a genre. Nor does he display the influence of those who have been advancing it in the West. That he is a significant figure in world literature, worthy of a Nobel Prize, is due to the fact that, besides being acutely sensitive to the issues confronting his native land, his themes and his treatment of them transcend local conditions and have a universal relevance in the latter half of the twentieth century. Perhaps most important of all, he is a remarkable artist with words and, at his best, an impeccable stylist.

Solzhenitsyn has recalled Tolstoy's remark that a novel can deal with either centuries of European history or a day in a man's life. While still in the camps, he made up his mind to describe one day in prison life. From his statement that he 'wanted to expose the false image of the prison camps',[5] it is clear that his immediate purpose in writing *One Day* was a plea for *social* justice. Solzhenitsyn composed his story over a period of several years and it went

3. *Ibid.*, p. 7.
4. *Ibid.*, p. 84.
5. *Ibid.*, p 7.

through at least four drafts, each one paring down the last, before the final version was reached. *One Day* was published exactly one hundred years after Dostoevsky's *Notes from the House of the Dead*, in which he described his own experience during a four-year term in a Siberian penal colony. The coincidence is fortuitous, but a comparison is instructive on both literary and historical grounds. The similarities between the two works are in fact superficial, but both writers had the avowed aim of exposing, as never before, the camps to the Russian public. Dostoevsky chose to present a broad view of the camps, through the eyes of an aristocrat, an intellectual who could rationalise his experience and philosophise about crime. Solzhenitsyn's hero Shukhov, however, is a simple peasant, innocent of any crime and able to comprehend little beyond the day-to-day problems of survival. Although, unlike Dostoevsky's story, *One Day* is not a first person narration, the point of view and even the language are consistently Shukhov's. Solzhenitsyn himself does not interpose extended comment, and thus the deeper thoughts of the more sophisticated prisoners are left unexpressed. Such questions as how communists and other thinking people explain to themselves the injustice which has condemned them to the camps, or how they have become reconciled to a twenty-five-year sentence, are left unanswered. There is no explicit generalisation in *One Day*. There are no politically motivated characters and Solzhenitsyn refrains from any overt political statement on the burning issues raised by the very existence of the camps.

The most striking conclusion to be drawn from Dostoevsky's and Solzhenitsyn's accounts of Russian penal colonies, is the extent to which conditions have worsened and inhumanity increased during the last one hundred years. Dostoevsky's prisoners enjoyed adequate food and spare time. They could indulge in private activities and make contact with the neighbouring population. Above all, they were sustained by the certain knowledge of freedom at the end of their terms. Shukhov and his comrades know in their hearts that they are doomed for life:

> Shukhov . . . didn't know whether he wanted freedom or not. At first he had longed for it. Every day he'd counted the days of his stretch—how many had passed, how many were coming. And then he'd grown bored

with counting. And then it became clear that men of
his like wouldn't ever be allowed to return home, and
they'd be exiled. And whether his life would be any
better there than here—who could tell?

Freedom meant one thing to him—home.

But they wouldn't let him go home.' (pp. 186-7)

Unlike Tolstoy, Solzhenitsyn does not build up his characters
or the episodes in their lives from an accumulation of minute
detail. The reader gains only a vague idea of Shukhov's appearance. Solzhenitsyn's technique of evoking a whole impression by
means of a few carefully selected, emotionally neutral, facts, is
Chekhovian. And the artistry with which he accomplishes his
effects is comparable with Chekhov's. He needs no more than two
laconic sentences to convey fully the sensation of the cold and the
early morning at the beginning of the story: 'The intermittent
sounds barely penetrated the window panes on which the frost
lay two fingers thick, and they ended almost as soon as they
had begun. It was cold outside, and the campguard was reluctant
to go on beating out the reveille for long.' (p. 9) And the simple
remark 'the snow creaked under their boots' conjures up the
entire image of the freezing snow-covered camp.

As Solzhenitsyn takes his little hero through every stage of an
ordinary camp day, he builds up a comprehensive account of all
the essential activities in a *zek*'s life and a picture of the camp itself
and of its inmates, both prisoners and guards. Without distorting
the simple central thread of the action he employs, though sparingly, the common devices of realistic narrative to give breadth
and perspective to his picture. From time to time, Shukhov and
his comrades reminisce. Shukhov's recollection of his previous
camp at Ust-Izhma enables Solzhenitsyn to emphasise that the
regime in this camp is relatively mild. At different points during
the day, Shukhov, Tiurin and Buinovsky have occasion to remember how each came to be arrested. Shukhov's punishment in the
guard-house, his short visit to the medical wing and Buinovsky's
imminent spell in the cells, provide an opportunity to describe
other facets of the camp.

On several occasions, Shukhov gives information which he has
only acquired himself through hearsay. He describes, for example,

the procedure when parcels arrive for the *zeks*. He mentions the
episode when knives were smuggled into the camp in vaulting
poles, about which he had only heard. Solzhenitsyn never indulges
in descriptions or digressions for their own sake. Comment is
generally confined to Shukhov's own frequently interposed remarks, which although reflecting a limited point of view, nevertheless impart a personal eye-witness quality to the story.
Solzhenitsyn, in fact, rarely intrudes at all in the capacity of
omniscient author. From time to time, he takes over from
Shukhov to speak about the Soviet intelligentsia among the
prisoners, the Captain and Tsezar, whose experience was beyond
the range of Shukhov's comprehension.

Many Russians would agree with Solzhenitsyn that 'of all the
drama that Russia lived through, the fate of Ivan Denisovich was
the greatest tragedy.'[6] Certainly there is no issue, except perhaps
the Second World War, which touches the emotions of Russians
more deeply than the memory of the labour camps. It was a
tragedy in which Solzhenitsyn shared and 'it is difficult to imagine
how one can remain simple, calm, natural, almost commonplace
when dealing with such a harsh and tragic theme'[7] as he manages
to do in *One Day*. Dostoevsky did not hesitate to convey the full
horror of life in his penal colony and give vent to his polemic
indignation: 'How much youth has perished between these walls
for nothing, what tremendous forces have perished here in vain
... Mighty forces have died here for nothing, died abnormally,
illegally, irretrievably. And who is to blame?'[8] This passage could
stand as an epigraph to Solzhenitsyn's story but it is a far cry from
his own approach. As Lakshin wrote:

> Were Solzhenitsyn an artist of smaller scale and less
> sensitivity, he would probably have selected the worst
> day in the most arduous period of Ivan Denisovich's
> camp life. But he took a different road, one possible
> only for a writer who is certain of his own strength, who
> realises that the subject of his story is of such importance
> and gravity that it excludes empty sensationalism and

6. *Ibid.*
7. V. Lakshin, *Novy Mir*, January 1964.
8. *F. M. Dostoevsky: Sobranie Sochinenii*, Vol. 3 (Moscow), 1956, p. 701.

the desire to shock with descriptions of suffering and physical pain. Thus, by placing himself in apparently the most difficult and disadvantageous circumstances before the reader, who in no way expects to encounter a 'happy' day in the convicts' life, the author thereby ensured the full objectivity of his artistic testimony, and all the more mercilessly and sharply struck a blow at the crimes of the recent past.[9]

In *The First Circle* there is a passage in which Nerzhin, obviously speaking for Solzhenitsyn himself, describes his reactions to prison camp life in a manner which is entirely appropriate to the situation in *One Day*, but beyond the artistic range of that story.

> Descriptions of prison life tend to overdo the horror of it. Surely it is more frightening when there are no actual horrors; what is terrifying is the unchanging routine year after year. The horror is in forgetting that your life—the only one you have—is destroyed; in your willingness to forgive some ugly swine of a warder, in being obsessed with grabbing a big hunk of bread in the prison mess or getting a decent set of underwear when they take you to the bath-house.
>
> This is something that cannot be imagined; it has to be experienced. All the poems and ballads about prison are sheer romanticism; no one need have been in prison to write that sort of stuff. The feel of prison only comes from having been inside for long, long years on end . . . (p. 200)

There is not a trace of romanticism in Solzhenitsyn's description of Ivan Denisovich's day. He had himself been inside for 'long, long years on end'.

It is unlikely that had Solzhenitsyn tried to emulate Dostoevsky, and elaborated his own opinions, *One Day* would have been published. But it was an artistic choice which led him to describe the undramatic experience of such an ordinary hero (he has even been called an anti-hero) as Shukhov. Shukhov is a simple, even

9. Lakshin, *op. cit.*

40

naïve, man whose perception of the world is purely physical. He does not search for meanings or draw conclusions. He doesn't possess the mental equipment to do so. He happily accepts the folklore explanation of the behaviour of the moon and stars. His one cry of protest is very muted by comparison with Dostoevsky's: 'You see, Alesha,' Shukhov explained to him, 'somehow it works out all right for you: Jesus Christ wanted you to sit in prison and so you are—sitting there for His sake. But for whose sake am I here? Because we weren't ready for war in forty-one? For that? But was it *my* fault?' (p. 187)

The choice of detail in Solzhenitsyn's picture of the labour camp is effectively Shukhov's. Things are presented as they appear to him. The language is colourful and rhythmical because it reflects the cadences of Shukhov's peasant speech, with frequent use of aphorism. But there is no sentimentality in the descriptions, no lyricism such as Turgenev might have brought even to this harsh scene. The narrative is confined to the unembellished facts, conveyed dispassionately in spare prose with an elliptical economy of words. Lukács has called this method 'non interpretative description'. It is a measure of Solzhenitsyn's self-discipline and control over his medium that he is able to maintain a consistent tone and pace from the first page of his story until the last.

Soviet critics complained at the apparent absence of indignation and civic protest in *One Day*. They were unable to appreciate that Solzhenitsyn's restraint, his unpretentious and even artless simplicity, were a more eloquent protest than emotionally charged rhetoric, that his artistic detachment disguised a passionate engagement.

Another Soviet critic, Lidia Fomenko, wrote that Solzhenitsyn's story 'for all its artistic mastery and harsh bitter truth . . . does not rise to the philosophy of the times, to a broad generalisation capable of encompassing the antagonistic phenomena of that era.'[10] Lakshin disputed this assertion, asking: 'Is it not an axiom, that an artist, if he is a true artist, is able to reflect the entire world in a small drop?' Solzhenitsyn's two big novels *The First Circle* and *Cancer Ward*, do contain material for a broad historical generalisation and it is remarkable the extent to which

10. L. Fomenko, *Literaturnaya Rossia*, 11 January 1963.

One Day, so narrow in time and space, also depicts as in a micro-cosm Soviet life 'in that era' and after. Solzhenitsyn's method rarely involves deliberate symbolism. But his stories as a whole, and also separate episodes within them, do nevertheless exert a strong symbolic effect. He could scarcely be unaware of the implications in this passage: 'they wanted to shift the 104th from the building shops to a new site, the "Socialist Way of Life" settlement. It lay in open country covered with snow-drifts, and before anything else could be done there, they would have to dig pits and put up posts and attach barbed wire to them. Wire themselves in, so that they wouldn't run away. Only then could they start building.' (pp. 11–12) *One Day* appeared just a year after the erection of the Berlin Wall.

Georg Lukács has written a paragraph which sums up succinctly the social and political significance of *One Day*:

> Solzhenitsyn's achievement consists in the literary transformations of the uneventful day in a typical camp into a symbol of a past which has not yet been overcome, nor has it been portrayed artistically. Although the camps epitomise one extreme of the Stalin era, the author has made his skilful grey monochrome of camp life into a symbol of everyday life under Stalin. He was successful in this precisely because he posed the artistic question: What demands has this era made on man? Who has proved himself a human being? Who has salvaged his human dignity and integrity? Who has held his own—and how? Who has retained his essential humanity? Where was his humanity twisted and destroyed? His rigorous limitation to the immediate camp life permits Solzhenitsyn to pose the question simultaneously in quite general and quite concrete terms.[11]

As in the big novels, though to a lesser extent, the camp in-mates represent something of a cross-section of Soviet people, the workers, peasants, intellectuals and nationalities. They are a roll-call of the successive waves of prisoners who were sent to the

11. Georg Lukács, *Solzhenitsyn* (London), 1969, pp. 13–14.

camps throughout the 1930s and 1940s, the Kirov wave in 1935, the families of the Kulaks, deported religious believers and nationalities, the former prisoners of war and alleged spies, like Shukhov himself, and finally those after 1949 with a uniform sentence of twenty-five years. Only the victims of the purges of 1937–8 are noticeably absent. Since *One Day* is fictionalised autobiography, many of the characters are based upon real life. Former camp inmates who wrote to Solzhenitsyn have claimed to be able positively to identify the camp and the characters in the book. 'Ivan Denisovich? That's me, SZ-209. I can give all the characters real names, not invented ones.' 'We were the 104th brigade with you, lived in the same hut.' 'Solzhenitsyn has not even changed Tiurin's name. I knew him and worked in the 104th brigade.'[12] Captain Buinovsky's story follows closely that of Commander B. V. Burkovsky who lived in the camp with him for three years. By 1964 Burkovsky had been released from the camps and had taken up an appointment as chief of the naval museum on the cruiser *Aurora*, on the river Neva in Leningrad. In an interview which he gave to the correspondent of *Izvestia* he also testified that the general picture of camp life, as well as many details, corresponded exactly with the reality. Some of the characters, he said,—Tiurin, himself, Tsezar Markovich and the Baptist Alesha—bear a close resemblance to actual persons. Most, however, were composites. And as for Shukhov, 'there was one like him in every brigade.'[13]

In February 1964 a meeting called to discuss the Lenin Prize nominations brought to light the real-life prototype for Tsezar Markovich. He was the poet Lev Kopelov who spoke out strongly in favour of *One Day* being awarded the Lenin Prize.[14]

A Soviet reader of *One Day* might identify many practices familiar in Soviet life—the callous attitude of authority and the need to outwit it (the worksheets), the self-seeking, scrounging and working on the side. A comparison between human behaviour in

12. Labedz, *op. cit.*, pp. 14–28.
13. *Izvestia*, 15 January 1964.
14. Priscilla Johnson, *op. cit.*, p. 75. In his open letter of 12 November 1969 Solzhenitsyn supported Kopelev when he was again in difficulties. 'They are also threatening to expel Lev Kopelev, the front line veteran, who has already served ten years in prison although he was completely innocent . . .' Labedz, *op. cit.*, p. 160.

the camps and in *Matryona's Home*, which depicts life beyond the wire, is revealing. Solzhenitsyn shows how many of the negative features of camp life have their exact counterparts among the inhabitants of an ordinary Russian village. There one finds a heartless collective-farm management, the authorities confiscating the peasants' fuel, falsified school records, unsympathetic medical services and a general lust for private gain. This comparison of a place of confinement with the outside world is a favourite source of irony with Solzhenitsyn. Shukhov wonders whether life will be any better if he is released and several times in *One Day*, Solzhenitsyn underlines the paradox that in general, it will not be. The central theme of *The First Circle* is built on such a paradox. When Shukhov goes to the medical wing he finds the former student of literature, Vdovushkin, 'writing in prison what he'd been given no opportunity to write in freedom,' (p. 30) Things can be said in the camps, as in the cancer ward and at Mavrino, which would be inadmissible outside. More good humour and comradeship is displayed in camp than in Matryona's village, where she herself is the only exception to the overall scene of vice. And the prisoners can at least rely on their rations if they fulfil their quotas, while the collective farmers in Shukhov's village and Matryona's cannot be certain of receiving theirs.

The area of Soviet life beyond the camp which receives the most detailed attention in *One Day* is the collective farm. Solzhenitsyn uses the letters from Shukhov's wife as a pretext for marshalling the depressing facts about another subject which exercised him personally. The picture of a depopulated countryside incompetently administered and riddled with graft is really only a preliminary sketch for his next story *Matryona's Home*. Matryona's village is Shukhov's village. There is the same undermanned collective farm with its reduced individual plots where Matryona is obliged to help out, the same peat-processing works which had attracted the younger workers. *Matryona's Home* is an indictment of life in the Russian village in the tradition of Chekhov and Bunin. Solzhenitsyn shares Chekhov's horror at the peasants' animal-like behaviour, drinking and knifing each other. And critics also rightly saw the story as an unfavourable comment on the Soviet agricultural achievement. The labour camps could be explained as a temporary aberration, monstrous, but capable, along with other direct consequences of what was euphemistcially called the 'cult of (Stalin's) personality', of being speedily rectified. But *Matryona's Home* was set in 1956, five years after *One Day*, and exposed a fundamental weakness in the Soviet system and in the mentality of a section of the Soviet people.

Matryona's Home is narrated in the first person by a returning prisoner and teacher of mathematics, a character close to Solzhenitsyn himself. Like Solzhenitsyn, his narrator has a Slavophile longing to return to the true legendary Russia and settle deep in the Russian provinces. He is fascinated by the vestiges of old Russia, the village names, the funeral rituals and the scene, which he wants to photograph, of Matryona at the spinning wheel. But besides these romantic survivals, he discovers other less attractive ones. He finds that the attitude of the collective farm to the workers is little different from the attitude of the pre-revolutionary landlords to their serfs. The chairman has simply replaced the *barin* and his wife continues to put on airs and order her inferiors about. As the peasants used to steal the landlord's wood, now they steal peat from the Trust. If anything, they now have less claim to the land than formerly. Their individual plots are uneconomical and they are forbidden to collect hay from the woods and railway side. There are shortages, the village is run down and there are no horses with which to plough. A Soviet critic complained: 'When you read this story you get the impression that the peasants' psychology has remained the same as it was sixty years ago. This is not true!' Solzhenitsyn is convinced that it *is* true.

By choosing peasants as the central protagonists of his first two stories, Solzhenitsyn was upholding one of the enduring traditions of Russian literature. For the aristocrats of the nineteenth century, the peasant held an almost mystical fascination. He was idealised by Tolstoy, Turgenev and Nekrasov in their search for truth, as the repository of natural wisdom and simplicity. It was this wishful image which Chekhov and Bunin attempted to correct with their ruthlessly objective glimpses of peasant life at the end of the century. Soviet critics were quick to see both these views reflected in Solzhenitsyn's stories. 'Reading the story,' wrote one about *One Day*, 'I involuntarily compared it with Lev Tolstoy's folk tales, with their admiration of passive saintliness and the meekness of the "simple folk". Solzhenitsyn even selected his hero on the principle that holy simplicity is higher than any wisdom.' Another, however, complained that Shukhov's way of life was little better than that of an animal, 'a total egoist, living only for his belly.' Similar views were expressed about the righteous and suffering Matryona on the one hand and the coarse peasants on the other.[15]

There is a superficial resemblance between Shukhov and Tolstoy's Platon Karataev, skilfully sewing a shirt for the French corporal. Karataev 'knew how to do everything, he was always busy', while Shukhov 'knew how to manage everything.' But the parallel between the two is confined to their external characteristics. In Shukhov there is nothing of 'the unfathomable, rounded, eternal personification of the spirit of simplicity and truth' which Pierre thought he had found in Karataev. Nor is Shukhov in any meaningful sense a religious believer. Solzhenitsyn does not idealise Shukhov or hold him up as the embodiment of some abstract principle. It happens to be Shukhov's nature that he is simple and submissive. Such qualities were cultivated as the essential prerequisites for survival even by more assertive characters like Tiurin. It is the lesson of the camps which Buinovsky must learn. And Shukhov's practical wisdom and adroitness are no more than refinements in a man accustomed to earn his living by the use of his hands.

During the early discussions between the 'friends and foes of Ivan Denisovich' opinions were divided as to whether Shukhov had managed to retain his pride and personal integrity or whether 'in reconciling himself to the camps he (had) surrendered his human traits entirely to his basic instincts.' One critic concluded that 'the regime of the special camps destroyed the souls of all the inmates and left them only a single goal—to stay alive by any means at all.' It was true that as Lakshin described it, 'the entire system of imprisonment in the camps through which Ivan Denisovich passed was calculated to suppress mercilessly, to kill all feelings of right and legality in man, to demonstrate in matters

15. For a detailed study of the Soviet response to Solzhenitsyn's earlier works see N. Tarasova, 'Vkhozhdenie Solzhenitsyna v sovietskuyu literaturu' in *Alexander Solzhenitsyn: Sobranie sochinenii*, Tom 6 (Frankfurt-am-Main), 1970, pp. 197–242.

large and small an impunity for arbitrariness against which any outburst of noble indignation was powerless. The camp administration did not allow the convicts to forget even for a moment that they were deprived of rights, and that arbitrariness was the only judge.' In such a situation, there must have been many who gave in and succumbed to the degradation inflicted upon them. This is not true of Shukhov and his fellow prisoners who, with the exception perhaps of the informers and Fetiukov, are shown not only adapting well enough to survive, but also maintaining their self respect. But for prisoners who had been in so long that they had forgotten their past and with so little hope of release that they could conceive of no future, it was inevitable that they should lose the habit of planning ahead: 'scrape through today and hope for tomorrow.' All the happenings which make Shukhov's day 'almost a happy one' refer to that day alone. Tomorrow he must begin all over again. The moments Shukhov lives for, on which he focuses his whole being, are the meagre sensual pleasures a prisoner can enjoy. Meals, those sacred moments for which a *zek* lives, are eaten with slow concentration, 'you had to eat with your whole mind on your food.' When he manages to scrounge a cigarette 'the smoke crept and flowed through his whole hungry body, making his head and feet respond to it.' Keeping warm is a primary concern of all the prisoners but the horizons of many no doubt extend beyond Shukhov's preoccupation with food. The narrator in *Matryona's Home*, an ex-prisoner and an intellectual, has learned from experience 'not to regard eating as the main object in life.'

By nature a timid man, it is easier for Shukhov 'who knew of no way of standing up for his rights' to learn the necessary degree of servility, than for some others: 'better to growl and submit, if you were stubborn they broke you.' The Captain, the only one who tries to hit back at his persecutors, has only been in camp a few weeks. But he too will learn to survive by emulating the other *zeks*, 'inert but wary.'

Shukhov is ready to run errands for his fellow prisoners and perform services which will bring him some small advantage, but not at the sacrifice of his own sense of personal worth. 'He wouldn't take on any old job.' He keeps himself tidy and clean. He is prepared to scrounge a smoke but 'he would never lower himself like that Fetiukov, he would never look at another man's mouth.' He retains his dignity, 'he couldn't eat with his hat on', and certain little personal fads such as, for instance, not eating fish eyes.

On several occasions throughout his 'happy day' Shukhov exhibits a compassion and humanity which a murderously inhumane environment has not crushed out of him. In spite of his longing to receive a parcel, he has selflessly forbidden his wife to send one so that his children may be better fed. He feels genuine sorrow for the Captain, and for Tsezar when he risks having his parcel stolen. He shares his cigarettes with the deaf Senka and his biscuits with Alesha, two characters who are even less equipped than he to stand up for themselves. Shukhov's integrity and ingrained sense of right and wrong have also survived in camp. He deplores the idea of saving his own skin at the expense of someone else's blood, like the squealers. And he'd never take a bribe, 'even eight years as a convict hadn't turned him into a jackal.' On the contrary, he has even acquired an inner strength, 'the longer he stayed in the camp, the stronger he made himself.'

The portrait which emerges of Ivan Shukhov, is of an unexceptional little man, wielding the practical guile native to the Russian peasant, simple but not innocent, sly but not dishonest, insulted but not a weakling, and submissive but not degraded. A man with sufficient force of character not only to preserve his primitive moral sense and feelings of common decency but even to benefit in some small way from his ordeal. Shukhov commands pity but also respect. Those who complained that his behaviour in camp was unworthy of a Soviet man were doing him less than justice. But if they meant that none of the qualities exhibited by Shukhov and the other prisoners were particularly attributable to their Soviet or socialist upbringing they were right. A year after *One Day*, at the height of the controversy it generated, a short novel entitled *They Endured*, by Boris Dyakov, was published. It was an undisguised polemic against *One Day*. 'The figures of the communists are central in the story,' wrote a sympathetic critic, 'unbending faith in communist ideals, in the durability of Soviet power, in the triumph of justice, and a warm love for the homeland—that is what enabled them not only to survive physically, but to preserve their ideological staunchness and their human qualities.'[16] In *One Day*, there is no suggestion that the virtues which enabled the prisoners to endure came from anywhere but their own inner being. As in *The First Circle* and *Cancer Ward* each prisoner is ultimately thrown back on his own personal resources. Rubin and Rusanov, the communists in the big novels, do not cope better than the rest. In *One Day*, the only character to invoke the name of communism is the Captain, a camp novice. And he must learn to sublimate his ideals, not parade them. If there is a doctrine which fortifies the prisoners in the camp, it is the camp itself. It is the camp which has toughened Shukhov just as it made Kostoglotov in *Cancer Ward* 'sharp as an axe.' The hardy Tiurin is also 'a true son of Gulag'. It was this lack of clear ideological orientation which finally disqualified *One Day* from official favour when a more orthodox interpretation of socialist realism began to be applied after Khrushchev's departure.

Solzhenitsyn has observed that 'Russian literature has always been sensitive to human suffering.'[17] In a sense all his own works are studies in human suffering and of differing responses to it. Shukhov's submissiveness is partly a cultivated quality, but in other ways he is a positive character who actively resists suffering by the exercise of certain sturdy, down to earth virtues. In Matryona, on the other hand, the righteousness and meekness of 'the insulted and the injured' are elevated to a moral plane. Her meekness is not an expedient, like Shukhov's, but is a part of her nature. Her lack of interest in personal property, in contrast to the grasping lust of the village peasants, recalls Tolstoy's teaching that private possessions are the chief cause of human isolation and are an obstacle to brotherhood. Matryona is a kind of holy innocent, a Christ-like figure reminiscent of Dostoevsky's Myshkin. She labours for others for no reward and helps even those who are robbing her. Everything in her life has gone wrong. Yet she retains her saintliness and serenity and feels neither envy nor bitterness. She has fewer sins to answer for than her lame cat. Even though her sister-in-law acknowledges Matryona's kindness and simplicity, she does so with scorn and pity. Matryona brings to mind also a character from a story by Leskov, a

16. N. Sergovantsev, *Oktyabr'*, no. 10 (Moscow), 1963.
17. Labedz, *op. cit.*, p. 8.

nineteenth-century writer with whom Solzhenitsyn has many affinities. Leskov's Golova Baraninya 'was so called because she was considered a fool, and a fool she was deemed because she was more mindful of others than herself.'[18]

In most of her essential characteristics, Matryona is the opposite of Shukhov. She is dirty, a bad housekeeper, and has never practised thrift. She has no skills and is foolish. Shukhov would never allow himself to be put upon by others as Matryona does. She is too lazy even to keep a pig. Matryona's lack of the virtues considered admirable in Shukhov, however, is of no consequence. Her worth does not lie in her capacity for physical adaptation, but in certain ideal qualities, traditionally loved by Russians, with which Solzhenitsyn endows her. Matryona is a unique figure in Solzhenitsyn's literary creation. Although movingly human, she seems also to be an embodiment of that mystical feeling for Russia which occasionally intrudes itself into the specifically Soviet experience in most of his writing. In the story she is a point of moral reference, represented in orthodox socialist realist literature by the communist hero whose virtues throw into relief the shortcomings of those around them. But Soviet critics, not unexpectedly, could find nothing in common between Matryona's 'uncomplaining patience and humility' and an ideology which demands 'protest, if not struggle' in such a situation as hers. They disliked, in particular, Solzhenitsyn's concluding comment on Matryona, that none of those who were close to her had realised that she was the one righteous person without whom no city can stand, nor the whole world. This is, in effect, a restatement of the moral of the story. Although probably no general analogy was intended by Solzhenitsyn, Matryona, like Christ, is despised and finally brought to her death by those too blinded by their own vices to perceive her true worth. Matryona unconsciously and instinctively embodies those values central to the ethical socialism preached by Shulubin in Cancer Ward. Despite material accomplishments, and these are modest enough in Matryona's Home, neither Russia, nor the world can hope to prosper without their Matryonas. The problem which Solzhenitsyn's stories set for Soviet critics was noted by an American writer, Priscilla Johnson:

18. See Ludmila Koehler, 'Alexander Solzhenitsyn and Russian Literary Tradition', The Russian Review, no. 2 (New York), 1967, p. 177.

It was odd, in a country so haunted by its classics, to see Solzhenitsyn accused of being at once too Tolstoyan and too Dostoevskian: told that Ivan Denisovich and Matryona are two sides of a single character, Platon Karataev and Sonya Marmeladova, alike a celebration of 'holy' passivity. At one level the question was: Should literature dedicate itself to the 'positive' hero who will show man how he ought to live, or should art be democratised, should it describe 'little', broken men as well as big, not merely leaders but the led?[19]

Soviet defenders of Ivan Denisovich and Matryona were able to quote one feature of the characters' personalities which coincides entirely with the requirements of socialist ideology, namely their attitude to work. The work ethic in Soviet literature has been much emphasised, but that it was also a nineteenth-century tradition may be seen in such writers as Chekhov and Tolstoy. One of the features of Karataev admired by Pierre was his love of work. Both Shukhov and Matryona, like the peasant Spiridon and his wife in *The First Circle*, feel and are seen at their best while working. For both work is a liberating force.

Dostoevsky discussed the nature of work in considerable detail in *Notes from the House of the Dead*. He pointed out that the same work may be either slavery or freedom, depending on the circumstances. 'The prisoner sometimes even gets carried away by his work and tries to do it as skilfully, rapidly and efficiently as possible', as did Shukhov. But forced labour is deadening 'not so much in its difficulty or continuity, as in the fact that it is forced, obligatory, performed under the lash.'[20] Solzhenitsyn himself elaborates on this theme in *The First Circle*. When the engineer Bobynin is summoned in the middle of the night by Abakumov to explain why the secret telephone they are making is behind schedule he retorts boldly:

'You and your schedule! It never occurs to you, does it, that it's no use issuing orders unless the men on the job have peace of mind, enough to eat and freedom? . . .

19. Priscilla Johnson, *op. cit.*, p. 77.
20. Dostoevsky, *op. cit.*, p. 409.

Ever thought about the poor devils who have to do all the work? They slave away for twelve or sixteen hours a day—yet only the senior engineers get a proper meat ration and the rest are lucky if they find a bone in their soup. Why don't you let the fifty-eighters have visits from their relatives? By right it should be once a month—but you only allow it once a year! What do you think that does to people's morale? . . . Rules and regulations, that's all you can think about. We used to be allowed out into the grounds all day on Sundays— now it's been stopped. What's the point—to get more work out of us? Like hell you will. You won't improve results by keeping us cooped up. Come to that, why did you have to drag me here at this time of night? What's wrong with the daytime. I've got to work tomorrow. I need sleep.' (pp. 88–9)

In another scene in *The First Circle*, Solzhenitsyn underlines the contrast between forced and voluntary labour. Nerzhin and Sologdin have asked to be allowed to cut wood for the exercise and spiritual satisfaction the work gives them:

Nerzhin picked up the saw and handed one end to Sologdin. They had cooled off and set about their task with a will. The saw spat brown powdered bark and cut into wood—not as easily as when Spiridon held it, but smoothly all the same. The two men were used to working together and tolerated each other's mistakes. They worked in silence and with that special zest and enjoyment that go with a job unforced by compulsion or need. (p. 129)

The prisoners in Stalin's special camps were subjected to a refinement in torture, by having to perform forced labour for their very food, and hence their very lives were made to depend on the work of each individual. In such circumstances, work became a backbreaking chore, to be avoided whenever possible. 'Work was like a stick. It had two ends. When you worked for the knowing, you have quality, when you worked for the fool, you gave him eyewash. Otherwise you croaked, they all knew that.' (pp. 20–1) They also knew that you worked to keep warm and pass the time. But Solzhenitsyn does not idealise creative labour in *One Day*. Only Shukhov among the prisoners adopts a genuinely conscientious attitude to work. When reading of the idleness prevailing in his native village, he reflects that 'easy money weighs light in the hand and doesn't give you the feeling you've earned it. There was truth in the old saw: pay short money and you get short value. He still had a good pair of hands, capable hands. Surely, when he was out, he'd find work as a stone-setter or carpenter, or tinker?' (p. 52) Solzhenitsyn makes a further discrimination between constructive work and pointless, humiliating work. When he is ordered to mop out the guardroom, Shukhov does as shoddy a job as he can get away with. When doing something meaningful, however, as on the building site, he is ready to make an effort and enjoys his work. But of all his team only he can muster real enthusiasm and pride in what he is doing. For Shukhov alone does work offer a liberation. Before the war he had been a builder and so the opportunity to exercise his skill even under the machine-guns of the guards is an act of freedom. It increases his sense of personal worth: 'after working like that he felt equal to the team leaders.' For most of the others, especially the intellectuals, physical labour was the most burdensome part of their bondage. And even for Shukhov his enthusiasm is the euphoria of the moment. In camp he thinks to himself of the doctor who recommended work as the antidote for illness: 'you can overwork a horse to death. The doctor ought to understand. If he'd been sweating blood laying blocks he'd quieten down, you could be sure of that.' (p. 29)

For Matryona, work is an activity free from compulsion. She works without pay or reward, but she works willingly. For her, too, creative work is not demoralizing, but liberating. Work is an infallible way of restoring her spirits. As in *One Day*, Solzhenitsyn draws a pointed comparison between Matryona's attitude to work and the collective farmers'. But also, like Shukhov's, Matryona's creative labour is not the application of a moral principle. By nature, she is lazy. It is not so much her conscience as her inherent good nature which prompts her to work for others. She works for herself because it is her only means of escape.

Solzhenitsyn has made his attitude to those who confine themselves to narrow topical interpretations of his work clear:

> It is not the task of the writer to defend or criticise one or another mode of distributing the social product or to defend one or another form of government organisation. The task of the writer is to select more universal, eternal questions (such as) the secrets of the human heart, the triumph over spiritual sorrow, the laws of the history of mankind that were born in the depths of time immemorial and that will cease to exist only when the sun ceases to shine.[21]

The intense experiences of Solzhenitsyn's own life have given him ample material for reflection on such problems as these, and at their most serious level, his writings embody the conclusions he has drawn. They receive their fullest treatment in the novels, but the main themes are found in embryo in *One Day* and *Matryona's Home*. Like Dostoevsky, Solzhenitsyn depicts his characters *in extremis*, but the situations in which they find themselves are all such as Solzhenitsyn has himself experienced or witnessed. The dilemmas they face are the fundamental problems of human existence, in *One Day* how to live, and in *Cancer Ward* how to die. But Solzhenitsyn's characters are also social beings and he identifies and examines the values which govern human relationships. Political values are ultimately irrelevant and Solzhenitsyn would surely agree with Yuri Zhivago that 'those who wield power are so anxious to establish the myth of their own infallibility that they turn back on truth as squarely as they can. Politics mean nothing to me. I don't like people who are indifferent to the truth.'[22] Nor is it possible to discover a metaphysical dimension to Solzhenitsyn's thinking, beyond the occasional glimpses of mystical intuition. Christianity, although it attracts Solzhenitsyn's sympathy, is practically irrelevant too. The saintly Alesha

21. Labedz, *op. cit.*, pp. 97–8.
22. Boris Pasternak, *Doctor Zhivago*, trans. Max Hayward and Manya Harari (London), 1958, p. 235.

in *One Day* has found his own peace of mind and earns the respect of Shukhov but it is Shukhov himself and the hardy Tiurin who, at this stage, come closer to Solzhenitsyn's own ideals. Even the righteous Matryona, whose virtues Solzhenitsyn expressly extols, pays only lip-service to religious practice: her real beliefs are as pagan as Shukhov's. Solzhenitsyn shows that the ethical forces at stake in his books—justice, truth and the powers of good and evil —are socially based. In 1967 he wrote a letter to three students which is of vital importance to an understanding of his ethical standpoint.[23] This, along with the ideas expressed by Shulubin in.*Cancer Ward*, is the fullest and most explicit exposition of the ethical convictions which motivate all Solzhenitsyn's writings. Like his literary manner, they are intrinsically Russian, deriving from deeply ingrained Russian literary and philosophical traditions.

The destinies of all Solzhenitsyn's characters are in their different ways subject to the interplay of good and evil, which are in turn the product of the presence or the absence of conscience and justice; conscience at a personal level and justice as the expression of the communal conscience. The all-pervading theme of Solzhenitsyn's work at every level is the quest for justice.

Together *One Day* and *Matryona's Home* provide a picture of goodness and truth at the mercy of evil and falsehood. In *One Day* the innocent are inexorably crushed by the evil of the camp regime, to which the icy grip of winter adds symbolic reinforcement. The story becomes a parable of everyday life in Russia. And it is also, as Max Hayward has suggested, 'a moving statement of universal application about the human lot ... It is symbolic of human existence as is Kafka's *Trial*. The day in the life of Ivan Denisovich is a day in *anybody's* life. The majority of the human race are trapped in a monotonous daily routine which differs from the concentration camp only in the *degree* of its unpleasantness and hopelessness.'[24]

23. Labedz, *op. cit.*, p. 101.
24. Max Hayward and Edward L. Crowley, *Soviet Literature in the Sixties* (London), 1965, p. 206.

3   Language and Style

Since the decline of the Formalist school in the 1920s Soviet literary criticism has paid little attention to style. Regarding literature first and foremost as a medium for transmitting ideas and moulding moral attitudes, official critics have always emphasised the primacy of content over form. In *The First Circle*, Solzhenitsyn writes that the teaching of literature in schools consists 'entirely of forcible instruction in the meaning of . . . writers' works, their political attitudes and the ways in which they responded to the pressure of the laws of the class struggle.' (p. 237) It is significant that in *For the Good of the Cause* the teacher of literature, arguing the need for style, talks about psychological depth. She doesn't understand the real meaning of the word.

In this atmosphere it is not surprising that in response to works as politically novel as *One Day* or as contentious as *Matryona's Home* or *For the Good of the Cause* the comments of Soviet critics were confined almost exclusively to the subject matter of the stories. The critics' awareness of Solzhenitsyn's stylistic importance was summed up in such general phrases as the 'writer gifted with a rare talent.' Only one short article devoted entirely to the style of *One Day* eventually appeared in the Soviet Union, some three years after it was published, when the short summer of official approval was already over.[1] In the West, where they were read mainly in translation, the critical approach to Solzhenitsyn's early works generally echoed the Soviet commentators'. And the same tendency has prevailed with the big novels, namely to regard them primarily as social and moral documents, albeit written with great power and authority. Russian-speaking critics abroad have drawn attention to the stylistic virtuosity of Solzhenitsyn's writing, but since their articles have appeared only in

1. T. G. Vinokur, 'O yazyke i stile povesti A. I. Solzhenitsyna "Odin den' Ivana Denisovicha"', *Voprosy kul'tury rechi*, no. 6 (Moscow), 1965, pp. 16–32.

emigré Russian language journals, the foreign reader is still very much in the dark. And there he must be content to remain, for Solzhenitsyn's unique style can be no more than hinted at in translation. It is a measure of his stature as a writer that, having had to leave behind so much, good translations can still claim attention as commanding literature.

So vital a part of his art, however, is Solzhenitsyn's style and his use of the Russian language, and so important is this aspect of his work for modern Russian literature as a whole, that even a study based on translations cannot omit to take some account of them. Moreover, some of the significant features of Solzhenitsyn's style can be described without its being essential to illustrate them from the original. Solzhenitsyn's approach to the use of language and style is consistent throughout most of his works and it is not feasible to attempt an analysis of all of them. But in many respects his first stories, *One Day* and *Matryona's Home*, are typical and a discussion based on these will serve as a guide to the language of everything else he has written.

One of the attractive features of Soviet writing in the 1920s, which was largely destroyed when socialist realism became mandatory after 1934, was the experimental and creative use of the Russian language. There were a few writers such as Sholokhov, Leonov, Platonov and Paustovsky who preserved their belief in language as an end in itself and continued to write vividly and expressively. But the majority, discouraged from verbal experiment, declined into cliché and rhetoric. As bureaucratic jargon proliferated in everyday communication, writers not only failed to combat it, but fell into the habit of imitating its sterile drabness. Their vocabulary became colourless and devoid of originality. It was against this background that Pasternak's rich poetic language would have made such an impact, if he had been able to publish *Doktor Zhivago* in the Soviet Union; indeed, it has since led many of the younger poets to claim him as their master.

The early 1960s saw an awakening of interest in the language of literature matched in several writers, notably Aksyonov and Kazakov, by genuine linguistic talent. The most original attempt to renew and enrich the Russian language, however, has been Solzhenitsyn's. While Aksyonov has enlivened the speech of his characters with foreign words and slangy expressions of modern

57

Soviet youth, Solzhenitsyn has sought to do virtually the opposite. The language of his stories is based upon the vocabulary, imagery, and rhythms of popular, predominently peasant speech, the wealth and freshness of which he shows is still far from exhausted. On this material he exercises his own astonishing verbal inventiveness.

In 1965 there appeared an article, the only one Solzhenitsyn has published, in which he analysed the shortcomings of the Russian literary language and offered a programme for reforming it. This piece is the key to Solzhenitsyn's own literary language, for he puts the programme vigorously into practice in his fictional works. It thus repays close examination.[2]

In the article Solzhenitsyn specifically links himself with the nineteenth-century lexicographer and fabulist Vladimir Dal.[3] B. V. Burkovsky recalls that when he was in the labour camps Solzhenitsyn 'would often be on his bunk reading a tattered copy of Dal's Dictionary and jotting down something in a large notebook.'[4] Nerzhin, the semi-autobiographical character in *The First Circle*, also had a copy of the Dictionary when he was in a labour camp. Solzhenitsyn now refers to two articles by Dal on language which he regrets have not been reprinted. He observes that since Peter the Great's time (early eighteenth century) the vocabulary, grammatical structure and above all the configuration (*sklad*) of the Russian written language have suffered through being used by an educated nobility thinking in French, through the caprices of translators and writers, who know the value only of ideas and time and not of words. Thus vocabulary has become emaciated because writers are too lazy to find suitable Russian words, are too shy of their coarseness or reject them for their inappropriateness to the nuances of modern thought. There are, Solzhenitsyn says, too many words adopted from foreign languages, some of which are quite unsuitable—'birdwords', as Sologdin, who deliberately avoids contaminating his speech with them, calls them in *The First Circle*. Solzhenitsyn also attacks the

2. A. I. Solzhenitsyn, 'Ne obychai degtem shchi belit', na to smetana', *Literaturnaya Gazeta*, 4 November 1965.

3. V. I. Dal (1801–72) was important for his *Dictionary of the Russian Language* (1861–8) which is still the best dictionary of popular spoken and dialect Russian.

4. *Izvestia*, 15 January 1964.

practice of deriving multi-syllable neuter nouns from verbs where the shorter more flexible masculine and feminine forms would be more expressive. And he draws attention to the wealth of prefixes which could be used, but which, except for a few set forms, would startle the modern reader. To illustrate the poverty of the modern Russian *sklad*, Solzhenitsyn points to the comparison between the phraseology of any contemporary literary documents and the special liveliness which echoes in a Russian proverb. Although the contemporary spoken language is less sterile than the written form, it too is declining in quality through the frequent repetition of a small number of words. 'This is an age,' Solzhenitsyn concludes, 'when the pace of life has quickened, but the vocabulary of conversational language used by society is a wedge, narrowing as time goes on. This is alarming. We must be able to reverse the wedge, put the narrow part the other way round, so that in future it will grow wider.' Solzhenitsyn then goes on to outline some of the ways in which this might be done. Oral speech 'gives us a not yet exhausted source for freshening and resurrecting our language . . . It seems to me that writers should be able to assist the written language to discharge a small debt to oral speech. By this I mean conscious broadening of vocabulary, the carefully thought out use (in author's speech) of those words which are *not* alive in the contemporary spoken language . . .' By way of illustration, he suggests fresh prefixes for verbs and the formation of new expressive forms of words. 'Do this—and no doubt the cry will be raised that this is word coining, the invention of some other new word. But in fact it is only a careful selection from the riches spread all around us, right beneath our feet . . . I believe that maybe the decisive decades have arrived when it is still within our power to correct the fault . . . to improve the *sklad* of our written authors' speech so as to return to it the lightness and freedom of conversational folk speech.'

Solzhenitsyn has emphasised that he was brought up on Russian literature. The influence of Tolstoy as both artist and thinker and certain affinities with the work of Dostoevsky, Turgenev and Chekhov have already been mentioned. None of the major realists, however, from Tolstoy to Bunin, managed to 'get beneath the skin' of simple people and part of the reason for this was that none of them attempted to cultivate popular speech.

Of Solzhenitsyn's earlier stories, on the other hand, it has been said that his most important achievement is that he has broken 'through a barrier as an interpreter of the popular mind'.[5] The authenticity and expressiveness with which he conveys the idiom of the common people, and particularly peasants, is one of the ways in which he has managed to do it. Solzhenitsyn owes his mastery partly, of course, to the eight years he spent in the company of ordinary Russians in the labour camps. He heard the speech of the common people all around him to an extent which no other Russian writer, not himself of peasant origin, has enjoyed. And by all accounts he put his opportunity to good use, making careful notes of what he heard and verifying it with Dal.

Dal however was not the only, or perhaps even the most important inspiration behind Solzhenitsyn's passionate enthusiasm for the untapped natural resources of the Russian language. Bukhanov[6] reports that among Solzhenitsyn's books in his house at Ryazan were four volumes of the works of Melnikov-Pechersky.[7] A Western critic, Roman Gul'[8] has suggested that Solzhenitsyn's writing can be linked with the ornamental prose of Alexei Remizov.[9] It is true that both writers were anxious to cleanse Russian of foreign bookish terms and restore to archaic forms their original freshness. Remizov would have heartily endorsed most of the points made in Solzhenitsyn's article. And Solzhenitsyn shares Remizov's love for 'the mystery and magic in the names of things', especially native Russian things. In *Matryona's Home*, for instance, the narrator delights in the names of the local villages, which wafted over him like a soothing breeze, holding promise of the true, legendary Russia. Like Remizov, Solzhenitsyn is sensitive to the sound of the Russian language. His prose is often rhythmical and he is particular about marking the stress on unfamiliar words, as was Remizov. But these similarities do not go far enough to sustain Gul's assigning of Solzhenitsyn to the Remizov 'school'. Solzhenitsyn's style is ornamental only in that

5. Max Hayward, *The Slavic Review*, vol. 23, no. 3 (Washington), 1963, p. 436.

6. *Literaturnaya Rossia*, 25 January 1963.

7. P. I. Melnikov-Pechersky (1819–83), an ethnographer and writer of novels describing the lives of old-believers and the remote parts of Russia.

8. R. Gul', 'Alexandr Solzhenitsyn) i shkola Remizova', *Novy Zhurnal*, no. 71 (New York), 1963, pp. 58–74.

9. A. M. Remizov (1877–1957).

he makes use of colourful vocabulary and turns of phrase from popular speech. But in his work these are alive and genuine and an essential part of his general design. Remizov's involved and artificial sentences were created for their own sake and recall Gogol, with whom Solzhenitsyn has little in common.

It is unlikely that Solzhenitsyn was influenced either consciously or unconsciously by Remizov. He may never have read him. The comparison is of value in that it helps to illuminate Solzhenitsyn's approach, but not as an attempt to categorise it. The same may be said of the comparison Zavalishin[10] has drawn between Solzhenitsyn and the critic and prose writer Sergei Leshenkov (Klychkov).[11] As Zavalishin points out, Leshenkov made a distinction between the ornamental prose of such as Remizov and Zamyatin and that of the later ornamentalists like himself and Artem Vesely:

> This latter trend, according to Leshenkov, was characterised by greater naturalness, a closer link with folklore, with the colloquial language of the people and its vivid use of images and the like. The idea of cultivating words and expressions, as it were, in a hothouse, of artificially rearing unexpected figures of speech as though they were orchids, was, according to Leshenkov, alien to the latter trend as it was characteristic of the former . . .

Klychkov (Leshenkov) entered the literary arena at a time when the folk element in this speech had not yet exhausted its traditional resources, while Solzhenitsyn wrote his story at a stage where these traditional forms of Russian folklore were already becoming degenerate. Nevertheless, he was able to show that their complete extinction is still far away in the future— Ivan Denisovich is a peasant and mixes mostly with peasants, but in the camp there are also officers, soldiers and criminals. Moreover the world they live in is cut off from the outside world. It is

10. V. Zavalishin, 'Solzhenitsyn, Dostoevsky and Leshenkov-Klychkov', *Bulletin of the Institute for the Study of the USSR*, no. 10, 1963, pp. 40–8.

11. S. A. Leshenkov (1889–?) wrote under the pseudonym of Sergei Klychkov.

not surprising therefore, if the language they speak has grown wild, so to speak, and primitive; what is noteworthy is that it has managed to preserve its traditional expressiveness, its power of inventing new words and images, and its popular humour—now become macabre.[12]

Whether or not, as Zavalishin suggests, Solzhenitsyn has deliberately 'applied Leshenkov's methods of polishing popular words and phrases to newer forms of Russian and colloquial speech', there can be no doubt that both writers were partaking of the same literary tradition which leads back to Dal and, what is even more important, to Leskov. Solzhenitsyn's links with Leskov are both specific and vital to his art.[13]

It was Leskov who in his fables raised the linguistic ideas of the ethnographical writers Melnikov-Pechersky and Dal to the level of high art. His writing abounds in such devices as dialect and slang expressions, aphorisms, proverbs, ellipsis and the use of unusual prefixes, and so does much of Solzhenitsyn's. Leskov's language is so unusual in Russian nineteenth-century literature that it attains a kind of autonomy as such. This cannot be said of Solzhenitsyn's. Solzhenitsyn is a virtuoso linguist and a genuine innovator. But he is first and foremost a literary artist for whom language is a means of communication. In his article he speaks of the need for innovation always to be accompanied by taste. It is a mark of his own taste that the style of his writing harmonises perfectly with the incidents and characters it is required to portray.

Many of Solzhenitsyn's dialectisms can be found in Dal's Dictionary, where he either found them or verified them. They are not confined to any particular region of central Russia, but it is noticeable that a high proportion are listed by Dal under the area around Ryazan where he wrote his earlier stories. Other dialect words taken from Dal are used by Solzhenitsyn with certain variations, which could be the result of his own creative imagination, or are otherwise forms he himself heard. Many words of dialectal colouring are not to be found in Dal at all and it is impossible to be sure where they came from. It can be said with some certainty however, that, unlike Remizov, Solzhenitsyn

12. Zavalishin, *op. cit.*, pp. 44–5.
13. N. S. Leskov (1831–95).

does not invent words. The unusual forms he brings out are either archaisms, regionalisms, words of a specific milieu or words which he has adapted in some way. The last numerous category includes the employment of unexpected prefixes and suffixes on nouns, adjectives and particularly verbs. The result of all this creativeness is that expressiveness and warmth are supplied to the language, and so sure is Solzhenitsyn's feeling for Russian that it is nearly always successful, although native critics have pointed to instances where the result is not completely felicitous. Among those who have expressed reservations, Roman Gul' has drawn attention to many unsuccessful word forms in *August 1914*, including the use of words of recent origin which could not have been heard in the Russia of 1914.[14]

A further device which Solzhenitsyn inherits from Leskov is folk etymology, foreign or technical words misused by ordinary people. But the most striking feature of Solzhenitsyn's style, which can occasionally be caught by a good translation, is the use of aphoristic expressions, often with a proverbial ring about them. Solzhenitsyn speaks of the importance of Russian proverbs through the lips of Nerzhin in *The First Circle*: 'Russian proverbs were always down-to-earth and direct; they meant what they said with no high moral overtones. In its vast treasury of proverbs the Russian people has always been much franker about itself than even Tolstoy or Dostoevsky had ever been.' (p. 577)

Some of Solzhenitsyn's proverbial expressions are taken straight from Dal. But others he has adapted. Thus in *One Day* there are two similar proverbial expressions: 'How can you expect a man who is warm to understand a man who is cold' (p. 30), and 'A man who is warm can't understand a man who is freezing' (p. 129), while Dal has 'A satisfied man can't understand one who is hungry'. Similarly Dal has slightly different versions of Ivan Denisovich's remark 'folk say God crumbles up the old moon into stars' (p. 126), and of the saying 'you've only to show a whip to a beaten dog.' (p. 71) The lore of the camps generated a new treasury of aphoristic sayings based in local conditions. Many of these depend for their crispness on rhyme and are consequently untranslatable, but others can be approximately conveyed. For

14. R. Gul', 'Chitaya avgust chetyrnadtsatogo', *Novy Zhurnal*, no. 104, 1971, p. 68.

example: 'Work was a stick. It had two ends. When you worked for the knowing you gave them quality; when you worked for a fool you gave him eyewash' (pp. 20-1) and 'as for the Russians, they'd forgotten which hand to cross themselves with.' (p. 22) In *The Love-girl and the Innocent* Khomich refers to campland as the country where ninety-nine men weep while one laughs and in *Cancer Ward* the saying is repeated by Kostoglotov. At the Union of Writers meeting in 1967 one of Solzhenitsyn's critics wondered whether the phrase 'twenty-nine (sic!) weep and one laughs' was meant to refer to the Soviet Union as a whole. To this Solzhenitsyn replied: 'twenty-nine weep and one laughs' was a popular camp saying addressed to the type of person who would try to go to the head of the queue. Kostoglotov comes out with this saying only so that he may be recognised, that's all.'[15]

The flavour of the Russian folktale is strong in these early stories of Solzhenitsyn's, as the following examples from *One Day* show: 'Stitch, stitch, stitch and the little tear in the mattress was mended, with the thread concealed beneath it' (p. 33); 'wonder of wonders! How time flew when you were working.' (p. 75) There are many comparable examples in *Matryona's Home*—'Here, both before and for some time after the Revolution had stood a thick impenetrable forest.' (p. 196)—and even the teacher of literature in *For the Good of the Cause* uses archaic incantatory language when she tells the students, 'a book stands as a record of our contemporaries, ourselves and our great achievements!' (p. 247) Passages of *Zakhar Kalita* recall the ancient Russian heroic songs: '. . . look around and behold—as the sun rises Telebei and Peresvet are joined in single combat. Like sheaves of wheat they lean upon one another. The Mongolian horsemen release their arrows and brandish their spears and with contorted faces they hurl themselves upon the Russian infantry. Trampling the Russians beneath their hooves they burst through the line and drive them back the way they came, to where a milky cloud hangs above the Nepriadva and the Don.' (p. 293) Similarly, in *Lake Segden* Solzhenitsyn writes of a secret lake in a secret forest.

Solzhenitsyn makes only sparing use of conventional figures of poetry such as metaphor and simile in any of his works. In his similes there is no attempt to create the unexpected effects by

15. Labedz, *op. cit.*, p. 98.

means of striking comparisons which often shock the readers of Babel's stories. Solzhenitsyn's similes are simply apt and reinforce an effect which is already present. Thus in *One Day*, for example: 'they all rushed out in a crowd, tumbling down from the bunks as if they were bears ...' (p. 177); 'men sitting shoulder to shoulder like seeds in a sunflower' (p. 157); 'men surrounded (the stove) as if it was a saucy wench' (p. 81); '(Tiurin's) skin was as tough as the bark of a tree' (p. 54); 'The air was as thick as in a bath-house.' (p. 21) From time to time Solzhenitsyn creates a memorable phrase, for example his description of the local Party secretary in *The First Circle*: 'He is a genie out of an ink-well with the soul of a printed form.' (p. 453)

One Day is packed with detailed information about the camp and description of life in it. But this does not, as might perhaps be expected, slow down the tempo of the story. Nor does the rhythm become monotonous. Maximum detail is combined with a lively pace of narration by means of the common elements of conversational speech—broken phrases, a wealth of emotionally coloured interrogatory and exclamatory figures, expressive parenthetical words and phrases, ellipses and unusual word order. Whenever events are viewed through the eyes of Shukhov this conversational style prevails. Two short passages will suffice to illustrate the point:

> The thoughts of a prisoner—they're not free either. They keep returning to the same things. A single idea keeps stirring. Would they feel that piece of bread in the mattress? Would he have any luck at the sick-bay that evening? Would they put Buinovsky in the cells? And how did Tsezar get his hands on that warm vest? He'd probably greased a palm or two in the store for people's private belongings. How else? (pp. 47–8)

and:

> Even from the two letters a year they write you don't get to know much. The Kolkhoz had a new chairman—they had a new one every year. They'd joined up some of the Kolkhozes—they'd done that before as well, but

they'd split them again later. And what else? Some
people weren't fulfilling their work-day norms and the
kitchen gardens had been cut down to fifteen hundred
square metres, some right back to the cottage walls.
(p. 49)

In Solzhenitsyn's vocabulary in *One Day* it is possible to distinguish several lexical categories. The basic language of the
narration from the author is contemporary literary Russian,
although at first sight it may seem to be otherwise. When the
author, as distinct from Shukhov, comments on the action the
language is almost purely literary Russian. For example, Captain
Buinovsky sitting in the canteen at lunch time:

> He had long finished his kasha. He didn't know the
> team had two extra portions to dispose of. He didn't
> look about to see how much Pavlo still had left to
> hand out. He was simply relaxing, warming up. He
> was not strong enough to rise to his feet and go out
> into the cold or into that frigid warming up point. He,
> like the very people he had just hounded out of the
> canteen with his rasping voice, was occupying a place
> he had no right to and getting in the way of the next
> team. He was a newcomer. He was unused to the hard
> life of the *zeks*. Though he didn't know it, moments
> like this were particularly important to him, for they
> were transforming him from an eager, confident naval
> officer with a ringing voice into an inert, though wary,
> *zek*. And only in that inertness lay the chance of
> surviving the twenty-five years of imprisonment he'd
> been sentenced to. (pp. 91–2)

This impression of Buinovsky comes straight from the author and
is rendered in literary prose with none of the characteristics of
Shukhov's conversational style. There are several such passages in
One Day where the subject is the intelligentsia, who are outside
Shukhov's limited range of comprehension. But even Shukhov's
own speech is not purely peasant dialect. It is basically standard
colloquial Russian with a liberal, but measured sprinkling of

vocabulary from the different social regions in which he has found himself. Apart from dialect and common speech, there is in *One Day* a limited quantity of archaic and Old Church Slavonic vocabulary, modern slang and swear words and, most interestingly, vocabulary deriving from the specific milieu of the labour camps.[16] Camp language is found, of course, in all Solzhenitsyn's works where the characters are either prisoners or ex-prisoners.

Over a period of twenty years during which the hard-labour prisoners constituted a significant proportion of the Soviet population, there grew up a special camp language. Some of the vocabulary and expressions originated in an even earlier era, from the Tsarist prisons, and much of it was later infused into ordinary Russian slang by prisoners, released at last after Stalin's death. Solzhenitsyn knew the language intimately and a veritable glossary can be compiled from his works. Solzhenitsyn's camp slang consists of new words, ordinary words with new meanings, special prefixes and suffixes, and camp sayings. One particular category consists of neologisms derived from abbreviations. Hence 'GULAG' meaning the camps in general is formed from the Russian G.U. Lag. (Main administration of camps), and 'BUR' refers to the strict regime barracks. From these basic words new nouns and adjectives are formed, such as 'burovets' (noun), an inmate of such a barracks. To this type of newly coined word belongs '*zek*' or '*Z/K*', the abbreviation of the Russian for an internee.

The overall narrative strategy on which *One Day*, and to a much lesser degree *Matryona's Home*, are based is a continuation of the same traditions which inspired Solzhenitsyn's approach to language. In Russian it is called *skaz* and again the acknowledged master is Leskov. Elements of *skaz* were already evident in Gogol's stories of the 1830s, but it was Dal and after him Leskov who developed the technique to the greatest extent in connection with ethnographical material in the following decades. Remizov was among those who brought it back into vogue in the early twentieth century and it enjoyed great popularity in the 1920s, being employed by such writers as Pilnyak, Zamyatin and Babel. At the same time critics of the Formalist school ascribed great importance to *skaz* in tracing the evolution of Russian literature.

16. See E. Shilyaev, 'Lagerny yazyk po proizvedeniam A. I. Solzhenitsyna, *Novy Zhurnal*, no. 95, 1969, pp. 232–47.

The *skaz* manner of narration was derived by Dal from the folktale and it employs the speech habits and point of view of a fictionalised narrator other than the author for part or all of the story. Usually a *skaz* narrator comes from a milieu low on the social scale, such as that of a peasant or a military man, or in the tales of Zoshchenko in the 1920s, of a Soviet petty-bourgeois figure. In Gogol's *Evenings on a Farm near Dikanka* (1831-2) the narrator, Rudi Panko, stands between the author and the stories he introduces, while in Zoshchenko's tales the narrator is himself the protagonist. The value of the *skaz* technique is that it endows the narration with an eye-witness quality and introduces the effect of an oral commentary, often humorous or sardonic. There is thus usually a strong flavour of oral speech using the phonetic, grammatical and lexical patterns natural to the narrator personally. Leskov's narrator uses dialect and provincial terms, popular etymology, folk-songs and puns. The narration in *One Day* is also based upon these devices with the added ingredient of camp slang. Zoshchenko's narrator, as befits his social environment, uses Soviet jargon and slangy substandard expressions.

The re-emergence of the short story and the novelette as the principal literary prose forms in the Soviet Union in the second half of the 1950s and the 1960s was also accompanied by a revival of *skaz*. In the first place, it offered a means of revitalising the turgid prose of the Stalin Prize novel. But the presence of a fictional narrator was perhaps also seen as a device for putting some distance between the author and his subject and so enabling him to adapt a more flexible attitude towards it. When in 1967 Valisii Aksyonov remarked that 'indirect–direct discourse, a deliberate blending of the author's speech with the speech of the hero, is one of the characteristic peculiarities of contemporary prose',[17] he could have added that the outstanding example of the technique is *One Day*.

In *One Day* there are two narrative voices—the author's and Shukhov's. But there is no clear syntactical or lexical dividing line between them. Just as Shukhov's language is not exclusively dialect and jargon, so the author's is seldom purely literary. The

17. V. Aksyonov, 'Literatura i yazyk', *Voprosy Literatury*, no. 6, 1967, p. 89, quoted by Deming Brown in *Contemporary European Novelists*, ed. Siegfried Mandel (Southern Illinois), 1968, p. 27.

voices interchange so imperceptibly that the reader is often uncertain which is speaking. Apart from the dialogues, the story
sometimes gives the impression of simply being an extended
interior monologue from Shukhov. A careful analysis is required
to reveal that this is not so.

Solzhenitsyn's infrequent interventions as omniscient author in
order to present people and happenings beyond Shukhov's range
have been referred to above. The author also takes up the narration from time to time in order to show the intelligentsia without
the good humoured and slightly condescending smile with which
Shukhov regards them. The entire impression of the sick-bay, for
instance, is relayed through Shukhov's thoughts except for two
paragraphs when the author steps in to speak about the orderly
Vdovushkin:

> Vdovushkin went on with his writing. He was, indeed,
> doing some work 'on the side', but it was something
> beyond Shukhov's ken. He was making a fair copy of
> a long new poem that he'd finished the previous
> evening and had promised to show that day to Stepan
> Grigorych, the doctor who advocated work therapy.
> (pp. 29–30)

The second paragraph is a typical comment by Solzhenitsyn
on camp life in general:

> As can only happen in the camps, Stepan Grigorych
> had advised Vdovushkin to describe himself as a medical
> assistant, and had taken him on at the infirmary and
> taught him how to make intravenous injections on
> ignorant prisoners, to whose innocent minds it could
> never occur that Vdovushkin wasn't a medical assistant
> at all. Vdovushkin had been a university student of
> literature, arrested while still in his second year. The
> doctor wanted him to write when in prison what he'd
> been given no opportunity to write in freedom. (p. 30)

In these paragraphs there are no popular speech elements or
emotional colouring. When the intelligentsia are shown through

Shukhov's eyes, there is not only mild humour, but also an effect of alienation (*ostranenie*). Shukhov's view of the conversations of educated men presents them in a new and unexpected light. All the comments on the following conversation are Shukhov's own:

> A queer fellow with glasses was standing in the queue, his head buried in a newspaper. Tsezar at once made for him:
> 'Aha, Pyotr Mikhailych'.
> They blossomed like a couple of poppies. The queer fellow said: 'Look what I've got! A fresh *Vechorka*. They sent it by airmail.'
> 'Really,' said Tsezar, sticking his nose into the newspaper. How on earth could they make out such tiny print in the glimmer of that miserable lamp?
> 'There's a most fascinating review of a Zavadsky première.' Those Muscovites can smell one another at a distance, like dogs: they sniff and sniff when they meet, in a way of their own. They jabber so fast too, each trying to out-talk the other. When they're jabbering away like that you hear practically no Russian: they might as well be talking Latvian or Rumanian. (pp. 150–1)

Unlike most of Zoshchenko's stories which are told in the first person, the narration of *One Day* is basically third person, even when the point of view is Shukhov's. But the prose is full of exclamations, comments, reflections and remarks in Shukhov's manner, and often there is a shift into the second person as if he was addressing the reader directly. In the following passage there are two commentators on the action. The first sentence and the second short paragraph are from the author alone, but the remainder is Shukhov addressing the reader.

> The coals were gradually glowing red-hot and throwing out a steady heat. But you felt it only when you were near them—everywhere else the shop was as cold as ever.

They took off their mittens. All four men held their
hands up to the stove.

But you never put your feet near the flame if you're
wearing boots. You have to remember that. If they're
leather boots the leather cracks, and if they're valenki
the felt gets sodden and starts to steam and you don't
feel any warmer. And if you hold them still nearer the
flame then you scorch them, and you'll have to trail
along 'till the spring with a hole in your boot—getting
another pair can't be counted on. (p. 77)

On another occasion a conversation of which Shukhov is only
a witness is reported by him and not by the author. In the original
Russian the commentary and dialogue is too saturated with
dialectisms for it to be mistaken for the author:

Shukhov went on working—working and listening.
'What d'you think you're doing?' *Der spluttered.*
(italics mine—C.M.) 'This isn't a matter of the
lock-up. This is a criminal offence, Tiurin. You'll get
a third term for this . . .'
*Ugh! What a mug Tiurin pulled. He flung down that trowel
of his and took a pace towards Der. Der looked round. Pavlo
lifted his spade . . . Der blinked, gave a sort of twitch, and
looked round for a way of escape. Tiurin leaned up against
him and said quite softly, though distinctly enough for
everyone to hear.*
'Your time for giving terms has passed, you rat. If
you say a word, you blood-sucker, this is your last day
on earth. Remember that!
Tiurin shook, shook uncontrollably. (pp. 113–14)

A very frequent arrangement in *One Day* is for the author to set
a new scene and for Shukhov to take over to describe what is
happening there:

The air was as thick as a bath-house. An icy wave
blew in through the door and met the steam rising
from the skilly. The teams sat at tables or crowded the
aisles in between, waiting for places to be freed. Shouting

> to each other through the crush, two or three men
> from each team carried bowls of skilly and porridge on
> wooden trays and tried to find room for them on the
> tables. Look at that bloody stiff-backed fool. He
> doesn't hear, he's jolted a tray. Splash, splash! You've
> a hand free, swipe him on the back of the neck. That's
> the way. Don't stand there blocking the aisle, looking
> for something to filch. (p. 21)

Here, up to 'tables' the scene is described in almost pure author's neutral literary language. Then there is a sharp change-over to Shukhov's speech, full of popular oral devices. Shukhov addresses first the reader then his fellow prisoners.

Rzhevsky[18] even distinguishes the presence of a third narrator, an unknown personage, although obviously a fellow prisoner, who stands beside Shukhov and supplies the third person descriptions of him. Thus in the following passage the first two sentences as far as 'zone' could have come from either the author or the unknown narrator since they contain varied speech elements, but the remainder clearly switches to Shukhov's own confiding oral speech style:

> The sky was still quite dark. The camp lights drove
> away the stars. The broad beams of the two search
> lights were still sweeping the zone. When this camp,
> this 'special' camp, had been organized, the security
> forces had a lot of flares left over from the war, and
> whenever there was a power failure they shot up flares
> over the zone—white, green and red—just like real
> war. Later they stopped using them. To save money,
> maybe. (pp. 24–5)

In another instance, however, the quality of the language indicates that it is the unknown narrator alone speaking up to 'they'd given him', before Shukhov takes over again:

18. L. Rzhevsky, 'Obraz rasskazchika v povesti Solzhenitsyna "Odin den' Ivana Denisovicha"' in *Studies in Slavic Linguistics and Poetics in Honor of Boris O. Unbegaun* (New York and London), 1968, pp. 165–78. Several of Rzhevsky's examples have been quoted. See also L. Rzhevsky, 'Tvorcheskoe slovo u Solzhenitsyna', *Novy Zhurnal*, no. 96, 1969, pp. 76–90.

> Then Shukhov removed his hat from his clean-shaven
> head—however cold it might be, he could never bring
> himself to eat with his hat on—and stirred the cold
> skilly, taking a quick look to see what kind of helping
> they'd given him. The average one. They hadn't
> ladled it from the bottom either. Fetiukov was the sort
> who when he was looking after someone else's bowl
> took the potatoes from it. (p. 23)

In moments of special intensity, or when Shukhov has a strong experience of fellow feeling with the other *zeks*, he openly takes over as narrator, using the first person 'we':

> Now there was not a soul in sight. Only the six sentries
> on their watch-towers were visible—and some people
> bustling round the office. That moment belonged to *us*.
> (italics mine—C.M.) The senior works-superintendent,
> it was said, had long been threatening to save time by
> giving the teams their work-rosters the evening before,
> but for all his efforts they never got round to it . . .
> So that moment still belonged to *us*. While the
> authorities were sorting things out *you* stuck to the
> warmest place *you* could find. Sit down, take a rest,
> *you'll* have time enough to sweat blood. (p. 56)

While he is using the first person Shukhov is speaking to the reader, but in the last three sentences he switches back to advising his fellow prisoners. After a brief passage of description from the author Shukhov takes over again in the first person on behalf of his team.

> The 38th, naturally, wouldn't let any stranger near
> their stove. Their own men sat round it, drying their
> footcloths. Never mind, *we'll* sit here in the corner,
> it's not so bad. (p. 57)

At the end of the day the *zeks* become absorbed in the race back to the camp and Shukhov again identifies himself with the common cause:

> When the rear of the column spilled over a rise
> Shukhov saw: to the right, far away across the steppe,
> another dark column on the move was marching
> diagonally across *our* course. They, too, seemed to be
> forcing their pace . . .

> It was easier for *us* now, we were running down the
> middle of the street. And the escort had less to stumble
> over at the sides. This was where *we* ought to gain
> ground. (pp. 137–8)

One Day is the most sustained and skilfully constructed example of the *skaz* technique in modern Russian literature. Solzhenitsyn makes use of the *skaz* in some of his other works. In *Matryona's Home* for instance, although the story is recounted in the first person by an educated man, his narration frequently lapses into the speech patterns of Matryona herself. While Shukhov is a modern peasant and speaks with the accents of the camps, Matryona's speech, as befits her character, abounds in archaisms, in the language of the folktale and even in church slavonicisms.

Recapitulating his ideas for the reform of the Russian literary language, Solzhenitsyn concluded his article in *Literaturnaya Gazeta* with a quotation from Dal. Dal demanded 'that all must help to make everything bad good, longwinded brief, diffuse direct, obscure clear, vulgar (*poshloe*) expressive and flabby strong'. This quotation is also an appropriate summary of the contribution which Solzhenitsyn's stories and novels have already made towards the forging of a new Russian prose.

4   Stories and Plays

In addition to *One Day* and *Matryona's Home*, Solzhenitsyn's two finest shorter works, several other stories have become available in the West, and two plays. Of these, three, the stories *For the Good of the Cause*, *An Incident at Krechetovka Station* and *Zakhar Kalita* (also translated as *Zakhar the Pouch*) were published in the Soviet Union. Two other short stories, *The Right Hand* and *The Easter Procession*, and sixteen poems in prose, some only half a page in length, have only been published abroad. One of the plays, *The Love-Girl and the Innocent*, was rehearsed in Moscow before being banned. The other, *A Candle in the Wind*, was never submitted for staging by Solzhenitsyn. A third play, *The Feast of the Victors*, written in 1949, which he repudiated at the meeting at the Union of Writers in 1967, has not been published. All these, with the three major novels and *The Gulag Archipelago*, which began to appear in the West in 1973, constitute Solzhenitsyn's literary output to date.

Since 1966 he has abandoned writing fiction in smaller genres and has devoted himself wholly to novels. His stories and plays were composed during the 1950s and early 1960s.

Like *One Day* and *Matryona's Home*, it is possible to consider *An Incident at Krechetovka Station* (hereafter referred to as *Krechetovka Station*) and *For the Good of the Cause* as a pair. While the first two describe the lives of Russian peasants, the second pair is about more-educated Russians, although not really, as some critics have stated, about the intelligentsia. For the setting of *Krechetovka Station* Solzhenitsyn goes back to Autumn 1941, to the Soviet Union at the beginning of the war. The story is not directly auto-biographical, but it is the only story to come from Solzhenitsyn's four years of active service and is unusual in Soviet war literature. Soviet authors were required to dwell on the heroism of the soldiers and the spirit of endurance and self-sacrifice of the

75

people. These qualities *are* present in some of Solzhenitsyn's characters also, in Lieut. Zotov and the long suffering little escort Corporal Dygin. But in *Krechetovka Station* there are also glimpses of other less edifying aspects of wartime behaviour. There are people at the station prepared to profiteer at the expense of the evacuees. The storekeeper considers his own comfort before the convenience of the fighting men he is supposed to serve. Many of those working around Zotov are more concerned with their own daily cares than the fortunes of the war.

> They listened to the reports as gloomily as he did and walked away from the loudspeakers in silence with the same feeling of pain. But Zotov could see a difference: those living around him had something else to live for than the news from the front—they lifted potatoes, milked their cows, cut firewood and sealed up their window-frames. These were the things they talked about and they cared much more about them than about what was happening at the front.
> Stupid woman. She's got her coal—and now 'there's nothing to fear'. Not even Guderian's tanks? (p. 141)

One aspect of the war in the East never openly referred to in the Soviet Union even today, which arouses vehement indignation in Solzhenitsyn, is the treatment accorded to returning Soviet P.O.W.s and those who managed to break out of encirclement. He never lets pass an opportunity to publicise what Stalin permitted to happen to them. The trainloads of returnees who pass through Krechetovka are among the thousands of former soldiers who were sentenced to long prison terms for espionage and were still in the camps ten years later. Ivan Denisovich was one of them. Solzhenitsyn takes up the subject of the injustices practised on these men in *The First Circle*, and in *The Gulag Archipelago*.

Krechetovka Station describes three or four hours in the life of Lieut. Zotov, the deputy station commander at Krechetovka, a railway junction not far behind the front line. Even here beyond the range of the guns an acute sense of discomfort and oppression is created by the slanting, soaking rain and the mud. Zotov's time is occupied with a succession of routine events until the minor incident which gives rise to the title. The kernel of Solzhenitsyn's war story is a sensitive character study of Lieut. Zotov. The narrative follows one line of development with flashbacks only to fill in the background and not to broaden the range as in *One Day* and the novels.

Because of his short-sightedness Zotov is declared unfit for active service and has to suffer the shame of watching all his friends depart for the front, while he is assigned to an unheroic but important post in the rear. To make up for this he tries to do his job with the utmost efficiency. Solzhenitsyn portrays Zotov as a dedicated young communist whose mind has been totally conditioned to show 'correct' attitudes and to think the 'correct' thoughts. Unlike other soldiers, he does not hide the fact that he is married and will take no liberties with the women with whom he has to live and work, in spite of their undisguised blandishments. In his spare time he is studying *Das Kapital* for it was 'Vasya's (Zotov's) belief that when he had mastered even this first volume and had memorised it in its noble entirety he would be invincible, invulnerable, irrefutable in any ideological argument.' (p. 157) It might seem that with these attributes Zotov is nothing more than the conventional stereotype in socialist realist literature of a positive hero. But from the outset Solzhenitsyn hints at another side to Zotov's character which gradually unfolds as the story progresses. His severe look is only a façade which his glasses give to his gentle features. Brought up to believe unquestioningly in Stalin's pre-war propaganda he is unnerved by the course the fighting seems to be taking. 'Why,' he asks himself, 'was the war going like this? Not only was there no revolution all over Europe, not only were we not advancing virtually without losses and against any combination of aggressors, but instead there was this muddle—and for how long would it go on?' (p. 139) He is scarcely able to admit such thoughts even to himself: 'It was blasphemy, it was an insult to the omnipotent, omniscient Father and Teacher, who was always in the right place, who could foresee everything, would take all the necessary measures and prevent it from happening.' (p. 139) But he is less and less able to ignore the evidence of his eyes and ears. The rumours of panic in Moscow, the confused news reports, the tramloads of returnees persuade him that all is not as it should be. Zotov, becomes so miserable that all he wants to do is to howl out loud.

Zotov is a member, like Volodin and Ruska Doronin in *The First Circle* of the same generation of Russian youth which according to Solzhenitsyn, 'had been taught to believe that "pity" and "kindness" were concepts to be despised or derided, that the word conscience was only part of the cant used by priests.' (p. 261)

Zotov, however, has managed to preserve his sense of decency and honesty. For him conscience is not simply mindless adherence to sterile social principles, as it is for the communist bureaucrat Rusanov in *Cancer Ward*, but is a token of genuine humanity. He adopts, for instance, a tolerant attitude to the trading which goes on at the station. 'This trade greatly embarrassed Lieut. Zotov ... but it could not be forbidden because no goods had been released for the evacuees.' (p. 137)

The conflict between Zotov's inherent kindliness and genuine anxiety to help everyone and the strict requirements of his duty is brought into focus when there suddenly enters his office a person of unusual appearance. The man, a gentle educated actor from the Moscow Dramatic Theatre, has volunteered for service, been sent to the front and, along with the rest of his unit, managed to break out of encirclement. Rounded up again, this time by his own side, he has become separated from the train taking them to the rear and applies to Zotov for assistance. Tveritinov, as the actor is called, has no papers and as Zotov questions him the two fall into conversation. For Zotov this is a rare opportunity to meet an intelligent and cultured man, and their conversation shows up the limitations to Zotov's own horizons. His enthusiasm for Gorky as 'the wisest, most human, the greatest writer we have' only meets with silence from the actor. They also display contrasting attitudes to the year 1937, the height of Stalin's great purge. For Zotov it was the year of the Spanish Civil War, and he fails to grasp Tveritinov's hint that to him it meant something entirely different. Kostoglotov in *Cancer Ward* also has difficulty in convincing the doctors and nurses about the labour camps and his life as an exile, which are new and incomprehensible to them.

The question of who knew what was really behind the purges in the 1930s was the centre of a serious controversy in the Soviet Union when *Krechetovka Station* was published in January 1963.

Khrushchev maintained in his 'secret' speech at the Twentieth Congress of the Party in 1956 that not one of the rest of the Soviet leadership knew at the time that most of the purge victims were entirely innocent. Ilya Ehrenburg hinted in his memoirs that this was not so, that many people realised that the purges were illegal and that Stalin himself was responsible for them. In February 1963 Ehrenburg was attacked in the press for these insinuations and Khrushchev himself joined in the argument.[1] Solzhenitsyn echoes Ehrenburg's view. People such as Zotov, to whom until now it never occurred to question the official version of events, no doubt *were* unaware of what was happening. But the independent heroes of Solzhenitsyn's big novels, Nerzhin and Kostoglotov, guessed the truth when they were teenage boys, as did Solzhenitsyn himself. By his readiness to discuss such a delicate and dangerous topic as 1937 with an unknown army officer, Tveritinov is displaying a *naivéty* which, had Zotov been able to grasp it, would have allayed his suspicion when Tveritinov makes his fatal mistake over the former name of Stalingrad.

But Tveritinov's hesitation instantly switches Zotov's mind back into the channel of official duty from which it has been distracted by Tveritinov's cultured manner and their interesting conversation. The actor's other peculiarities click into place—his lack of papers, his asking for a map and his travelling alone. Zotov believes that he must be a spy, a Russian emigré who has infiltrated the returning Soviet soldiers. Zotov has no doubt about the man's guilt or his duty to hand him over to the security police, although he knows what that will mean. But the humane side of his nature is ashamed that he too is practising a deception. As Tveritinov is detained by the sentry, 'Zotov could not stop himself looking back once more, for the last time in his life—to catch a glimpse of that face by the dim light of the lantern, the despairing face of Lear bound for the grave.' (p. 192)

Tveritinov remains on Zotov's conscience; twice he attempts to find out what happened to him, but gives up when he sees that he is attracting suspicion himself. But for the rest of his life Zotov could not forget that man.

Lieut. Zotov is one of Solzhenitsyn's most sympathetically

1. See C. Moody (ed.), *Ilya Ehrenburg. Selections from People, Years, Life* (Oxford), 1972, pp. xxii–xxiv.

drawn characters. In spite of his acceptance of the conventional Stalinist assumptions about life, he also possesses human qualities which Solzhenitsyn admires. The conclusion of the story is, however, ambiguous. As an army officer in charge of a sensitive sector of the war, Zotov was right to be suspicious of odd-looking strangers without papers. In this particular case his suspiciousness has nothing to do with the atmosphere of distrust which was normal in Stalinist society. To Zotov the evidence is conclusive. It is not his fault that his narrow upbringing and limited knowledge of human beings prevents him from sharing the reader's belief that Tveritinov is innocent. Later, when he has had time to reflect, his regret at having had to hand over such an attractive character mingles with a suggestion of doubt about his guilt. He cannot entirely allay his conscience with the thought that it is all part of the inevitable inhumanity of war. If anyone is to blame for the tragedy it is, after all, the system which condemns both the innocent and the guilty. Like Shchevronok, who is arrested with Volodin in *The First Circle*, once Tveritinov has fallen into the hands of the security police 'the mistake can never be put right.'

Published in the same number of *Novy Mir* as *Matryona's Home*, *Krechetovka Station* was overshadowed by both the political implications and the literary merits of the former and attracted attention neither in the Soviet Union nor abroad. But *For the Good of the Cause*, published some six months later, although much less important artistically than any of the three stories discussed so far, immediately caused a lively debate in the Soviet press. Solzhenitsyn takes as his subject the characters and conduct of Party officials.

Set in a provincial town, allegedly Ryazan, *For the Good of the Cause* is the only one of Solzhenitsyn's stories, apart from the short piece *The Easter Procession*, which describes contemporary happenings, that is to say of the 1960s. It is also unusual for Solzhenitsyn in that the situation is a normal everyday one and that there are no allusions to the labour camps or exile. The story is simple and centres on a technical college, the students of which have volunteered to speed up the building of their new premises by doing most of the work themselves. When the decision is suddenly handed down from above that the freshly completed building is to be used for a new scientific research institute instead, the principal of the college does his best to have the decision reversed, without success. The students must be satisfied that all their labours are 'for the good of the cause.'

This is an overtly political story. It is an undisguised attack on the undemocratic manner in which decisions are taken by the all-powerful central bureaucracy without reference to the opinions or interests of the people, whose lives are involved. It also reveals that the motives of those entrusted with authority are not always consistent with the philosophy they profess. The story was perfectly in accord with the policy of democratising public institutions which Khrushchev was putting forward at the time it was written. Although composed with an artistry which lifts it into the category of significant literature, *For the Good of the Cause* is for all that a political polemic and was treated as such by the Soviet press.

In his letter of protest at being expelled from the Union of Writers in 1969 Solzhenitsyn complained: 'Were we not promised fifty years ago that never again would there be any secret diplomacy, secret talks, secret and incomprehensible appointments and transfers, that the masses would be informed of all matters and discuss them openly?'[2] This is the political point he is making in *For the Good of the Cause*. No attempt is made to explain to the college director, let alone to the students who have done the work, why the new building must be converted into a research institute. The decision to hand it over was taken by the regional Party secretary, to oppose whom the political system gives to those beneath him no effective power. The machinery of consultation need not be and has not been used. The portrait of Knorozov, the regional Party secretary, is a failure because Solzhenitsyn does not endow him with a human character. He is conceived simply as a political symbol:

> Even sitting behind his desk Knorozov was an imposing figure. His long head made him seem very tall. Although he was far from young, his lack of hair did not age him. On the contrary it made him look younger. He did not make a single superfluous movement and even the skin on his face did not move unnecessarily. For

2. Labedz, *op. cit.*, pp. 160–1.

this reason his expression seemed to be permanently
fixed and didn't show the tiniest hint of emotion.
Were a smile to spread across his face, its balance
would have been disturbed and its perfection destroyed.

Knorozov took pride in the fact that having once
given his word he never retracted it. Just like Stalin
at an earlier time in Moscow, so Knorozov now in
this region never changed or went back on what he
had said. And although Stalin was long since dead,
Knorozov lived on. (pp. 281–2)

Knorozov is Solzhenitsyn's contribution to the 'heirs of Stalin'
debate in the Soviet Union.

Knorozov's vices go beyond his manipulation of arbitrary and
unbridled power. He is also corrupt. His inflexible rationalisations
of his actions are a camouflage for predatory self-interest. He is
one of the hierarchy of little Stalins ruling his own fiefdom as his
master had once ruled the country. As he explains to his sub-
ordinate Grachikov who has come to plead the college director's
case:

'Do I have to tell you how to fight for the honour of the
town? In our town there is not and never has been a
scientific research institute. And it wasn't so easy for our
people to get one. We must take our chance, before the
Ministry changes its mind. If we get it we'll automatically
rise into a different class of town—on the scale of Gorky
and Sverdlovsk.'

He frowned. Either he could already see his town transformed
into Sverdlovsk, or he was inwardly measuring himself up for
some new higher position. (p. 282)

Grachikov, who once before stood up to superior authority
when 'right had come face to face with wrong,' voices Solzhenitsyn's own argument against Knorozov:

'In the last resort, what is more important to us—stones
or people? Why are we bothering with these stones? . . .
We can't build communism with stones, but with people,
Victor Vavilovich," he shouted excitedly. "It's harder
and will take longer, but if we finish building tomorrow
out of stones it certainly won't be communism.' (p. 283)

Neither Grachikov nor Fyodov Mikheyich, the director, who is in awe of Knorozov, can make any impression upon him. But their anger and despair is redoubled when it is discovered that the director of the nearby factory, who should have been collaborating with Fyodor Mikheyich, has in fact been conspiring with Knorozov and will probably head the new institute. The title of the story becomes ironical. The exploitation of the students' goodwill is not for the good of any cause save the personal gratification of the local Party personages. Solzhenitsyn ends the story, which has all the characteristics of a classical socialist realist plot, in a totally unconventional manner. As in Dudintsev's *Not by Bread Alone* (1956) the Drozdovs, the corrupt authorities, are permitted to triumph. The little man, in the case of Fyodov Mikheyich with uncertain Party affiliation, loses. Justice succumbs to injustice, humanity is defeated by politics. The question of the justification of the means by the ends and the individual's right to be considered is treated in profounder, non-political terms in *Cancer Ward*.

In *For the Good of the Cause* Solzhenitsyn demonstrates another facet of the theme of work. In Stalin's time and later, those who had avoided the labour camps were urged to undertake extra voluntary labour under the slogan 'Enthusiasm'. That there was immense genuine enthusiasm for socialist construction and after the war reconstruction is beyond question. But by the beginning of the 1960s 'enthusiasm' had lost some of its magic. When Lydia Georgievna explains to the new teacher how the new college was built by the students in their free time, he comments in reply: ' "Probably enthusiasm is a natural human quality and is one of the best. But the word has become worn out and hackneyed in our country. It's used too loosely even on the radio." ' (p. 236) He has learned from experience in the factory that more recognisable motives dominate the thinking of the workers. ' "At the factory I usually hear: What am I going to get out of it? What's the rate? Fill in an overtime claim. Not that it's surprising—it's just a question of material incentives. It's quite normal." ' (p. 236) Lydia Georgievna herself finds it amazing that no one had to be coerced to build the college. The college is the only instance in Solzhenitsyn's work of a genuine Soviet collective based not upon coercion and fear, but on mutual trust. The tone is set by the leadership of Fyodor Mikheyich:

> A moderate, unambitious man, his idea of a leader was
> not an arbitrary or capricious figure, but one who
> coordinated the efforts of people who trusted each
> other and worked for a common cause. (p. 252)

Furthermore the college is the only labour undertaking Solzhenitsyn describes which produces results. Far from encouraging
the students and rewarding their enthusiasm the regime cheats
them: Grachikov argues with Knorozov:

> 'Victor Vavilovich.' He was no longer speaking
> normally, but pronounced his words more sharply than
> he intended. 'We are not mediaeval barons vying with
> each other over our coats of arms. The honour of
> our town lies in the fact that these young people erected
> this building themselves and enjoyed doing it and it is
> our responsibility to help them. But if we take the
> building away from them they will remember for the
> rest of their lives that we have deceived them. And if
> they've been deceived once, they'll know that they
> can be deceived again.' (p. 283)

In keeping with the polemic design of *For the Good of the Cause*,
Solzhenitsyn employs the standard socialist realist device of
distinguishing very clearly between the good and the bad characters. In the first few pages he generates a strong feeling of sympathy for the college students and teachers. Throughout the story
he makes liberal use of dialogue. This is a device to which
Solzhenitsyn resorts from time to time with good effect. *Krechetovka Station* begins with two pages of pure dialogue without
explanation or comment. There are entire chapters in this form in
The First Circle. The whole of the first section of *For the Good of the
Cause* is straight dialogue and Solzhenitsyn thereby creates an
atmosphere of liveliness, spontaneity and mutual affection among
the students and staff. The principal himself, despite his modest
ability and personality, is devoted to his job and the interests of
all under him. He served and suffered, together with Grachikov,
the only official who tries to help him, in the army. Solzhenitsyn
always reserves special sympathy and respect for those of his

generation who like himself proved their mettle at the front, and barely disguises his contempt for those who did not. He develops the theme most fully in the character of Shchagov in *The First Circle*. Fyodov Mikheyich dresses in a plain, slightly worn suit and makes his appearance swaying about in the battered college jeep. His welcome betrays the affection in which he is held by the college.

The arrival of the bureaucrats and the commission of inspection creates a very different impression: 'The cars drew up at the entrance and five men wearing hats stepped out of them: two in stiff green felt hats as was the custom among the local leadership and the rest in light-coloured ones.' (p. 253) The leader Khabalygin is grossly overweight and his every action is 'a struggle with his vast form, the unsightly flabbiness of which was concealed by his skilful tailors'. Among those with him is the comrade from the Ministry who allows Fyodor Mikheyich to 'hold the tips of three of his soft white fingers for a brief moment' and a young man fashionably dressed down to the last detail. Obviously none of these has seen the front line. Solzhenitsyn even uses a device which he employs rarely, in spite of the efforts of some critics to demonstrate the contrary, to characterise the villains in *For the Good of the Cause*. Both Khabalygin and Knorozov have names which reflect their natures. Khabalygin means 'coarse' or 'crude', while a knoros is a kind of ox in Russian.[3]

Lydia Georgievna's conversation with groups of students in the street, which develops into a debate about literature, is fully in harmony with the general picture of life in the college. The students possess a self-confidence and readiness to express their own irreverent opinions which contrast significantly with the demoralised girl students in *The First Circle*. The difference between the two generations is an eloquent indication of the changes which had taken place between 1949, the height of Stalin's last purges, and 1962. Solzhenitsyn is also creating an opportunity to publicise opinions about literature which are certainly his own. The condition of Soviet literature in the 1940s and 1950s is an aspect of Stalinism which attracts his particular indignation and contempt and to which he constantly returns in his fictional works as well as his polemic letters. The target of

3. P. Pletnyov, *A. I. Selzhenitsyn* (Munich), 1970, p. 30.

Solzhenitsyn's scorn is the Soviet literary 'establishment' which he regards as bureaucratic and hypocritical. He has no time for socialist realism. His own works contradict most of its central dogmas and his literary minded characters ridicule its stock situations. He has summed up Soviet literature as 'cosmetics'. He doesn't mention writers by name in this story, the censor would not have permitted it. But he exercises no such restraint in his novels. Writers of whom he speaks disparagingly on more than one occasion include A. Tolstoy, Panferov, Babaevsky, Gribachev and even Gorky. Ehrenburg is mentioned as a writer, whom orthodox communists like Rusanov and Zotov cherish. But the independent Sologdin in *The First Circle* uses Ehrenburg's volumes to prop the window open.

In *For the Good of the Cause* the students draw attention to the piles of books, by writers highly praised in the newspapers, which are only sent back to be pulped. They express their disapproval of the current vogue of memoirs (another swipe at Ehrenburg) and of the excessively long novels which seem to be printed only for the benefit of the critics:

> ... What do they write in the *Literary Gazette*? 'The images are conventional, the composition is formless, but what lofty ideas!' It's just like telling us, 'there's no current, the mechanism won't work, but how well the condensers have been selected!' Why don't they say: 'This novel ought to be ten times shorter'? Then people wouldn't get bogged down trying to read it.' (p. 246)

Solzhenitsyn's assessment of modern Russian literature is very close to the widely prevailing view of it in the West. With reference to his own work he would probably endorse Lydia Georgievna's statement that a book should be 'a record of our contemporaries, of ourselves, and our great achievements'—but he would add 'and of our failures'.

Solzhenitsyn's short prose works contain in embryo ideas which receive fuller treatment in the big novels. *The Right Hand*, which was written in 1964, is in a sense a preliminary sketch for the second part of *Cancer Ward*, where Kostoglotov is recovering from cancer. The novel was only commenced some two years later. *The Right Hand* is told in the first person by Solzhenitsyn himself, but virtually everything about the narrator and his ideas applies equally to Kostoglotov. The story provides another reason for regarding Kostoglotov as in all essential characteristics an autobiographical figure. The new patient and the assistance which the narrator gives him are reminiscent also of Shulubin in the novel.

In *The Right Hand* Solzhenitsyn makes a point which he often makes elsewhere—about the callousness of the (hospital) system in which regulations are put above the humane interests of the individual, about the lack of recognition accorded to those who, by their lights, have served society. As a short story, *The Right Hand* is a sensitive glimpse of life from an unexpected angle. In the context of Solzhenitsyn's work as a whole, it is reduced to insignificance by *Cancer Ward*.

Solzhenitsyn's two remaining stories, *Zakhar Kalita* and *The Easter Procession*, and the sixteen small poems in prose, may be considered in conjunction since all are thematically connected and form a part of the same artistic conception. The first to be written were the prose poems. Most of them were composed and jotted down during the 1950s and the set was finally put together in about 1962 without, so far as is known, Solzhenitsyn's making any attempt to publish them at home. None more than about four hundred and fifty words in length and the majority much less, these little compositions contain in emblematic form random thoughts which Solzhenitsyn develops later. In *The Old Bucket*, for instance, he recalls the friendship of the war years. *The Bonfire and the Ants* symbolises, perhaps, the Russian soldiers cut off by the enemy.

Solzhenitsyn wonders in *The City on the Neva* whether the sufferings of his generation will nevertheless produce something as lastingly beautiful as did the thousands who died in the swamps to build St. Petersburg. In *We will never Die*, he poses a question which he raises at several levels in *Cancer Ward*—fear of death and respect for the dead. In *Cancer Ward* Vadim complains of the neglect of Russian cemeteries: Why, he asks, do people not look after graves? Is it part of the Russian national character? And he is obliged to admit that it is a new phenomenon, that it never used to be so. At the end of this little story Solzhenitsyn reminds his readers that all nations dedicate one day to remembering those who gave their lives for their country. More men died for Russia than for any other country, yet she has no day of remembrance.

As works of art the poems in prose are of small importance, although some of them such as *Lake Segden* have the haunting fabulous quality which is found in passages of *Zakhar Kalita*. There is also a suggestion of the influence of the Soviet nature writer Prishvin. *Zakhar Kalita*, the story of a bicycle trip which Solzhenitsyn made to the battlefield of Kulikovo where the Russians defeated the Tartars in 1380, and the description of *The Easter Procession*, were written in 1965 and 1966 respectively. Nearly all these stories have in common a quality present in *Matryona's Home*, namely Solzhenitsyn's nostalgic love for the Russian countryside and the traces of old Russia which, romantically, he discovers there. The behaviour of the villagers in *In Yesenin Country* (the Ryazan district) is no better than in *Matryona's Home*, their main concerns are still the crops, how to make money, how to keep up with the neighbours. Yet Solzhenitsyn seems to believe in a pristine innocence and purity lingering in the countryside which modern materialist life has destroyed in the cities. The embodiment of this old Russian spirit in his stories is, curiously, the Church.

It was noted in the last chapter that Solzhenitsyn is not a religious writer. Only one of his earlier characters, the Baptist Alesha in *One Day*, is a believer and a practising Christian. The saintly Matryona pays only lip service to the Church. Neither Nerzhin nor Kostoglotov, men who embody Solzhenitsyn's own quest for the purpose of life, find themselves drawn towards formal religious belief. And a religious believer is conspicuously absent among the patients faced with the problems of life and death in *Cancer Ward*. It is true, as he makes clear in the latter novel, that his basic philosophy does stem, at any rate partly, from religious influences. His rejection of materialism and politics in favour of a society founded on ethical premises such as Shulubin advocates in *Cancer Ward* was inspired by the Russian religious thinker Vladimir Solovyov. But Solzhenitsyn does not stress the specifically religious aspect of Solovyov's thought. The nearest he comes to a religious interpretation of human life is the kind of vague eternalism with which Dr. Oreshchenkov sustains himself in *Cancer Ward*: after the death of his wife he came to realise that the purpose of life is as far as possible to keep alive and untarnished the image of eternity with which every individual is born.

In recent years, however, after having written most of his stories and novels excepting *August 1914*, Solzhenitsyn has turned more and more towards the Russian Orthodox Church. He was baptised in childhood and in spite of moving away from the Church, he seems to have preserved a vivid impression of his early religious observance. He had his own child baptised and in 1971 received his first communion. It is now possible to describe Solzhenitsyn as a deeply religious man and a moving prayer which he has written has become available in the West:

> How easy it is for me to live with you, Lord!
> How easy for me to believe in you.
> When my spirit is lost, perplexed and cast down,
> When the sharpest can see no further than the night,
> And know not what on the morrow they must do
> You give me a sure certainty
> That you exist, that you are watching over me
> And will not permit the ways of righteousness to be
>   closed to me.
> Here on the summit of earthly glory I look back
>   astonished
> On the road which through depths of despair has led
>   me here
> To this point from which I can also reflect to men
>   your radiance
> And all that I can still reflect—you shall grant to me.
> And what I shall fail you shall grant to others.

He is here ascribing a religious purpose to his writing.

In March 1972 Solzhenitsyn spoke out directly for the first time about his religion and his profound concern for the condition of the Russian Orthodox Church. He addressed an open Lenten letter to Pimen, Patriarch of all Russia. In his Christmas message in 1971 Pimen said that it was the duty of Russian parents living abroad to bring up their children with a love for the Church, but he made no mention of any similar obligation upon Russians living in his own country. Solzhenitsyn responded sharply to this omission:

> Why do you address this honest appeal only to Russian emigrés? Why do you appeal only for those children to be brought up in the Christian faith? Why is it only the distant flock that you warn to be 'discerning of slander and falsehood' and to gird itself with righteousness and truth? What about us—are we to be discerning? What about our children—should we inspire in them a love of the Church or not?[4]

He goes on to attack restrictions placed by the state on religious worship:

> We are robbing our children when we deprive them of something which they can never experience again—the pure angelic perception of worship which as adults they can never recapture nor even realise what they have missed . . . We have to hand over our defenceless children, not into neutral hands, but into the domain of atheist propaganda of the most primitive and dishonest kind.

And he expresses his anxiety for the future of Russia where such circumstances prevail:

> In the final analysis the fate of our country, in the true and profound sense, depends on whether the idea of the RIGHTNESS OF FORCE becomes finally embedded in the national consciousness, or whether it will be purged of obscurantism and will shine forth once again with the FORCE OF RIGHTEOUSNESS . . . Shall we succeed in reviving in ourselves, at length some elements of the Christian faith, or are we going to lose the very last of them and abandon ourselves to

4. *The Sunday Telegraph* (London), 9 April 1972. Trans. Michael Bordeaux.

considerations of self-preservation and personal gain . . .

We have lost the radiant ethical atmosphere of
Christianity in which for a millennium our morals
were grounded; we have forfeited our way of life, our
outlook on the world, our folklore, even the very name
by which the Russian peasant was known. We are
losing the last features and marks of a Christian
people . . .

In the light of this last passage it seems that now Solzhenitsyn
would give his Slavophile love for the traditional Russian way of
life a religious connotation which is not apparent from the texts
of the stories themselves.

There is one point in Solzhenitsyn's Lenten letter which does
repeat in almost precisely the same terms a passage from his
literary work, in *The First Circle*. In the novel Yakonov's girl friend
of twenty years ago argues vehemently against the manner in
which the Church is persecuted:

'What makes you think the Church is being persecuted?'
Yakonov protested. 'Nobody stops them ringing their
bells, baking their Communion bread, holding their
Easter processions—as long as they keep out of civic
affairs and education.'

'Of course they're persecuted,' Agnya protested, in
her usual low voice. 'If people are allowed to say and
write what they like about the Church, without it
being able to answer back, if Church valuables are
confiscated and priests banished—isn't that persecution?'

'Have you seen any priests being banished?'

'That's not the sort of thing you see in the street.'

(p. 130)

Solzhenitsyn repeats all of this in his letter. But he also reproaches
the Church itself for the spineless way in which it has submitted,
not only under the Soviet regime but throughout its history, to
the demands of the state:

'A study of Russian history over the last few centuries
convinces one that it would have followed an incomparably

more humane and harmonious course if the church had
not renounced its independence and the people had
listened to its voice . . . In order to preserve its existence
the church has abandoned its spiritual function, its rights
and its property to the dictatorial rule of atheists. The
impression is created that 'for the bishops of the Russian
Church earthly power is more important than heavenly
power . . . their temporal responsibilities are more awesome
to them than their responsibility before God'.

In *The First Circle* Yakonov asks the unworldly Agnya whether
it has ever occurred to her how the Russian Church managed to
survive 240 years under the Tartar Yoke? And he tells her:

> The church survived because, after the Tartar invasion
> the Metropolitan Cyril was the first Russian to go and
> pay homage to the Tartar Khans and beg guarantees
> for the safety of the clergy. So it was Tartar armed
> force that the Russian clergy used to protect their
> lands, their serfs and their ritual. (p. 130)

In several of his stories Solzhenitsyn invokes the image of the
Tartar Yoke to symbolise Stalin's atheistic tyranny. And the role
of the Patriarch Pimen is no more glorious than the behaviour
of the Metropolitan Cyril.

The old churches scattered through his stories are also symbolic. They embody for Solzhenitsyn the dying spirituality of the
Russian people which he values and appeals for in his letter. In
The Journey along the Oka he writes that the angelus echoing from
village to village used to serve as a reminder that earthly cares are
ephemeral and to call men to give up an hour to thoughts of
things eternal. It was into the building of their churches that the
ancient Russians put the best they had to offer—all their knowledge and their faith. In his letter Solzhenitsyn complains: 'we
do not dare even to raise the question of the ringing of church
bells—yet why has Russia been deprived of its ancient adorn-
ment, its finest voice?'

In *The First Circle* Agnya tells Yakanov of the impression
churches make upon her:

'How well the Russians chose the places to build their churches and monasteries! ... I remember when I went down the Volga and Oka, it was just the same there—they were always built in the most superb places.' (p. 129)

Solzhenitsyn takes up the same theme again in his prose poem *A Journey Along the Oka*. This is a poem to the immemorial tranquillity of the Russian countryside. The sensation of calmness which the traveller experiences on the roads of central Russia springs from the churches. Their carved belfries tower above the wooden huts and everyday life and greet each other in sonorous tones. The traveller is never alone but is constantly beckoned by some Borki Lovetskie, Lyubichi or Gavrilovskoe. From the author of *The First Circle* such lyricism and nostalgia for Old Russia is perhaps unexpected. But it is an expression of something essentially Russian in Solzhenitsyn himself and a vital part of his art. It is a source of great pain to him that so many of the Russian churches, such as the one at Kulik in the prose poem *Ashes of the Poet* or the church which Yakanov visits in Moscow are neglected and in ruins. In *A Journey along the Oka* he regrets that so many of the churches have been desecrated, used for other purposes, or simply locked up.

With the destruction of these churches something vital in the Russian people has been destroyed by the materialist order. Solzhenitsyn returned to the theme again in his Lenten letter:

Is there a sight more heart-rending than these skeletons now taken over by the birds or the store-keepers? ... The northern regions of our country, the age-old repository of the Russian spirit where possibly the future of Russia most truly lies, is now completely without churches.

Originally the Orthodox Church was pillaged and suppressed by the Tartars who returned after the Battle of Kulikovo, but even they did not persecute it as the communists are now doing. In *The Easter Procession* the marchers are even more intimidated than in the days of Tartar rule; at least the Tartars did not

93

interfere with the faithful at the Easter morning service. Nor did Khan Bahty destroy the monastery of the Assumption described in *The Ashes of a Poet*. But under Stalin it was transformed into a prison. The modern heathens who destroy the churches and persecute the people who use them are for Solzhenitsyn a new visitation from the 'Tartar hordes' who are over-running Russia. The final words of *Zakhar Kalita* that the Russians would be foolish to neglect this place are intended as a timely warning that invasions do not always come from the West. In *The Easter Procession* he shows the hordes in action. He contrasts the pure bright faces of the young girls in the procession with the arrogant hooligans who come to watch and mock the ancestral rites of the Church.

Again he concludes his story with words which sum up the portentous meaning of this for Russia. What can she expect from her rising generation? The truth is that they will destroy everything worthwhile, nor will those who have encouraged them be spared.

Solzhenitsyn's picture of the Easter Procession, suggested by Ilya Repin's famous genre painting on the same theme, is a frightening image, not only of modern Soviet youth, but of the prospects for humanity as a whole.

The young people who molest the procession with their immature moronic expressions of totally unfounded self confidence are the generation brought up in the amoral climate of Stalinism. They are encouraged in the same mentality as is apparent in the drunken knife-wielding peasants of *Matryona's Home*. The cynicism of the fourth-year students in *For the Good of the Cause*, compared with the trusting idealism of the younger ones, is another facet of this problem. Disenchanted by experiences such as the betrayal over the institute, they lose their enthusiasm and confidence in their 'cause' and degenerate into the idle hooligans of *The Easter Procession*.

The Easter Procession itself is a symbolic re-enactment of the Passion of Christ—the pathetic little procession, with the worshippers too intimidated to participate and the church warden terrified that he will be set upon and beaten up by those very people who claim to be building the new society. It is interesting that here Solzhenitsyn uses the same Christian imagery as did Pasternak to convey an essentially similar message in *Doktor Zhivago*. The message is valid today as it was at the time of the Revolution and 2,000 years ago. It is as true of the Soviet Union as of amoral materialist cultures anywhere else.

The first of Solzhenitsyn's two published plays *The Love-girl and the Innocent*, sometimes translated as *The Tenderfoot and the Tramp*, was also the first of his published works to be written. He wrote it in exile in 1954, the year following his release from prison. The play was accepted by the *Sovremennik Theatre* in Moscow at the end of 1962, immediately after the success of *One Day*, and it was rehearsed with the author's advice during the early months of 1963. Changes in the political climate, however, prevented the production from reaching the stage and it remains unperformed in the Soviet Union. The première finally took place in the Sir Tyrone Guthrie Theatre, Minneapolis in 1970 and received favourable reviews from the American critics.

Solzhenitsyn regards *The Love-girl and the Innocent* as the best of his earlier works. If he is including *One Day* and *Matryona's Home* in this assessment it is difficult to agree with him. The setting is similar to that of *One Day*, one of Stalin's labour camps in 1945 just after the war has ended. The camp is a mixed one with women prisoners and warders working together with the men. The action occupies a period of a few weeks and covers several facets of camp life. The main character is an ex-army officer, Nemov, just in from the front, who has been sentenced for the usual 'crime' of the time—anti-Soviet activities. But neither he, nor his relationship with the female prisoner Lyuba which gives the play its title, dominate it. There is in fact little dramatic development and Solzhenitsyn's aim seems to have been to give a powerful overall picture of camp life. This an elaborate production would probably succeed in doing, but it would be a considerable theatrical undertaking. The named cast numbers nearly sixty and at least another dozen extras are needed. Solzhenitsyn is meticulous in his description of the sets which amount virtually to a realistic reconstruction of the camp itself with separate scenes depicting different areas.

Solzhenitsyn is anxious to achieve the maximum possible audience participation. The stage is dominated by camp watch towers continuously manned throughout the play. At the end of each act the sentries are changed and the guard party crosses the auditorium. Solzhenitsyn's instructions are that if members of the audience get in their way, the officer must shout at them rudely and order them back from the wire. In the production on which the Sovremennik Theatre was working, presumably with the author's agreement, it was intended that after the first act the audience would not be permitted to leave the auditorium. An armed guard would stand by each door pointing a rifle at the audience. The effect of this device would be to assist the spectators to identify with the prisoners on the stage. It might also serve as a reminder of the captive society in which they live—hemmed in by force and with the ever-present threat of the labour camps behind them.

Solzhenitsyn uses a subsidiary curtain to provide a graphic illustration of one of the dominant themes of his writings—the absurd discrepancy between the Stalinist dictatorship's propaganda image of itself and the reality behind the façade. The big curtain is raised at the beginning of the play and is not used again until the end. Behind it there is a second curtain which is brought down to hide the scene at the end of each act. This second curtain represents a poster depicting the typical figures of industrial propaganda—cheerful men and women working happily and easily. There is also a procession of children bearing flowers and the ritual portrait of Stalin.

In *The First Circle* Solzhenitsyn develops this idea in the brilliantly satirical story of Mrs. Eleanor Roosevelt's visit to a Soviet special prison (Chap. 54). And he restates it symbolically as the conclusion to the novel, when Nerzhin and his fellow prisoners are being transferred back to the labour camps:

> ... the gaily painted orange and blue truck drove on through the streets ... There, halted by a red traffic light, stood the dark-red car belonging to the Moscow correspondent of the Paris newspaper *Liberation*, on his way to a hockey match at the Dynamo Stadium. On the side of the van the correspondent read the words:
>
> МЯСО, VIANDE, FLEISCH, MEAT.
>
> He remembered having seen several trucks like this

today in various parts of Moscow. Taking out his
notebook he wrote with his dark-red fountain-pen:

'Now and again on the streets of Moscow you meet
food and delivery vans, clean, well designed and
hygienic. One must admit that the city's food supplies
are admirably well organised.' (p. 581)

Solzhenitsyn uses one of Chekhov's favourite structural devices
for introducing movement into an otherwise static situation. The
play begins with the arrival of a new transport and ends with
the departure of one. In all four of Chekhov's major plays at the
beginning new characters are just arriving on the scene of a big
house, and the plays end as they leave. Turgenev's novels are
built on the same idea and Solzhenitsyn uses it himself again in
The First Circle, where transports arrive and depart, and in *Cancer
Ward* in which Rusanov is admitted on the first page and Kostoglotov goes out into the world at the end.

The ex-officer Rodion Nemov has also just arrived. The central
conflict in the play is between his still uncorrupted humanity and
idealism and the savage law of the camps to which he must submit if he is to survive. Nemov is a combination of Capt. Buinovsky
and Vasya Zotov. He is humane, feels sorry for everyone, but
preserves his officer's bearing. He tries to increase productivity
in the camp by means of genuine improvements. He is scrupu-
lously honest, refusing to take or offer bribes or steal from the
other prisoners. Nemov is motivated in fact by his conscience,
which he elevates even above life itself. He is asking the big
question posed by their lives for Nerzhin and Kostoglotov as well
—is there a degree of moral surrender which is too high a price
to pay for life?

Contrasted with the gentle intellectual Nemov is the practical
Khomich, an engineer who has been sentenced for thieving and
who arrives on the transport. Khomich is a typical camp professional—a man who knows how to fix things so that he doesn't
have to do a single day's general duties. He outbids Nemov
for his job as work allocator by invoking the very principles on
which camp life is based—forced labour and lust for booty.
Nemov achieves an increase in productivity of 8 per cent simply
by being fair. Khomich promises an increase of 60 per cent by

introducing draconian regulations and he gets the job. He won't get the results, but he knows that promises and an appeal to the instincts of his superiors by means of bribery will ensure his survival.

By comparison with *One Day, The Love-girl and the Innocent* is an immature work. It possesses several features the absence of which in *One Day* marked the stature of Solzhenitsyn as an artist. Although the horrors of camp life are again not accentuated, and this is not the worst type of labour camp, some of the prisoners, the 'goners', have fallen lower than any of Shukhov's fellow prisoners. Nemov is an intellectual, who tries to rationalise his own and the general situation. He voices for instance Solzhenitsyn's anger at the favour shown to the criminal prisoners as against the treatment meted out to innocent politicals. He himself spent four years fighting the fascists, but as soon as he was captured he became an enemy. In contrast, the deserters and those who led a criminal life in the rear are regarded by Stalin as social allies.

Most significant of all, however, is the difference between the quality of life in the two camps. In *One Day*, for all the critics' complaints, Solzhenitsyn shows the positive side of the prisoners —their stoicism, humanity and even comradeship. In this camp he shows the full consequences of the regime's attempts to destroy everything decent in people. Adapting to every bestiality perpetrated upon them, the prisoners are divided, by a cynic's count, into two groups, professionals and whores. Each uses his talents to help himself, whoever else may suffer. Romantic love is sullied, for Nemov can only keep Lyuba if he is prepared to share her. Far from bringing out the best in the people, the camp brings out the worst. Shurochka wonders why people in the camps become horrible? Were they any different outside? Or did they just keep out of sight? And Granya complains that she's seen so much cruelty and meanness in the camps that she could never rest content, even if she were freed. *The Love-girl and the Innocent* is the other side of the medal, which Solzhenitsyn chose not to reveal in *One Day*. *One Day* would have been a lesser work of art and would not have been published if he had.

The Love-girl and the Innocent is not a good play. There is some dramatic tension in the earlier scenes when Nemov is still prepared to struggle. But when he loses his job and feels relief at being an ordinary prisoner, the tension goes slack. Nemov can only spell out meanings which he can no longer act out. The critic of the *New York Times* wrote of the American production:

> The evening, painting a picture of gradual but inevitable disintegration, is built horizontally rather than vertically. No upward thrust is at work to give it a spine; it must therefore catch its prizes randomly, in bits and pieces, wandering the outskirts of the endlessly labouring group to overhear snatches of night time conversation, fragments of life histories dropped into the common pool.[5]

Solzhenitsyn wrote his second published play *A Candle in the Wind* in 1960 and later both the Vakhtangov and Komsomol theatres in Moscow wanted to produce it, but neither was able to do so. Solzhenitsyn described the purpose of his play:

> I wanted to write a play that had nothing to do with politics or the larger problems. The action of the play takes place in an unknown country, the time is not precisely defined, and all the characters are given international names. My purpose was not to camouflage. I was interested in the moral problems of highly civilised societies, whether capitalist or socialist.[6]

The setting of *A Candle in the Wind* is a university town somewhere by the sea. The time is towards the end of the twentieth century in a country which bears some resemblance to the Soviet Union, but also has features of the Western democracies. There is no list of *dramatis personae*. The action mainly involves the personnel of the science faculty of the university.

In *A Candle in the Wind* Solzhenitsyn purports to deal with very modern problems, but in fact he is resurrecting an idea which had a brief popularity in Russia in the 1920s. The play has an anti-utopian theme reminiscent of Zamyatin's novel *We*, the model for Orwell's *1984*, and Olesha's *Envy*. The resemblance in situation to *Envy*, which was also made into a play, is quite strong. Like Philippe, with his technique for controlling human emotions,

5. *New York Times*, 25 October 1970, pp. 1 and 22.
6. Labedz, *op. cit..* p. 7.

Ivan Babichev, one of the protagonists of *Envy*, imagines an Institute of Emotions and a machine which will be able to implant psychological characteristics into the patient on demand. There is some similarity between Alda and Valya, the two girls who are to be subjected to personality change, while aunt Christine and Olesha's Anechka both live in squalor and keep a large number of cats. The basic idea behind the two works is the same, the threat posed to human individuality and feelings by the onset of the age of machines.

A Candle in the Wind is a thesis play and presents in almost abstract form the moral ideas which Solzhenitsyn develops in human terms in his novels. As he admitted himself, it is not a particularly good play,[7] but it is of interest for what his characters have to say on the matters which exercise the heroes of his novels. The main character, Aleks, is the autobiographical figure. He has just returned after spending eighteen years successively in the army, the labour camps and exile in a mud hut on the edge of the desert. There, like Solzhenitsyn, he taught mathematics and astronomy. He has now been rehabilitated. Aleks is tormented by the questions about the quality of life which later preoccupy Nerzhin and Kostoglotov.

The play contains several of Solzhenitsyn's seemingly obsessive ideas—that life in prison had its value, even its blessings; that affluence deprives people of the faculty for appreciating food; that a man without material possessions has nothing to lose; that those who served throughout the war and suffered in the camps have acquired a moral superiority. The central idea, however, is the question posed in *Cancer Ward* by Tolstoy's book *What Men live by*. It leads to a conflict between the scientist Philippe, who expresses the values of technological society, and Aleks, also a scientist, who voices Solzhenitsyn's doubts.

Philippe maintains that science is the spirit of the twentieth century which has brought all its material wealth. It is their duty to hand on the torch of science to the twenty-first century. Even in exile, while teaching science in school, Aleks has been worried by the question *zachem*—Why? How, he asked himself, does one prepare people to oppose the heartlessness and calculation awaiting them in life? And he asks Philippe why people want wealth

7. *Ibid.*, p. 8.

anyway. It doesn't seem to improve a man. He wonders whether people will remember the cost in spiritual and intellectual terms of the material blessings they are so anxious to attain. The general whom Philippe hopes will provide a military subsidy for their research has already discovered how computers have replaced human leaders in the army and navy. Aleks envisages the day when scientists will be able to read human thoughts and the uses to which this facility will be put by corrupt oppressors. Such a vision is foreshadowed in *The First Circle*, where the prisoners invent devices of oppression for Stalin.

Significantly, Philippe, who proclaims pure science, has within himself the seeds of its perversion. He is a cynical materialist who enjoys the ducats which his science brings and readily submits to his own selfish interests.

The experiment, which Philippe and his team carry out on Alda, helps to convince Aleks that he can no longer participate in their kind of science. The scientists have devised a method of identifying and controlling biocurrents which are the media of all human sensations and actions. They use their technique to transform Alda, who is highly-strung and unstable, into a self-confident, unemotional character who is none the less only half a person. Eventually Aleks rebels. He accuses Philippe of taking a marvel of nature and turning it into a stone. This is precisely what Grachikov accuses Knorozov of doing to the students. Aleks decides to devote himself to defending the spiritual side of man against the encroachments of materialism and science.

The candle of the play's title symbolises the human spirit. When Alda's father dies, aunt Christine (perhaps the name is significant) appears and reads verses from the Bible:

> No one lights a lamp and puts it in a cellar, but rather on the lamp-stand so that those who enter may see the light ... see to it then that the light that is in you is not darkness. [Luke 11 : 33, 35 (N.E.B.)]

And she adds two more verses:

> Man, you have plenty of good things laid by, enough for many years: take life easily, drink, and enjoy

> yourself. But God said to him, 'you fool, this very
> night you must surrender your life; you have made
> your money—who will get it now?' [Luke 12:19–20
> (N.E.B.)]

These last two verses are the basis of the story from Tolstoy's
What Men live by which makes such an impression on Podduyev in
Cancer Ward. Like Podduyev, Aleks is also groping towards what
men live by. He doesn't discover the answer, but he finds himself
drawn towards the social scientist Terbolm, whom the others
despise and who gets no subsidies from anyone.

Aleks perceives the contrast between Philippe's idea of biocybernetics which he regards as an unwarrantable interference in
man's nature and the social cybernetics preached by Terbolm.
Terbolm himself maintains that it is science which will enable
man to understand the world and himself. He believes that science
is as necessary to man as conscience. Terbolm is stating Solzhenitsyn's own view that the development of science, but under the
direction of moral conscience, is essential if man is to have a
future. The play, however, is an expression of Solzhenitsyn's
doubts as to whether science is in fact progressing in a desirable
direction. In his Nobel lecture he reiterates his doubts more forcibly as part of his general dissatisfaction with the state of the
world:

> It would appear that the shape of the modern world is
> entirely in the hands of the scientists, for all mankind's
> technological steps are determined by them. It would
> appear that the direction the world ought to take should
> depend, not on the politicians, but on the co-operation
> of scientists the world over, particularly since the
> example of individuals shows how much they could all
> achieve by joining forces. But no, the scientists have
> made no definite attempt to become an important,
> independently-motivated force among mankind. They
> shy away in congress-loads from the sufferings of others:
> it is more comfortable for them to remain within the
> frontiers of science. The same Munich spirit has spread
> its enervating wings over them.[8]

8. *The Listener* (London), 14 September 1972, p. 337.

Philippe wants to hand on to the twenty-first century the torch of physics—science as he understands it. Aleks realises that the torch he will hand on must be different—the flickering candle of the spirit. In the twenty-first century they can do with it what they like. But amidst the scientific materialism of the twentieth century its light must not be permitted to be extinguished. Aleks' task is to keep alive that tiny fragment of the universal spirit of which Shulubin in *Cancer Ward* becomes aware on his death bed.

5   *The First Circle*

Solzhenitsyn's two major novels on contemporary themes, *The First Circle* and *Cancer Ward*, were written successively over a period of twelve years. Together they represent the core of his literary achievement and his most searching commentary on the times he has lived through. *The First Circle* was begun in 1955, when he was still in exile, and the first draft was completed by 1958. Encouraged no doubt by the success of *One Day* and by the expectation that the leadership was now embarking upon a thorough re-appraisal of the Stalin era, he enlarged and revised the novel and submitted it for publication to *Novy Mir* in 1964, just before Khrushchev fell. He was considering further alterations when the manuscript was confiscated a year later. But this was probably a last attempt to satisfy the censor rather than an artistic revision. The version which soon appeared abroad was the one which had already been edited by *Novy Mir*. A fuller and in some ways superior version of *The First Circle* is still in the possession of the author. *Cancer Ward* was begun in 1963 in the same heady atmosphere of the Khrushchev renaissance. The first part was discussed at a friendly and constructive meeting of the prose section of the Union of Writers in November 1966. Solzhenitsyn accepted that parts of the novel should be rewritten, but the manuscript was sent to the West before this could be done. The second part was completed in 1967.

Like *One Day* and *Matryona's Home*, the two novels complement each other in several important respects. *Cancer Ward* may be regarded as a sequel to *The First Circle*. *The First Circle* is set in 1949, during the last years of Stalin's reign, as the old dictator, sinking into senility and insanity, was preparing to launch a new round of purges. It depicts life in the terrorist bureaucracy as it approached its final climax.

By 1955 when the events portrayed in *Cancer Ward* took place,

Stalin was dead and times had already begun to change. The purgers were themselves being purged, while the former denizens of the camps and the special prisons, the Buinovskys, the Nerzhins and the Rubins were coming back to the villages and the cities of Russia. Those like Matryona's Ignatich and Kostoglotov, who had served their sentences, were witnessing the first signs that their exile would shortly come to an end.

If in *One Day* Soviet society is glimpsed in a microcosm, in *The First Circle* it is magnified and revealed in precise, authentic detail. Both works derive their significance from a specific historical milieu. The author was concerned first and foremost to present life as it was, there and then, dominated by the immediate problems of physical and spiritual survival. *Matryona's Home* and *Cancer Ward* also, of course, have firm historical roots, but they depict a world in which restraints are diminishing. They record the hopeful beginnings of release from endless incarceration and relentless bureaucratic pressure, a time when men could start to look forward. In *Cancer Ward* Solzhenitsyn's inquiry broadens to embrace the purpose and quality of life in general and the values which must be found to replace the total moral corruption of Stalinism as the new society takes shape.

Formally, *The First Circle* and *Cancer Ward* are similar and are based on the structural method which Solzhenitsyn employed in *One Day*. The characters are placed in situations of unnatural confinement, the special prison and the cancer ward. The author is thus able to assemble people of widely diverse social origins, reduce them to a common level and confront them with common problems. When comparing *Cancer Ward* with Thomas Mann's *The Magic Mountain*, Georg Lukács describes Mann's method in a manner which is valid for both of Solzhenitsyn's novels:

> The characters of this novel are removed from the 'natural' location of their lives and movements, and are transplanted into new and artificial surroundings (here the sanatorium for consumptives). The major consequence of this is that the characters do not come into contact with each other, as so often in life and even more frequently in art, in 'normal ways', i.e. they are not limited by birth, occupation, etc.;

> rather this 'chance' common terrain of their present
> existence creates new fundamental forms of their
> intellectual and moral relations with each other.[1]

Both novels have a prominent central character who carries
the main burden of Solzhenitsyn's personal experience. But unlike the shorter stories, the novels do not proceed along a single
line of development. *The First Circle* is composed of a series of
separate narrative centres, held together by characters moving
from one to another. Solzhenitsyn adds further dimensions
through the conventional devices of realism which he used in
One Day; far-reaching lateral digressions, flash-backs and letters.
Solzhenitsyn has described his method (and it applies also to
August 1914) as polyphonic 'with concrete details specifying the
time and place of the action. The novels are without a main
hero . . . each character becomes main when the action reverts
to him.'[2] The result is a kind of literary mosaic, given cohesion
by consistent themes binding the varied parts into a syncretic
whole.

Most of the action of *The First Circle* takes place in Mavrino,
a special technical prison situated in an old house on the outskirts
of Moscow. Two-thirds of the eighty-seven short chapters are
devoted to the lives of the prisoners and their jailers, the Soviet
security police. Mavrino was set up in July 1946 as an institute
to exploit the talents of some of the highly qualified scientists and
technologists who were among the millions sentenced to the
labour camps. As a mathematician Solzhenitsyn spent three years
in Mavrino. In *The First Circle* he presents a portrait gallery of
some of the two hundred and eighty-one inmates of the *sharashka*
(a slang term for the prison meaning 'a sinister place') and of the
prison staff. The novel is, of course, fiction, but as in *One Day* the
characters are based on Solzhenitsyn's own former comrades.
Also like Ivan Denisovich's labour camp, the prisoners at Mavrino are the victims of successive repressions which scourged
Russia from the early 1930s to the return of the P.O.W.'s in
1945. Within the limited conception of *One Day* Solzhenitsyn
could offer only brief sketches of his characters and their ex-

1. Lukács, *op. cit.*, p. 37.
2. Licko, *op. cit.*, part of interview not included in translation in Labedz.

periences. Here some of the personal stories are several pages in length.

The purpose for which Mavrino has been lavishly equipped, from Soviet resources and materials requisitioned from Germany, is the development of special apparatus partly for the M.G.B., but mainly for the personal use of Stalin himself. The prisoners have already made him a huge television set and are now working on two new devices, a scrambler to render his telephone conversations immune from interception and a method of breaking down the human voice into its basic elements to enable recordings to be used for identification like finger prints. This latter device links Mavrino with the intrigue element in the novel and with the secondary sphere of action outside the prison, in Moscow itself.

In common with nearly all Solzhenitsyn's other works *The First Circle* is extremely compressed in its time sequence. It covers just three days over the Western Christmas 1949. At 4.05 p.m. on Saturday 24 December Innokenty Volodin, a promising young diplomat, makes a telephone call to warn a family friend that he is in danger of arrest. The call is monitored and a series of events is set in motion which results in Volodin's arrest on the night of 26 December. The tapes of Volodin's call have been sent to Mavrino where the prisoners are given the task of identifying the culprit. This, along with the many other things which happen at Mavrino over the weekend, they do with the aid of the 'new science' of voice printing. The novel is then incidentally a detective story but, as might be expected in circumstances as perverse as those of Stalin's Russia, the usual conventions of the detective story are turned upside down. Not only is the culprit known to the reader from the beginning, but it doesn't really matter whether he is positively identified or not. Arrests and a conviction will be carried out.

Several chapters describing Volodin's life in Moscow and his family connections take the story from Mavrino to the opposite end of the social scale, to the Soviet *haute bourgeoisie*, the new elite of the artistic establishment, overpaid state functionaries and their class-conscious wives. Ironically, it was the prisoners now in Mavrino who built the block of flats where they live and their neighbours are Mavrino officials. There are other narrative strands which lead the story beyond the walls of Mavrino. Gleb Nerzhin's wife, Nadya, constantly harried and persecuted because she is the wife of a prisoner, lives in a hostel together with some typical Soviet students struggling through the ideological minefield of the late 1940s to complete their theses. Nadya's friend Shchagov epitomises the bewildered ex-soldier trying to adapt to a society which has already forgotten the slogans and the loyalties which won the war. Finally Solzhenitsyn ascends through the hierarchy of the M.G.B., from deputy minister to minister, until he reaches another isolated house on the outskirts of Moscow, where Stalin himself keeps nocturnal vigil over his *univers concentrationnaire*.

At the end of Chapter two Solzhenitsyn explains what he had in mind when he chose *The First Circle* as the title of his novel. A detachment of prisoners arrives at Mavrino from the camps and one of the newcomers says to Rubin:

> 'Forty grams of butter! As much black bread as you like — *out on the table.* You can read books, you can shave and the guards don't beat you. This is a great day! It's like a mirage — or perhaps I've really died, and this is all a dream? I'm imagining I'm in heaven!'
>
> 'No, my dear Sir,' said Rubin, 'you are in hell, just as before. But you have graduated to its best and highest circle – the first circle. You asked me what sort of a place this is. Remember how Dante racked his brains to know where to put the Sages of antiquity? As a Christian he was in duty bound to send them to hell. But as a man of the Renaissance he was troubled in his conscience at the thought of throwing them in with all sorts of ordinary sinners and condemning them to all the torments of the flesh. So he designed a special place for them in the Fourth Canto . . .' (p. 14)

The title is clever, but it can equally well be applied to the place of the action outside the prison. For Abakumov and those immediately beneath him, and the members of the new elite who gather at the Makarygins', are also in the 'first circle'. They are the inhabitants of the innermost of the concentric rings which surround Stalin. All the episodes and all the characters in the novel are connected in some way to the invisible axis stretching between two suburban Moscow houses, the centres of the two first circles.

Central to *The First Circle* is a portrait of a society and its values. The chapters are selected so as to form a picture of Soviet life from the leadership to its most humble citizens. The action alternates between prison and the outside Moscow world, composing a sort of counterpoint enabling Solzhenitsyn to draw subtle and illuminating comparisons. Life in Moscow is no more agreeable than in prison. The prisoners in Mavrino enjoy privileges unheard of in the further rings of the *gulag archipelago* stretching out across the Soviet Union. But they are aware that they are poised on the brink of an abyss where a single false move could send them plummeting back to the lowest circle of Stalin's inferno. The pampered bureaucrats know that they too have entered a region of rich rewards and deadly dangers. As the pressure from the ministry on the research staff at Mavrino mounts Col. Yakonov, the Head of Research, wanders the streets of Moscow after a disastrous interview with Abakumov. Gazing down from a bridge at an ominous black hole in the ice he reflects:

> They had started the usual murderous game and it was
> approaching its climax. Yakonov knew all there was to
> know about this kind of lunatic scramble — it was more
> than flesh and blood could bear to be hopelessly
> caught up in impossible, grotesque, crippling schedules.
> You were trapped and held in a deadly grip. The
> system crushed you, driving you harder and faster all
> the time, demanding more and more, setting inhuman
> time-limits. . . . But until it dawned on someone that
> people were only human, there was no way out of this
> vicious circle for those involved . . . (p. 124)

Despite the almost limitless power of the successful bureaucrats and the wealth and privileges afforded to public prosecutors and favoured writers, Solzhenitsyn brings out the fantastic irony that only the prisoners, men who have nothing to their name but a pocket handkerchief, can call themselves free and think of happiness. The more they have acquired the more the elite have to lose and the greater the likelihood of their losing it. But the prisoners have been released from the ties of earthly goods and aspirations. Bobynin boldly informs Abakumov:

> 'You can tell old you-know-who up there that you only have power over people so long as you don't take *everything* away from them. But when you've robbed a man of everything he's no longer in your power — he's free again.' (p. 87)

Abakumov, immeasurably above Bobynin in the social hierarchy, is reminded of what Stalin might take away from *him* when he goes to report in an hour's time, and he restrains himself. Bobynin says:

> 'You can shout at your colonels and your generals as much as you like because they've got plenty to lose.'
> 'We can deal with your sort too if we have to.'
> 'No you can't.' Bobynin's piercing eyes flashed with hatred. 'I've got nothing, see? Nothing! you can't touch my wife and child — they were killed by a bomb. My parents are dead . . . you took my freedom away a long time ago and you can't give it back to me because you haven't got it yourself. I'm forty-two years old. You gave me twenty-five years. I've done hard labour, I know what it is to have a number instead of a name, to be handcuffed, to be guarded by dogs, to work in a punitive brigade what — more can you do to me?' (p. 87)

Bobynin is of course exaggerating. He knows that he can be sent back to the camps, which are infinitely worse than his cosy life at Mavrino. But it is a short drop compared with the fall which awaits the exalted Abakumov.

At the centre of the first circle of society at large presides the Leader of the Peoples, the Genius of Geniuses, the Greatest Strategist in History. The titles by which Solzhenitsyn sarcastically refers to Stalin punctuate the novel like a refrain, as the names of Jehovah punctuate the Bible. Solzhenitsyn has been accused of being obsessed with Stalin, whose spirit haunts nearly all his works like the unseen gods in a Greek play. There is no doubt that he holds Stalin directly responsible for all the nightmares which beset Russia from the death of Lenin onwards — collectivisation, the purges, the disasters of the war years and the monstrous injustices which condemned the flower of Soviet manhood, including Solzhenitsyn himself, to the labour camps. He has remained faithful to the words with which Tvardovsky introduced *One Day* to the world. The baleful figure of Stalin broods in *The First Circle* like a poisonous spider, spinning a web of mistrust and fear over his captive society.

Solzhenitsyn's portrait of Stalin is an attempt to get behind the public façade and show the nature of the man through the secret workings of his mind. With the exception of the interview with Abakumov, when the Leader is seen through the eyes of his terrified Minister of State Security, the four Stalin chapters are an extended reverie, an inner monologue in which Stalin flits lazily from subject to subject in search of relief from his boredom. There is insufficient published evidence for a psychological portrait of Stalin, particularly during his last years, to be composed on the basis of objective data. It is interesting that Roy Medvedev, in the most comprehensive compilation of information about Stalin to be attempted in the Soviet Union, using both printed and oral testimony, can add little in this respect to what is already known in the West.[3] Solzhenitsyn's portrait is an imaginative reconstruction, but is faithful to historical truth.

Like Tolstoy, with his portrait of Napoleon in *War and Peace*, Solzhenitsyn is setting out to explode a myth. In his secret speech and in subsequent utterances Khrushchev had already called into question many of the sacred beliefs about Stalin, but Solzhenitsyn wants to destroy the idol entirely. On the table beside Stalin's bed lie his favourite books, among them the *Short Biography*. Leafing through its pages he is captivated by the adulatory phrases:

> 'Strategist of Genius . . . wise foresight . . . mighty
> will . . . iron determination . . . his love for the

3. Roy Medvedev, *Let History Judge* (London–New York), 1972.

> people . . . his great concern for human beings . . .
> his astounding modesty (very true that bit about
> modesty).' (p. 91)

Stalin has written most of this himself! Solzhenitsyn underlines
the ludicrous self-delusion which allows Stalin to believe that all
this is true by having him pick up another book which has caught
his fancy, *Tito, the Traitor's Marshal*. Stalin has read it carefully
and reflects:

> 'To think of all the millions of people whose eyes it
> would open to this vain conceited, cruel, cowardly,
> vile, hypocritical, despicable tyrant! This sickening
> traitor. This unspeakable ignoramus!' (pp. 96–7)

No more appropriate words than these could be found to
describe the character of Stalin himself as he emerges from
Solzhenitsyn's pages. The gulf of self-deception which divides
reality from its official image at every level in *The First Circle*
begins in the mind of Stalin.

Solzhenitsyn is not content merely to show Stalin as a perverter
of all decent human values. He has become personally a nonen-
tity: 'He was just a little old man with a wizened fold of skin on
his neck (which was never shown in portraits), breath that
smelled of Turkish pipe-tobacco, and thick clammy fingers which
left their mark on books.' (p. 90) A few days after his seventieth
birthday he appears as a sick man with failing memory and
mental powers, trying desperately to retain his grip, but feeling it
inexorably slipping from him. In the final lines of a chapter or
story Solzhenitsyn likes to sum up and he does this for Stalin at
the end of Chapter twenty-one:

> He was an old man without any friends. Nobody loved
> him, he believed in nothing and he wanted nothing.
> He no longer even had any need of his daughter, once
> his favourite, but now only admitted on rare holidays.
> Helpless fear overcame him as he sensed the dwindling
> memory, the failing mind. Loneliness crept over him
> like a paralysis. (p. 120)

The paralysing loneliness with which Stalin infected the whole of Soviet society is not the chronic failure of personal communication which divides the characters in, for instance, Chekhov's major plays. Nor is it part of the labyrinth of the absurd of Beckett or Kafka. It is the loneliness of a socially dislocated world, the product of corroding fear and mistrust. The presence everywhere of informers, the constant threat of secret denunciation, has completely destroyed the concepts of the collective and of comradeship on which socialist society is theoretically based. Solzhenitsyn shows how the mechanism of suspicion and hatred isolates not only the wives of prisoners, the students, the diplomats like Volodin, but also the officials of the M.G.B. from the Minister downwards. When danger or difficulties threaten, each individual has only himself to rely on. Even in prison, where in spite of informers, real relationships and mutual trust are possible, the prisoners must make their final decisions alone. At the centre of his hideous web Stalin is the loneliest of all. Enclosed by bullet-proof windows and steel-plated doors, friendless, sterile, and bored, Stalin is imprisoned in solitary confinement of the spirit.

If, as Solzhenitsyn implies, Stalin in his declining years had lost the shrewdness and force of character which outwitted his rivals and defeated his enemies, it is legitimate to wonder how he was able to maintain his total ascendancy. Solzhenitsyn only suggests the answer – by his mediocrity. 'Just as King Midas turned everything he touched to gold, so Stalin's touch turned everything into mediocrity.' As Abakumov and all his subordinates who hoped to survive were aware:

> It was fatal to work for him at full capacity; instead one had to find the golden mean: while Stalin would not tolerate failure, he also hated it if people were too efficient. He saw in this a threat to his own absolute superiority in everything. Nobody else was allowed to achieve perfection. (p. 110)

As a realistic writer concerned with historical truth, Solzhenitsyn rarely strays into regions beyond his own experience or for which he does not possess a reliable witness. Apart from his novel of the First World War, he makes little use of conventional historical sources. He has no need of them. The chapters in *The First Circle* depicting Stalin *do* fall outside his own personal knowledge. Indeed there was probably no one save Poskryoby-shev, Stalin's personal secretary, who could furnish a first-hand account of the Leader's private life. For his reconstruction of Stalin's personal world Solzhenitsyn was obliged to make imaginative use of such sources of information as were accessible to him. He apparently regarded Stalin's manner of expressing himself in public as a useful guide to his habits of mind. The Stalin chapters in *The First Circle* closely reproduce the verbose and colourless style of Stalin's speeches, which even the Makarygins cannot bear to listen to and such a devoted admirer as Vadim in *Cancer Ward* feels to be a little insipid. Solzhenitsyn employs the same clichés and endless lists in the first paragraphs of Chapter eighteen even though they are still the direct narration of the author.

As a former prisoner Solzhenitsyn was thoroughly versed in the gossip of the camps. Many highly placed figures added their contribution to the fund of common knowledge which reached the ears of all *zeks* and among them were some who had known Stalin personally. Nerzhin records how, when he was brought to the Lubyanka, 'he had met a few survivors of the Great Purges; they were not surprised at how much he had pieced together, but were able to add a hundred times more.' (p. 204) Among the stories circulating about Stalin there was probably much that was exaggerated and fanciful, but a writer with an ear as finely tuned to the ring of truth as Solzhenitsyn had little difficulty in distinguishing the authentic facts from apocrypha.

Edward J. Brown has pointed out that certain features in Solzhenitsyn's portrait of Stalin recall Khrushchev's 'secret speech' of 1956.[4] Like Solzhenitsyn Khrushchev emphasised Stalin's belief in his own indispensableness, his vanity and his approval of the *Short Biography*. Both make much of Stalin's intellectual limitations and of his idiotic faith in Hitler. To his credit, however, Solzhenitsyn rejects Khrushchev's view of Stalin's shortcomings as a strategist. The story of his using a schoolboy's globe for his military plans has been authentically denied.

What other published and unpublished accounts of Stalin's

4. Edward J. Brown, 'Solzhenitsyn's cast of characters', *Slavic and East European Journal*, Vol. 15, no. 2 (Wisconsin), 1971, pp. 153–66.

character and behaviour were available to Solzhenitsyn can only be a matter of speculation. He has been denied access to the archives even for his work on the First World War, but so was Roy Medvedev, who nevertheless managed to assemble an immense quantity of material for his book on Stalin. Medvedev and Solzhenitsyn are friends and it is perhaps reasonable to assume that Solzhenitsyn was able to get hold of most of what Medvedev discovered. Medvedev was poorly acquainted with Western sources, but he does make use of Milovan Djilas' *Conversations with Stalin* and so, it seems, does Solzhenitsyn. Djilas, who last met Stalin in 1948 when he noted the decline in his intellect, imagines him thinking: 'Age has crept up on me and I am already an old man.' Djilas wrote that in Stalin's senility 'there was something both tragic and ugly. The tragic was invisible.'[5] In Solzhenitsyn's picture the suggestion of tragedy, or perhaps only pathos, is present as an undercurrent.

Both Tolstoy and Solzhenitsyn intended to denigrate the historical figure they were writing about. But while Tolstoy distorted the image of Napoleon in accordance with his own prejudice, Solzhenitsyn produces an impression which the reader instinctively feels is close to the real-life Stalin. As a work of art in itself the portrait is less successful. Solzhenitsyn's need to telescope a large number of separate memories and reflections into a short passage of time confers a certain caricature effect. And his all too frequent use of elementary irony sometimes degenerates into unsubtle sarcasm.

During one of his conversations at the Kremlin Djilas speculates on the moral convictions which motivated Stalin:

> His conscience was troubled by nothing, despite the millions who had been destroyed in his name and by his order. For what is conscience? Does it even exist? It had no place in his philosophy, much less in his actions.[6]

At the heart of Solzhenitsyn's critical examination of Soviet society is his concern for the moral standards which govern

5. Milovan Djilas, *Conversations with Stalin* (London), 1962, p. 146.
6. *Ibid.*, p. 98.

human conduct. The simple peasants and workers in *One Day* are not given to philosophical speculations, nor do the circumstances encourage them. In the labour camps it is basic instinct which is uppermost in the struggle for physical survival. If standards of individual behaviour vary, the prisoners and guards are merely responding to an innate moral sense without stopping to rationalise. Ivan Denisovich's sense of right and wrong springs from his nature and he is not aware of possessing a certain moral superiority, nor could he offer an explanation of why he acts as he does. In *The First Circle* the prisoners are released from the struggle for existence. They are warm, have enough to eat and are not crushed beneath the burden of physical labour. Moreover most of them are intellectuals with the leisure and the inclination for speculation. Unlike the labourers in the camps who have sunk as low as they can go, the Mavrino workers have an opportunity for real moral choice. In *The First Circle* Solzhenitsyn makes a thorough examination of his characters' moral responses, from Stalin downwards.

For Solzhenitsyn the cornerstone of morality is conscience. Conscience, he believes, confers on man a capacity to distinguish between right and wrong. Grachikov in *For the Good of the Cause* is responding to the demands of conscience when he takes the side of the college students against the Party secretary. Zotov, who is determined to remain faithful to his wife, regards his friend Paulina as the embodiment of his conscience and the guardian of his fidelity. Nemov in *The Love-girl and the Innocent* wonders, even in his fearful camp, whether conscience is not a more valuable possession than life itself. All Solzhenitsyn's principal characters are morally conceived and their dilemmas of conscience are the crux of all his stories. They are the central issue in *The First Circle*.

Solzhenitsyn believes that 'convictions based on conscience are as infallible as the internal rhythm of the heart',[7] but he seems to have had some difficulty in determining what, fundamentally, conscience is. In *A Candle in the Wind* the scientist, Philippe, observes that we don't know its composition or its formula. Some people consider it no more than a conditioned reflex. Conscience, he concludes, is an optional feeling.

7. Labedz, *op. cit.*, p. 101.

Later in the same play the doctor Sinbar argues that since a moral imperative in man cannot be proved scientifically it does not exist, absolute morality is just an old wives' tale. All truth is concrete, but all morality is relative.

Against this Aleks argues that there are certain things which are invariably crimes. Solzhenitsyn's own sympathies clearly lie with Aleks, but he is unable to refute the view of the scientists convincingly. In *Cancer Ward* he can only refer to conscience as an indicator which man has inside him and which continues to work even when it is short-circuited. In his letter to three students Solzhenitsyn wrote that justice, which he regards as the conscience of a community, 'has been the common patrimony of humanity throughout the ages . . . obviously it is a concept which is inherent in man, since it cannot be traced to any other source'.[8] The letter to the students confirms the general conclusion to be drawn from all Solzhenitsyn's literary writings, that man's moral sense, his conscience, is an innate quality the nature of which cannot be precisely defined. There is no suggestion that it can be explained in religious terms. None of the characters who in one way or another act morally exhibit religious convictions. While the novels of Tolstoy and Dostoevsky embody a search for the metaphysical origins of good and evil and justice, Solzhenitsyn's seem to show that they spring from purely social considerations and from man's nature as a social being.

In his Lenten letter, written at Easter time in 1972, Solzhenitsyn seems to have arrived at a new understanding of the nature of morality. There he writes: 'we have lost the radiant ethical atmosphere of Christianity in which for a millennium our morals were grounded.'[9] The implication is now that morality is indeed a religious matter. The general import of the letter is that the destruction of the Church is causing the erosion of the moral foundations of the nation, which the new socialist morality is conspicuously failing to replace. *The Easter Procession* was apparently written to illustrate this idea. Solzhenitsyn's view is close to that of Amalrik in his essay *Will the Soviet Union Survive until 1984?*[10]

8. *Ibid.*
9. *The Sunday Telegraph*, 9 April 1972.
10. *Survey* (London), Autumn 1969, pp. 63–4.

While the old forms of social structure both in town and countryside are being definitively destroyed, new ones are still only being formed. The 'ideological basis' on which they are being built is extremely primitive: there is the aspiration for material prosperity and the instinct of self preservation . . . It is hard to make out whether the bulk of our people have, apart from these purely material criteria, any kind of moral criteria — 'honourable' and 'dishonourable', 'well' and 'badly'; 'good' and 'evil', the supposedly eternal principles which constitute the restraining and guiding factor when the mechanism of social compulsion starts moving and an individual is abandoned to himself. I have formed the impression, possibly a wrong one, that the people do not have or almost do not have such moral criteria. Christian morality with its concepts of good and evil has been dislodged and effaced from the popular conscience and efforts have been made to replace it by 'class' morality which can be formulated more or less as follows: good is what is required at the present moment by authority. Naturally, this kind of morality and also the implantation and the instigation of class and racial discord have completely demoralised society and deprived it of any really permanent moral criteria.

Amalrik's use of the term 'racial' is significant in view of Kostoglotov's attacks on Rusanov in *Cancer Ward*. Both Solzhenitsyn and Amalrik attribute the moral disorientation of the Russian people under the Soviet regime to materialism and the decline in the influence of the Church.

Whether or not there is still some confusion in Solzhenitsyn's mind as to the origins of morality his published remarks give insufficient evidence to be sure. But he is in no doubt as to what conscience involves in practice and conscience is the criterion by which, as men, all Solzhenitsyn's characters are judged.

The conflict between good and evil is shown by Solzhenitsyn in acute forms. There could hardly be a severer test of the quality of conscience than the labour camps or, indeed, Stalin's society as a whole. Solzhenitsyn himself is the outstanding example of those who have passed the test. In *One Day* there are many who managed to — in *The Love-girl and the Innocent*, very few. In the society portrayed in *The First Circle* a man's chances of success or even of survival are in direct inverse proportion to the extent to which he heeds the voice of conscience. Like Djilas, Solzhenitsyn can find no trace of conscience in Stalin. Beneath him there are numerous gradations of conscience from those such as Abakumov and Makarygin, who are most closely linked to Stalin's system and who have become 'moral monstrosities', to men like Nerzhin, whose conduct depends entirely on conscience, and to Rubin and Volodin, who are not beyond the possibility of redemption.

When Lyubimichev was a prisoner of war in Germany 'the only people who survived were those who had gone the furthest in rejecting the relative and limited concept of good and of conscience . . .' (p. 470) The situation is the same in *The Love-girl and the Innocent* and Solzhenitsyn reveals in *The First Circle* that these are the laws which govern society in general.

At the level of society as a whole the exercise of conscience leads to justice. As Solzhenitsyn wrote to the students:

> There is nothing relative about justice, as there is
> nothing relative about conscience. Indeed justice is
> conscience, not a personal conscience but the conscience
> of the whole of humanity. Those who clearly recognise
> the voice of their own conscience usually recognise also
> the voice of justice. I consider that in all questions,
> social or historical, justice will always suggest a way
> to act (or judge) which will not conflict with our
> conscience.[11]

The political message of Solzhenitsyn's novel is the need to restore justice to a society where it has become almost totally perverted. Here Solzhenitsyn disagrees with Amalrik. Amalrik wrote in the same essay as the one quoted above:

> The Russian people has, as can be seen from both its
> past and its present history, at any rate one idea that

11. Labedz, *op. cit.*, p. 101.

is apparently positive: the idea of *justice*. A government which thinks and acts for us in everything must not only be strong but also just; all must live justly and act justly . . . However attractive, though, this idea may appear, when one makes a careful study of what lies behind it, it represents the most destructive aspect of the Russian's psychology. In practice, 'justice' is motivated by the wish 'nobody should be better off than me'. (I look upon this as one of the typical features of the Russian psyche.) This idea is motivated by hatred for everything that is outstanding, which they make no effort to imitate but, on the contrary, force into conformity with themselves, by hatred for any form of life that is more elevated or more dynamic than their own.[12]

If this is indeed all the Russian notion of justice amounts to, then it was the very instinct on which Stalinism was based. But Solzhenitsyn does not think so. His own ideas on social justice are outlined by Shulubin in *Cancer Ward*.

One day, Volodin, who has been brought up to take his place in the ranks of the Soviet elite and to live by its rules, came upon the diaries of his dead mother and from them he got to know her for the first time.

'Compassion is the spontaneous movement of the virtuous heart.'

Compassion? Innokenty frowned. He had been taught at school that pity is as shameful and degrading for the one who pities as for the one who is pitied.

'Never be sure that you are more right than other people. Respect their opinions even if they are opposed to yours.'

This was pretty old-fashioned! If my view of the world is right, how can I respect those who disagree with me?

He could almost hear his mother's brittle voice as he read: 'what is the most precious thing in the world? It seems to be the consciousness of not participating in

12. *Survey, op. cit.*, pp. 62–3.

injustice. Injustice is stronger than you are, it always was and always will be, but let it not be committed through you!

Yes, his mother had been a weak woman. He couldn't see her putting up a fight. The very idea of it was absurd.

If six years ago, he had opened her diaries, he would not even have noticed this passage. But now he read it slowly and it astonished him. Not that any of it was so extraordinary, and some of the things she said were plainly wrong. But it astonished him all the same. Even the words she and her girl-friends used to express their ideas were old-fashioned: 'Truth, Goodness and Beauty', 'Good and Evil' (all with capitals), 'the ethical imperative'. In the language he spoke and heard around him, words were more concrete and therefore easier to understand: rightmindedness, humaneness, dedication, purposefulness.

. . . Sitting on a low stool in front of the open cupboards, he felt he had discovered something that had been missing from his life. (pp. 346–7)

In this passage Solzhenitsyn uses the device of the diary to tabulate his own moral dogmas and set them against the facile precepts which have replaced them in the education of youth.

In time Volodin manages to identify the missing part of himself — his conscience. He discovers that 'we only have one conscience — and that a crippled conscience is as irretrievable as a lost life.' (p. 348) When eventually faced with the choice of suppressing his conscience or risking his own life, he realises that in fact he has *no* choice: 'If you always look over your shoulder, how can you still remain a human being?' (p. 9)

The moral dilemma which the peculiar circumstances of Mavrino present to the prisoners is daunting. The *zeks* in the camps work only to fulfil their norms and qualify for their rations. They can even console themselves with the thought that what they build is of direct benefit to the community. At Mavrino the prisoners enjoy vastly superior, even humane living conditions, but in return they must work at projects which they know will make the repression of their fellow countrymen even more efficient. Those who co-operate may stay, those who will not are returned to the camps. Each of the 281 men must choose. During the three days which Solzhenitsyn describes in *The First Circle* four of the central figures in the novel are confronted by the need to make the fateful choice. All four are offered the opportunity to earn themselves an early release by devising new instruments of evil. Paradoxically, it is the two who have most to lose who will not give in. Nerzhin and Gerasimovich are both married and have been made painfully aware of the position of their persecuted wives by their unexpected visits. Both recognise and heed the voice of conscience and, like Solzhenitsyn himself in a similar situation, they are unable to make a moral compromise. Gerasimovich thinks it over:

> He could keep quiet. He could cover himself. He could accept the job like any other prisoner, and then drag it out, not do it. But Gerasimovich rose and looked with scorn at the bloated belly, fat cheeks, blunt snout and general's hat.
> 'No, it's not in my line!' His voice rose to a shrill squeak. 'Putting people in prison is not in my line! I'm not a fisher of men. There are more than enough of us in prison as it is . . .' (p. 505)

The prison authorities bring in his old university professor to try and persuade Nerzhin. He holds out to Nerzhin the chance to win a pardon for himself:

> 'Pardoned?' Nerzhin cried angrily, his eyes narrowing. 'What makes you think I want such a favour of them? . . . you're putting it the wrong way round. Let them admit first it's not right to put people in prison for their way of thinking—and then *we* will see whether we can forgive *them*!' (p. 48)

Neither Sologdin nor Rubin has a wife waiting desperately for his release. Yet both agree to compromise and be compromised. Unlike Nerzhin who is still searching for the meaning of his experiences, Sologdin and Rubin have both worked out their philosophies of life. Sologdin, the anti-communist, embittered by his wife's desertion and with nothing to live for or depend upon but himself, embarks on a campaign of self-perfection. Difficulties he welcomes as opportunities to sharpen and perfect his willpower. 'In general the greater they are the more valuable. Not so much if they arise from your struggle with yourself. But if they come from an increased resistance of the object—that is splendid.' (p. 142) Sologdin resolves to confront the system on its own ground. Realising the power which the speech device he has invented gives him over his superiors whose own careers are at stake, he does not hesitate ruthlessly to exploit his advantage. His confrontation with Yakanov is an acute ordeal for him, but in the duel of wills he triumphs. In spite of his admirable personal qualities, however, Sologdin has in a sense been corrupted by Stalinism, and his conscience is untroubled by moral scruples about his action.

The tough, independent Sologdin acts only in accordance with precepts of his own devising. For Rubin 'a great hulk of man with the thick black beard of a biblical prophet . . . a Jew and a communist' (p. 15), the interests of the Party are sacrosanct. But Rubin is beginning to be troubled by the torments of conscience. He has never allowed himself to doubt the Party ends nor the means employed to realise them. 'For the first time in the history of mankind we have an aim which is so sublime that we can really say that it justifies the means employed to attain it,' he tells Sologdin when the latter reminds him 'that the higher the aim the higher your means should be as well. Wicked means destroy the end.' (p. 405) Rubin is indignant, 'wicked means? Who's using wicked means?' He himself did not refuse to denounce his own cousin and help to execute cruel measures during collectivisation. But recently the recollection of it has begun to disturb him:

> All this was imprinted in his mind, as though branded there by red-hot iron. And sometimes he thought that everything he had suffered—his war wounds, his imprisonment and his ill health—was punishment for it.
> True, he had only got his deserts, but since he now

> knew what a terrible thing he had done, and would
> never do it again, and had paid the price, was there
> no way of purging himself? He would have given
> anything to say it had never happened . . .
>   There is nothing a sleepless night will not wring from
> an erring soul in distress . . . (pp. 416–17).

Rubin is becoming ever more painfully aware that 'wicked means' *are* being used and is beginning to have doubts about the abstract phrases he uses to justify them. The task of applying his new science of voice-printing to identifying the person who has warned Dr. Dobroumov bring him face to face with his moral dilemma. Rubin's common humanity momentarily asserts itself when he realises that the man is plainly as innocent as he was himself. Rubin is forced to retreat behind his ideological shield:

> . . . objectively, although this man had imagined he
> was doing good, he was in fact working against the
> forces of progress. If it was considered part of the vital
> interests of the state to claim that all scientific
> discoveries had been pioneered in Russia, then anyone
> who thought differently was objectively standing in the
> way of progress and must be swept aside. (pp. 195–6)

When the final decision is made between the two suspects Rubin discovers the sort of travesty of justice in which he is being asked to participate. Both are arrested and Rubin is left to make his peace with his conscience. Had it not been for his science all five original suspects would have been taken; 'at least he had perhaps saved three of them.' He is a troubled man as he turns to a map of China which he has pinned to the wall, with the communist held territories pencilled over in red; 'It was the only thing that heartened him now. In spite of everything we were winning . . .' (p. 512)

Rubin is an ambiguous figure, the most complex of Solzhenitsyn's characters. As Helen Muchnic has written: 'He is a scholar who perverts his knowledge, an honest man who becomes an informer, a humane man who, because of his ideals, acts brutally, so that in him more eloquently than if he had been by nature false, petty and cruel, the basic principles of communism, the logic of dialectical materialism, and the official ethics of the Soviet State, stand condemned.'[13]

Solzhenitsyn observes in *Cancer Ward* that contrast reveals the truth. In the novels he organises the relationships between his characters into patterns of opposites and personal foils. In *Cancer Ward* Rusanov and Kostoglotov came into conflict at every point and the personalities of the two women with whom Kostoglotov strikes up friendships are deliberately contrasted. In *The First Circle* there are many pairs of opposites. At the Makarygins there are Makarygin himself and Dushan Radovic. The writer, Galakhov, comes into contact on the one hand with Volodin and on the other with Shchagov. At Mavrino there is the natural opposition of the prisoners to their jailers. The prisoners themselves are a very varied collection of men who constantly argue among themselves.

Gleb Nerzhin for all his independence and intelligence is a receptive character with a number of foils grouped around him, to all of whom he looks for guidance, people with whom he disagrees, but from whom he learns. The most important are Rubin, Sologdin, the peasant Spiridon and the old artist Kondrashov-Ivanov. *The First Circle* covers too short a period for there to be any significant development in the characters themselves or in the relationships between them. The three days witness the climax of much that has gone before. But in any case Solzhenitsyn does not attempt to show personal relationship in deep human terms. Men like Nerzhin, Sologdin and Rubin are differentiated intellectually, morally and culturally. Clashes between Rubin and the other two are over ideological questions. Where there is influence, such as Sologdin exerts over Nerzhin, it is only intellectual and not personal. This also goes for the inhabitants of the Makarygins' world.

A certain proclivity for theorising and moral disputation is, of course, part of the Russian realistic tradition and there is no need to look further than Tolstoy for Solzhenitsyn's inspiration. Like Tolstoy in his major novels Solzhenitsyn formulates the principal ideas in *The First Circle* in the debate between two or three central characters. Nerzhin is Solzhenitsyn's Pierre, trying to make sense

13. *The Russian Review*, Vol. 29, no. 2, 1970, p. 162.

of bewildering historical events. He is also the author's *alter ego* in the novel.

The outward circumstances of Nerzhin's life coincide at all the main points with Solzhenitsyn's own. His age, education, marriage, military service and prison experiences could all come from the author's autobiography. Complete identification between author and hero cannot be claimed on the strength of these details, but there can be little doubt that Nerzhin shares Solzhenitsyn's own attitudes and voices his thoughts.

Sologdin has taught Nerzhin to regard his prison sentence not as a misfortune, but as a blessing: 'Time to sort yourself out, to understand the part of good and evil in human life. Where could you do it better than in prison?' (p. 139) In the process of 'sorting himself out' Nerzhin also quarrels with Rubin. Rubin sticks tenaciously to his orthodox Party beliefs and Nerzhin accuses him:

> 'You've wilfully closed your eyes, plugged your ears,
> you're putting on an act and you think you're clever!
> You think it's a sign of intelligence to refuse to
> develop.' (p. 40)

He might have added Kostoglotov's motto—'a fool loves to teach, a wise man loves to learn.'

Rubin answers with his usual glib phrases and his faith in Stalin: 'He is wise. He is really wise. He sees far beyond what we can possibly see.' Nerzhin's retort is characteristic: 'Better to trust your own eyes.'

The debate between Nerzhin and Rubin is central to Solzhenitsyn's own political thinking. Rubin expresses in the distorted form characteristic of its official apologists the marxist-materialist philosophy which provided the rationale for Stalin's regime. Nerzhin counters this with the independent humanist view to which Solzhenitsyn subscribes. In contrast to the doctrinaire Rubin, Nerzhin is open-minded. He has Kostoglotov's habit of always using his eyes and ears to pick up anything that might broaden his mind. His life has taught him to 'suspect everything.'

Nerzhin's scepticism does not bring him comfort. Secretly he envies Rubin the latter's certainty. He is irritated when he finds his own doubting approach being thrown back at him by Ruska as nihilism.

> 'This kind of scepticism, agnosticism, pessimism—
> whatever you call it (says Nerzhin)—it all sounds very
> clever and ruthless, but you must understand that by
> its very nature it dooms us to futility. It's not a guide
> to action, and people just can't stand still, so they must
> have a set of positive beliefs to show them the way . . .
> I think scepticism is very important—it's a way of
> getting at people with one track minds. But it can never
> give a man the feeling that he's got firm ground under
> his feet. And perhaps it's what we need—firm ground
> under our feet.' (p. 72)

Obliged, like Sologdin, to depend only on himself, he has not yet worked out the positive values on which to build his life. Nor perhaps at this stage in his pilgrim's progress had Solzhenitsyn.

Sologdin's promptings have, however, led Nerzhin to the discovery of something positive. He believes that he has found a key to happiness. In one of his arguments with Rubin he insists that the word 'happiness' is derived from the Russian for 'fate' or 'lot'. 'You can't have any illusions if you know your etymology.' (p. 36) The key, then, is to be happy with what you have. Rubin accuses Nerzhin of being an eclectic, for he has culled his ideas from many sources. He quotes the books of the Sankhya: 'For those who understand, human happiness is suffering'—and the Taoists: 'whoever is capable of knowing when he has had enough will always be satisfied.' Nerzhin's favourite Russian proverb which he quotes twice, once early in the book and again at the end, is: 'you won't drown in the sea but you may drown in a puddle.' (pp. 158 and 568) These snippets from the accumulated wisdom of mankind help Nerzhin to formulate a quietist philosophy from his prison experiences. At various stages throughout the book he expounds it.

Nerzhin has reached the conclusion that only a man who has been purged of all his worldly goods and aspirations can attain peace of mind and know how to enjoy simple things:

It was only outwardly that he appeared ill-fated—
secretly, he found happiness in his very misfortune.
He drank from it as from a spring. Here in prison he
was discovering people and events he would not have
heard of anywhere else on earth . . . (p. 158)

Nerzhin reminds Rubin of their experience in the Lubyanka:

'To understand the nature of happiness we first have
to know that it means to eat one's fill. Remember how
it was in the Lubyanka and when the security people
were grillling us? Remember that thin barley or oatmeal
porridge without a drop of milk? . . . It was like Holy
Communion, you took it like the sacraments, like the
prana of the yogis. You ate it slowly, from the tip of a
wooden spoon, entirely absorbed in the process of eating,
in thinking about eating—and it spread through your
body like nectar . . . Can you compare that with the
way people wolf down steaks . . . It's not a matter of
how much you eat, but the *way* you eat. It's the same
with happiness—it doesn't depend on the actual
number of blessings we manage to snatch from life,
but only on our attitude towards them.' (p. 38)

He cites as an example of total happiness the occasional free
Sundays in the prison:

'I lie on my top bunk and stare at the ceiling . . . I
tremble from the sheer joy of existence! I go to sleep
perfectly happy. No president, no prime minister can
fall asleep so well pleased with his Sunday.' (p. 39)

Nerzhin the intellectual is describing the sensations of the peasant
Shukhov lying on the top bunk recalling the successes of his
almost happy day. By contrasting the state of bliss attainable in
prison with the miseries of life in the outside world Nerzhin
develops his idea into a comment of universal application:

'The happiness that comes from the total fulfilment of
desire, from success, from feeling completely gorged—

that is suffering! That is spiritual death, a kind of
unending moral indigestion . . . They exhaust themselves
in the senseless pursuit of material things and die
without realising their spiritual wealth.' (p. 39)

The secret of Nerzhin's inner contentment is that he has over-
come the fear of death. It is also this absence of fear which distinguishes Kostoglotov from the patients in the cancer ward.
Solzhenitsyn himself announced to the world on two occasions
that he was not afraid to die for what he believes in. Whether
Nerzhin and his friends will 'swim in the sea' or sink they cannot
be sure, but they will have the chance to realise something of
their spiritual wealth:

> . . . they were at peace within themselves. They were as
> fearless as men who have lost everything they ever
> had—a fearlessness hard to attain but enduring once
> it is reached. (p. 581)

In Chapter two it was argued that those critics who wanted to
see Shukhov as a latter-day representative of the People, romantically idealised by nineteenth-century writers, were mistaken. In
The First Circle Solzhenitsyn makes a serious investigation of the
matter himself. He creates an archetypal peasant figure in Spiridon, a man endowed with several characteristics reminiscent of
Shukhov. He then gives Nerzhin the task of putting the idea of
'the People' to the test on him.

Predictably, neither Rubin nor Sologdin have any sympathy
for Nerzhin's attempt 'to go to the People.' Rubin, as becomes a
Marxist, knows that the traditional concept of 'the People' is
meaningless in class terms. Only the proletariat embodies historical truth. Sologdin on the other hand regards 'the People' as
'just a general term for all those dull, drab, uncouth individuals
totally absorbed in their joyless daily routine.' For him 'only
outstanding individuals shine forth like lonely stars in the dark
firmament of our existence, could embody the higher meaning
of life.' (p. 387)

The evolution of Nerzhin's view of the people has already
passed through 'many extreme phases.' With its anguished view

of the peasants, Russian nineteenth-century literature created for Nerzhin in his youth 'an image of a venerable, grey-haired People which embodies wisdom, moral purity and greatness.' (p. 387) But as an ordinary soldier he discovered that the People were in reality 'scruffy, foulmouthed, callous and very disagreeable.' Then as a prisoner he loses faith in the intelligentsia 'among whom he had not long ago thought it honourable to be numbered', and turns again to the peasants and labourers who work with their hands 'to learn the wisdom of their skilled hands and make their philosophy his own.' And unlike his intellectual forebears of the last century there is nothing artificial in his 'going to the people': 'he was thrown among them in the shabby quilted trousers and the jacket of a prisoner and made to do his work quota side by side with them.' But again Nerzhin finds only disillusionment. The people have no inherent advantage, no great homespun wisdom. Like Shukhov they are naïve: 'if a camp officer smiles at them, they smile back and are much more eager for small material things ... few of them had the sort of beliefs for which they would willingly sacrifice their lives.' (p. 389)

Nerzhin reaches a conclusion, in one of Solzhenitsyn's key passages, which like most of the truths shining out of his work is simple and unsophisticated:

> One belonged to the People neither by virtue of speaking the same language as everybody else nor by being among the select few stamped with the hallmark of genius. You were not born with the People, nor did you become part of it through work or education.
>
> It was only character that mattered, and this was something that everybody had to face for himself, by constant effort over the years.
>
> Only thus could one make oneself into a human being and hence be regarded as a true part of one's people. (p. 389)

There seems to Nerzhin to be something 'deep' about Spiridon which, in spite of all his experiences, revives both his interest in the idea of 'the People' and the hope that he might conceal a source of special 'insight'. The story of Spiridon's life is one of the most successful sections of the novel and contains material enough for a novel in itself. The life story of this Russian peasant who was 17 at the time of the Revolution and over 40 when the war with Hitler began summarises the history of the Russian countryside in the twentieth century: 'During all those terrible years of his life, during all its cruel ups and downs, this stubborn red-haired peasant had never once paused to reflect at critical moments of decision.' (p. 396) Like Shukhov's, his ethics are straightforward. He never slandered anyone, never lied, swore only when he had to, could never bring himself to steal. His two main preoccupations in life, the land and his family, are typical of the Russian peasant mentality. There is no sign of mystical wisdom in Spiridon, no 'universal system of philosophical scepticism' such as Nerzhin hoped he might find—only, in spite of his terrifying ignorance, a consistent thread of straightforward good sense.

Finally Nerzhin resolves to ask Spiridon outright: '"Is there any way for a man to know who is right and who is wrong?" . . . "I can tell you," replied Spiridon . . . as readily as if he had been asked which of the warders had come on duty that morning. "I can tell you, wolfhounds are right and cannibals are wrong."' (p. 402) Solzhenitsyn is fond of summing up his meanings with a peasant aphorism or a saying of proverbial quality, not for the sake of artificial ambiguity, but for clarification. He has already provided clues in earlier works as to what Spiridon's astonishing reply means. In *Matryona's Home* there are the cockroaches which rustle, although there is nothing false or deceptive about them: 'It is their nature and they cannot help it.' (p. 16) And in *A Candle in the Wind* Aleks compares biocybernetics with social cybernetics (p. 202). Even the disease of cancer is not inherently evil. In *Cancer Ward* Vadim points out to Dyoma that it also wants to live, in its own way. In all of these instances Solzhenitsyn wishes to say that what is natural is right and what is unnatural is wrong. The wolfhound is right, for however savage he may seem, it is his nature. But the cannibal's savagery is unnatural to mankind. Significantly, in *Cancer Ward* Solzhenitsyn speaks of Stalin as 'the cannibal' (*lyudoyed*).

Perhaps the cruellest fate of all those who suffered under

Stalin's tyranny was reserved for the innocent wives of the prisoners. It was almost invariably assumed, and the practice has by no means been discontinued under his successors, as Solzhenitsyn's own experiences demonstrate, that the family of an accused man also shared his guilt. If they were not actually arrested as well, their punishment was often worse than his. Gerasimovich's wife, Natasha, unable to suppress her feelings any longer, blurts out during their meeting:

> 'You're among friends and you're doing the work you
> like. Nobody pushes you around, but I've been sacked,
> I've got nothing to live on. I won't get a job anywhere.
> I can't go on! I'm at the end of my tether. I won't
> last another month! I might as well die. The neighbours
> treat me like dirt—they've thrown my trunk out of
> the hall and pulled down a shelf I put up on the wall.
> They know I daren't say a word, because they can
> have me thrown out of Moscow . . . They keep telling
> me to divorce you and remarry. When is it all going to
> end?' (p. 228)

That his own wife, Nadya, has already waited nine years and is ready to go on doing so astonishes Nerzhin:

> He could not understand how Nadya could have
> waited so long for him. How could she move among
> those bustling, insatiable crowds, constantly feeling
> men's eyes on her—and not waver in her love for him?
> Gleb imagined that if it had been the other way round—
> if she were imprisoned and he were free – he would
> not have held out for as much as a year. (p. 201)

The tradition of constant wives, willingly enduring the fate of their exiled husbands, is strong in Russia. The wives of the Decembrist insurgents in the early nineteenth century are a national legend. But the lot of the prisoners' wives has deteriorated even more since the nineteenth century than that of the prisoners themselves. One of the women waiting at the prison with Nadya gives a poignant description of their plight (pp. 215–16). How in spite of this appalling persecution so many women did remain faithful, Solzhenitsyn does not explain. The prisoners' wives, finely and sympathetically drawn though they are, are introduced with the purpose of pointing to yet another facet of inhumanity.

In *Cancer Ward* relationships between men and women form a substantial part of the novel. If for no other reason, it would be unique in Soviet literature because of its treatment of sex. But in *The First Circle*, apart from Nadya, the female characters are not of great importance, either for themselves or for the attitudes of the men towards them. Solzhenitsyn washes his hands, as it were, of the need to probe deeply: 'There is nothing predictable about relationships between men and women—they have no set course and they have no laws to govern them. They sometimes reach such a dead end that there's nothing to do but sit down and howl . . .' (p. 408) At one point, no doubt under the influence of his impending meeting with his wife, Nerzhin talks about what it means to be separated from her: 'You know, I thought I could stand anything . . . But when they trample on the one live feeling that's left to me—my love for my wife—I just can't take it.' (p. 198)

In practice, Nerzhin can take it. Neither for him nor for the other prisoners are relations with women the most important of their aspirations. There are clandestine affairs between the prisoners and the free workers, but for the most part, like Sologdin's with Larissa or Nerzhin's with Sima, they are casual relationships. The unhappy wives outside are not well rewarded for their devotion. Nerzhin's philosophical preoccupations seem to be more important to him than Nadya, and neither she nor Gerasimovich's Natasha are seriously considered when their husbands are given the chance to win an early release. The wives put their relationships with their husbands above everything else, but the husbands do not return the compliment. Even Ruska, infatuated though he is with Clara, does not hesitate to consider that they will never see each other again if he persists with his plan to expose the informers.

In his open letter to the Congress of the Union of Writers in 1967 Solzhenitsyn voiced strong criticism of the narrow ideological framework within which Soviet literature and literary scholarship are required to function. He warned that:

> Literature cannot develop in between categories of 'permitted' and 'not permitted', 'about this you may write' and 'about this you may not'. Literature that is not the breath of contemporary society, that dares not transmit the pains and fears of that society, that does not warn in time against threatening moral and social dangers—such literature does not deserve the name of literature; it is only a façade. Such literature loses the confidence of its own people, and its published works are used as wastepaper instead of being read.[14]

This is the point the students are making in *For the Good of the Cause* and Solzhenitsyn returns to it in *The First Circle*.

It is sometimes difficult to avoid the impression that the episodes enabling Solzhenitsyn to attack Soviet literature are introduced rather too deliberately for the purpose. A literary discussion is a standard feature of his stories and novels on contemporary themes. In *One Day* for instance Shukhov interrupts a conversation about Eisenstein between Tsezar and the old *zek X 123* which has no connection with the current action of the story. Rusanov's daughter with her literary pretensions in *Cancer Ward* is, as Solzhenitsyn acknowledges, a caricature. So to some extent is the Stalin prize novelist Galakhov. Galakhov is not out of place in a broad survey of Soviet society, but the lengthy expositions of his point of view are disproportionate in *The First Circle*. He seems to be present at the Makarygin's party for the sole purpose of being interviewed by Volodin and then reflecting for a page or two. With Galakhov Solzhenitsyn falls into a socialist-realist habit which he himself decries, namely using a literary work as a platform for preaching and polemics.

Three characters in *The First Circle* who preserve their faculty for independent thought, Khorobrov, Clara and Volodin, pronounce judgements on contemporary Soviet literature close to Solzhenitsyn's own. In Khorobrov's view, the swelling crowd of writers are producing books 'for morons who had seen and knew

14. Labedz, *op. cit.*, p. 66.

nothing of life and were only too delighted to be amused with any rubbish. Everything which really moves the heart was absent from their books.' (p. 168) He prefers to read *The Count of Monte Cristo*.

For Clara literature has been killed by the teaching at school. When later at university she acquires the opportunity to see something of life she concludes that literature depicts a world 'made up of everything except what you could see with your own two eyes.' (p. 238) The writers to whom Solzhenitsyn disparagingly refers, Panferov, Babayevsky, Prokofiev, Gribachev and the barely disguised Vasilii Azhayev (his novel *Far from Moscow* is given as *Far from us* in *The First Circle*) all contributed in novels or poems to the false picture of life presented by literature in the post-war years.

The main debate on Soviet literature is between Makarygin's two sons-in-law, Volodin and Galakhov. Galakhov bears a close resemblance to the novelist and poet Konstantin Simonov. It may not be without significance that Simonov, whose review of *One Day* was among the most enthusiastic and who wanted to see *Cancer Ward* in print, expressed his opposition to the publication of *The First Circle*. Volodin pronounces a telling indictment of Galakhov and those who write like him. He has no ideas save 'the conventional ones you get from socialist realism'; his war novels resemble military textbooks. Finally, and significantly in view of Solzhenitsyn's own achievements, Soviet writers have failed to fulfil the traditional role of the Russian writer, to speak as the conscience of the nation. Volodin says:

> 'Anyway, writers always remind me of prosecutors, except that they get no leave and no rest. Wherever they are, they are always pursuing their enquiry into crime, real or imaginary.'
>
> 'You mean they are the voice of conscience.'
>
> 'Judging by what some of you write, I would say—not always.'
>
> 'Yet it isn't crime we look for in a human being—we look for his qualities, his better side.'
>
> 'That's just where you cease to play the part of conscience.' (p. 360)

Volodin continues:

> 'Aren't writers supposed to teach, to guide? Isn't that
> what I was always taught? And for a country to have
> a great writer—don't be shocked, I'll whisper it—is
> like having another government. That's why no regime
> has ever loved great writers, only minor ones.' (p. 361)

One of the most sympathetic and sensitively drawn of the
portraits in the 'first circle of hell' is that of the old painter
Kondrashov Ivanov. Solzhenitsyn adds a certain aura to his
personality by having him as a descendant of one of the Decembrists. Kondrashov Ivanov expounds his approach to art to
the guests at Nerzhin's birthday party wedged between their
bunks. Kondrashov's pictures are ugly in the eyes of his 'patrons',
because he refuses to emulate the academic genre painting of the
Wanderers who were held up as models for official Soviet art.
Were he to paint the Easter Procession his picture would be very
different from Repin's.

On his return from the meeting with his wife Nerzhin visits
Kondrashov's studio. He examines some of the landscapes amidst
the disorder of unfinished and neglected pictures. Whether in 'The
Ravaged Oak' and 'The Autumn Stream' Solzhenitsyn was remembering pictures which he had actually seen in Mavrino is not
known, but his description of them reveals his own sensitivity to
the Russian countryside and also a remarkable visual imagination.
The two pictures recall some of his own prose poems, such as
Lake Segden and *A Storm in the Mountains*.

Like the prose poems, the pictures have a symbolic resonance
which Solzhenitsyn deliberately invites the reader to perceive
although within the context of such a starkly realistic work as
The First Circle the device may seem precious. If *Lake Segden* is,
perhaps too obviously, a figurative evocation of Stalin's evil hold
over Russia, 'The Ravaged Oak' is also Russia or the Russian spirit
represented by the Church:

> The picture was of a lone oak tree, which by some
> mysterious fate was growing on an outcrop of a bare
> cliff-face. A dangerous pathway led up the precipice

towards the tree, carrying the eye of the viewer with it.
The tree was gnarled and bent by the hurricanes
which blew there. The stormy sky behind the tree was
a sky where the clouds never parted, the sun never
shone. Disfigured by unceasing combat with the winds
which constantly tried to uproot it from the cliff, this
obstinate, angular tree with its broken, claw like,
twisted branches, had never given up the struggle and
clung on to its precarious patch of ground over the
abyss. (p. 252)

Kondrashov himself comments on his picture: 'This Russia of
ours is not as tame as it looks. It will not submit! It has never
meekly accepted the Tartar yoke. It fights back.' (p. 257) In
Chapter four it was seen how Solzhenitsyn uses the image of the
Tartar hordes for the modern generation of Stalin-inspired van-
dals. In Yakonov's recollection of his visit to the little Moscow
church with Agniya the link between the oak tree and the church
as well as with *The Easter Procession* is established:

There was not much room inside the railings—a path
just wide enough for the priest and deacon walking
side by side to lead the Easter procession round the
church . . . in a corner of the churchyard grew an old
oak tree taller than the church . . . it stretched itself
protectively over the dome and the street making the
church seem even smaller. (p. 128)

Perhaps 'The Autumn Stream' with its 'chill water waiting for the
grip of the ice' is also a visual evocation of Russia. Solzhenitsyn
suggests this by the stream's 'power to absorb the change in
temperature (by which) it held in itself the balance between
autumn and winter and perhaps some other, less intangible
balances.' (p. 256)

The streak of romanticism which obtrudes from time to time
in Solzhenitsyn's work reappears in Kondrashov's idea for his
picture of Parsifal's first sight of the castle of the Holy Grail.
The old artist expresses to Nerzhin an instinctive belief in the
existence of the human soul:

> 'Man is invested from birth with a certain . . . essence.
> It is as it were the nucleus of his personality, his ego . . .
> he has something to measure himself with . . . he can
> look at an image of perfection, which at rare moments
> manifests itself to his inward ego.' (p. 258)

This is perhaps the same idea as Solzhenitsyn had in mind when
he had Doctor Oreshchenkov describe in *Cancer Ward* that image
of eternity with which every man is born.

Then Kondrashov shows Nerzhin his picture—'What a man
might experience when he suddenly glimpses the image of perfection.' The picture has a special meaning for Nerzhin. If the
prisoners can be thought of as the fraternity of the Grail in search
of a hidden truth, he is their leader. And Nerzhin is shortly going
out again from Mavrino. Perhaps Solzhenitsyn intended Parsifal's
glimpse of the castle of the Holy Grail to be Nerzhin's vision of
the happiness and understanding he is seeking.

The First Circle is a massive, crowded and convincing novel.
Solzhenitsyn is a ruthlessly honest writer, burning with indignation, but retaining an objectivity and sense of proportion not to
be expected in a man who has experienced what he has been
compelled to endure. His grasp of the true nature of Stalinism is
remarkable. The mirror he holds up to society does not lie and
the scales he uses are just. As 'a record of our times, of ourselves'
The First Circle is the most important work of literature to have
been written in the Soviet Union. It is also a social document of
immense value. The words which Edmund Wilson used to
describe *Doctor Zhivago* may as appropriately be applied to *The
First Circle*:

> Nobody would have written it in a totalitarian state
> and turned it loose on the world who did not have the
> courage of genius . . . His work is a great act of faith
> in art and in the human spirit.[15]

To say that *The First Circle* is a portrait of Soviet society, and a
brilliantly successful one, is also to suggest where its shortcomings
as a novel lie. For Soviet society was and is totally politicised.

15. Edmund Wilson, *The Bit between my Teeth* (New York), 1966.

Solzhenitsyn believes that only when politics, which encourage the basic materialist instincts in man, have been banished from ordinary Soviet life can humane values be restored and the spiritual wealth of the Russian people, symbolised in his works by the Church, begin to grow again. Being a combatant writer, Solzhenitsyn uses every means at his disposal to help bring these things about. Bureaucracy and the politicisation of life are his principal targets, but in attacking them he falls to some extent into the trap of himself adopting political methods. It has already been observed that the main characters are clearly distinguished intellectually, but are only sketchily realised in human terms. This limitation may be partly attributable to the short time-span which enables Solzhenitsyn to show how the characters react to one another, but precludes development in their relationships. Sexual encounters in *The First Circle* are too fleeting to be deeply significant. The only characters who come really to life as human beings are the old peasant Spiridon, Nadya and Volodin. Most of the others are either conceived ideologically in terms of their arguments with each other, are satirised like the Party secretary Stepanov, or even border on caricature as do Mishin and Shikin.

It can also be argued in criticism of *The First Circle* that Solzhenitsyn selects his material with the rather too deliberate intention of amassing the evidence for a comprehensive exposure of Stalinism. There is hardly an aspect of the injustice, incompetence or tyranny of the late 1940s which does not get an airing. Waste, work methods, the judicial system, anti-semitism, Party work, informing, literature and the less-publicised sides of the war—war correspondents, the treatment of prisoners—are all included. Solzhenitsyn's text is littered with small but telling asides on some subject or another he wishes to mention. The education system, for instance (p. 30), or the collective farms—'Spiridon could understand anything that had reason, but why they had got rid of the horses was beyond him. Then there had been all this talk about their work being done by tractors, but in the upshot the women had to do it.' (p. 430) Solzhenitsyn even refers to the behaviour of the Soviet troops in Germany at the end of the war—the subject of his first play *The Feast of the Victors*—in Nerzhin's confession to Sima: 'When I remember what I did during the war in Germany, what we all did.' (p. 518)

Solzhenitsyn continued to work on *The First Circle* after it had been published in the West and additional chapters have been circulating in *Samizdat* for some time. In 1972 he stated that the latest version was the one he preferred. But whether or when he will produce a definitive text is at present uncertain.

Maybe one day, too, he will write the continuation of Nerzhin's philosophical odyssey in the camps. In the meantime, he has provided the scenario in the pages of the massive *Gulag Archipelago*.

6 Cancer Ward

In *The First Circle* the moral and social pressures which weigh on the characters stem directly from the nature of the society in which they live. In one sense they occupy a position of unique detachment. There is a superb passage in which Solzhenitsyn likens Mavrino to an ark giving the prisoners a special vantage point from which to view the world around them: 'From this ark, serenely ploughing its way through the darkness, it was easy for them to survey, as from a great height, the whole tortuous, errant flow of history.' Yet at the same time they are really an integral part of the system, 'like people completely immersed in it, they could see every pebble in its depths.' (p. 296) In *Cancer Ward* Solzhenitsyn lifts his characters, as usual a varied assortment of Soviet citizens, out of the main stream of national life and isolates them in a hospital ward. The reasons for the patients being there have nothing to do with politics, and political considerations rarely intrude into the everyday life of the hospital. It is true that they often argue about political matters and both Kostoglotov and Rusanov realise that their futures will be profoundly affected by events taking shape outside. But so long as they remain in the cancer ward, social considerations do not apply to them. It is another of the perverse ironies of Stalinism that, as Ivan Denisovich and Col. Yakonov discovered, hospital is the surest and perhaps the only refuge from the dictator's tyranny. In the cancer ward Rusanov feels safe from the problems which await him on his discharge and Kostoglotov is able to play a role which his political status would never permit outside. *Cancer Ward* is set in Tashkent, a device which also assists in creating an impression of distance from the inner circles of Soviet life.

Solzhenitsyn's preoccupations in *Cancer Ward* are again questions of social and personal morality. And among his themes are those at stake in *The First Circle* and the stories—conscience and the nature of freedom. But here they are lifted to a level of universality which transcends local conditions. To some extent the reactions of each patient to his disease and the possibility of death reflect the area of the social environment from which he comes. Ultimately, however, it is as human beings that Solzhenitsyn puts them to the test, not as the bearers of some or other intellectual belief, as were Nerzhin and his friends. Kostoglotov's idea of freedom means refusing to surrender control over his own destiny. He is ready to fight against the malign tyranny of Stalinism and protest against modern societies which turn their subjects into helpless victims of omnipresent authority. So he opposes the benevolent tyranny of the doctors as well.

There is even less plot in the conventional sense in *Cancer Ward* than in *The First Circle*. The novel covers a longer period than any of Solzhenitsyn's other stories, four months, and there is an opportunity for the author to develop his characters. In practice he makes little effort to do so. Only the friendships between Kostoglotov and the two female staff, Dr. Gangart and Nurse Zoya, make significant progress during the course of the novel. The main substance of *Cancer Ward* is a comparison of the patients' attitudes and characters which are already fully formed. They interact, argue, agree and disagree, but they do not influence each other, either intellectually or personally.

Solzhenitsyn introduces the inmates of the cancer ward one by one through the eyes of their fellow patients. To Rusanov, the bigoted Russian bureaucrat, the patients are either apathetic wrecks or non-Russians. From the beginning he regards Kostoglotov as an uncouth lout and an anti-Soviet element. The noisy arguments they have in the succeeding weeks only serve to fortify his judgement. Vadim, like Rusanov a communist, also does not at first like Kostoglotov. But he soon perceives that his coarseness is only a façade. He concludes that it is only Kostoglotov's unhappy life and perhaps certain flaws in his temperament which have made him appear arrogant and hostile.

Vadim's more charitable opinion of Kostoglotov reflects his own more generous nature. There is also a review of the cancer ward patients by the author. Solzhenitsyn confines himself in these brief portraits to their external appearance and how they spend their time. But following Tolstoy, Solzhenitsyn is an acute observer of the outer signs of a man's inner condition. Rusanov's spectacles suggest his role in society, and his red ears express his injured surprise whenever he can hardly believe what he hears with them. Physical appearances point to the inner contrast between Vera Gangart and Nurse Zoya. The sensuous Zoya's figure is trim and healthy, while Vera's gentle hazel eyes and slender legs harmonise with the spirituality of her nature.

More than any of Solzhenitsyn's other larger works, *Cancer Ward* seems to invite metaphorical interpretation. If Ivan Denisovich's day in the labour camp contains the essence of Stalinist society as portrayed in *The First Circle*, the broader reaches of human experience find a certain parallel in the life of the cancer hospital. At his 1966 meeting with the Union of Writers, Solzhenitsyn was reproached, as he was by certain critics of *One Day*, for not actually showing the country outside the confines of the cancer ward, and in reply he explained his approach:

> Literature can never grasp everything in life. I will take an image from mathematics and explain it. Every work passes through one point. You choose this point according to your personal bias, your life history, your superior knowledge and so forth. The point which I chose, the cancer ward—was suggested by my own illness . . . But I do not feel the necessity to describe the territory of the republic beyond the limits of the cancer ward. You can't reflect everything, but that part of the whole picture which is essential can be depicted through that single point.[1]

The novel is full of little incidents and ironies which draw attention to the wider implications of the narrative. There is ample evidence, for instance, that Solzhenitsyn was himself conscious of the cancerous tumour as a symbol of the malignant disease of Stalinism which had beset the Soviet body politic. And he told the Union of Writers in 1966, that 'the prison camps were, of course, a tumour'.[2] At the same time there is no reason to

1. Labedz, *op. cit.*, p. 61.
2. *Ibid.*, p. 60. See also Chap. 8.

doubt that Solzhenitsyn was quite serious when he told his next meeting with the Union of Writers in 1967 that the subject of *Cancer Ward* is, first and foremost, 'specifically and literally cancer, (a subject) which is avoided in literature, but which those who are stricken with it know only too well from daily experience . . . perhaps soon, someone among those present will be confined to a ward for cancer patients, and then he will understand what kind of a "symbol" it is.'[3]

Much of the action of *Cancer Ward* is based on a similar episode in Solzhenitsyn's own life. He has said that he 'invented nothing.'[4] Like Kostoglotov, Solzhenitsyn developed cancer while still in the labour camp and the course of their disease and the treatment was the same, except that Solzhenitsyn is not known to have suffered from the repressive effects of hormone therapy. In 1953 Solzhenitsyn reached Kok Teren, his place of exile, having undergone an operation, and there his condition began to deteriorate. 'My cancer developed rapidly; at the end of 1953 I was at the brink of death, unable to eat or sleep and severely affected by the poisons of the tumour.'[5] Dying, Solzhenitsyn managed to reach Tashkent, where he was saved by his exceptional tolerance to X-rays. After a long treatment he was discharged from the hospital in 1954, and has not since been troubled by cancer.

Cancer Ward is, then, a study of cancer as a physical disease from the point of view of the patients and of the doctors who treat them. Solzhenitsyn shared Kostoglotov's sceptical turn of mind and was unwilling to commit himself unconditionally to the hands of his doctors. He was also a trained scientist, well equipped to acquire a firm grasp of oncology which he studied from medical books, 'in order to check up on the way they were treating me.' In *Cancer Ward* he records carefully his observations of the disease in himself and his fellow patients and the methods which were employed to cure it. Medical authorities have been unable to fault the accuracy of his descriptions.

But *Cancer Ward* is a novel, with its main focus on people. And cancer is not simply a painful physical affliction, it is a cause of death. The theme of *Cancer Ward* is 'the conflict of life against

3. *Ibid.*, p. 97.
4. *Ibid.*, p. 62.
5. *Sunday Times* (London), 20 June 1971.

death',[6] with all the attendant moral ramifications. For the doctors there are the crucial issues of medical ethics, to treat or not to treat, and what price can be asked of the patient for his cure. Their position becomes almost unbearably poignant when the most revered and humane of their number is herself laid low by cancer.

For the patients cancer brings the crisis of their lives. In the labour camps and prisons Solzhenitsyn shows people struggling in their different ways with the problems of how to keep going and what they can still make of themselves. The situation of the patients in *Cancer Ward* is altogether more acute. For most of them death, both imminent and unavoidable, is all they have before them. All that is left to them is to discover how to meet it. Cancer reduces them to a common level. The artificial distinctions of rank and wealth raised by society are now of no regard. The highly placed official must lie beside the social outcast, the Russian beside the non-Russian, the old beside the young. Rusanov in the space of a few hours discovers that all his plans for the future have become meaningless. Death and/or fear of death strips from each person the inessential layers of character, leaving only the basic resources of his being on which to rely. And like the prisoners, the patients can expect little comfort from each other. In Solzhenitsyn's cancer ward there are many wounding personal clashes, but no sustaining personal attachments. In *The First Circle* the Soviet philosophy of mutual aid and collective security is shown to be an absurd mockery, and it has nothing to offer a man confronted by death from cancer. Kostoglotov spells it out when he tells his fellow patients that they are only members of the collective when they are alive. As soon as they are about to die they are released from the collective to die alone. Although unable to admit it, even to himself, Rusanov has come to feel this already. Even the affairs of state to which he is normally devoted fail to sustain and cheer him.

Aleks in *A Candle in the Wind* believes that man's greatest task in life is to devise a philosophy which will equip him to meet death. (p. 185) This is the test which the cancer patients are now obliged to face. Released from the collective and from pressures towards conformity in thought and action they are

6. Labedz, *op. cit.*, p. 61.

revealed to themselves as individuals. Solzhenitsyn makes cancer a device for moral exploration through which each character exhibits his capacity for self-knowledge or self-deception. It is a mark of the subtlety with which he employs this device that he places no two characters in identical circumstances. Differences in personal background and in the nature and severity of the disease provide as many fine variations on the theme as there are sufferers. The older patients, Podduyev, Shulubin and Rusanov are induced to undertake a searching appraisal of their past lives, while the younger ones such as Vadim, Dyoma and Asya (only the first of whom expects to die) can still think of the future. Kostoglotov, who has no fear of death, and Chaly, who never thinks of it, are eccentric in their attitudes to cancer.

Podduyev and Shulubin are brought to terms with their past by cancer, which they come to accept as a form of natural justice. Both manage, if belatedly, to respond to the demands of conscience. Podduyev, a former K.G.B. man, lived all his life only for today. He knocked about the country going wherever his instinctive needs, women, vodka and the money in his pocket took him. Never knowing a day's illness and filling his life with work and rough pleasures, Podduyev had no occasion to stop and reflect on the right and wrong of what he was doing or what sort of a man he had become. His entire life has prepared him for living, not for dying, and when cancer unexpectedly struck him there was nothing in his character to help him cope with it. He had no strength of character with which to adapt to the change. He attempted a façade and people praised his willpower. But it was not willpower, it was blind, cold terror. Podduyev is the subtlest psychological portrait in the novel. Solzhenitsyn shows how he attempts to mask his fears by aggressive and disagreeable behaviour towards the other patients. He ridicules every hope they cling to as he tries to relieve his own loneliness and convince himself that they will all share his fate.

The book which Podduyev is persuaded to read is Tolstoy's *What Men live by*, with the simple message that men live not by worrying about their own affairs, but by the love of others. Under the book's stimulus Podduyev goes over his own life and realises how he has fallen short of Tolstoy's ideal. He is haunted by the reproach of one of the young prisoners whom he probably sent to their deaths. Now his turn has come and his past has caught up with him. But if it cannot save him or even bring him peace of mind, Tolstoy's book has taught Podduyev the lesson of his life. During a discussion in the ward on the possibility of self-induced healing Podduyev suggests that what is needed is something he knows he can never have—a clear conscience.

Ironically, it is Podduyev's tongue which has developed cancer—the tongue with which he lied and swore and told crude stories all over Russia. But for Shulubin, whose crimes against his fellow men have been more base, the retribution is more severe. He has a tumour about which he cannot even speak—cancer of the anus. And the operation to cure it will cause him to forfeit the company of his fellow beings. On the eve of his operation, which he is not sure he will survive, he makes his confession to Kostoglotov. In the old Bolshevik, Shulubin, the pangs of conscience which began to torment Rubin have become an obsession. He relates how he preserved his life by compromising at every turn. He knew what he was doing was wrong, but only on the edge of the grave can he bring himself to acknowledge his fault. Quoting Pushkin he observes that in his time all men were either tyrants, traitors or prisoners. And he knows he has never been either the first or the last.

Shulubin's conclusion from his fearful life is the same as Tolstoy's message to Podduyev. Happiness can only come to human society as a result of genuine brotherly love. Man is distinguished from animals, who can also be happy in their own way, by his ability to feel affection. Like Podduyev, Shulubin's realisation has come too late. There will be no second chance for him on this earth. But alone among Solzhenitsyn's cancer victims, Shulubin in his desperation reaches out towards something eternal. Again echoing Pushkin he expresses to Kostoglotov his conviction that not everything in him will die. He feels that in him as in all men there is some small piece of the universal spirit which will survive.

The most important victim of cancer for Solzhenitsyn's exploration of the moral foundations of Soviet society is Rusanov. Rusanov is a typical bureaucrat of the Soviet new class. Narrow minded, arrogant and status conscious, he is an archetypal *chinovnik* in the Russian nineteenth-century tradition, from Gogol's petty officials to Chekhov's *Man in a Box*. He also recalls the protagonist of Tolstoy's *Death of Ivan Ilyich*. There can be no doubt that Solzhenitsyn had Tolstoy's pioneering literary treatment of fatal disease in mind when he wrote *Cancer Ward*. The family situations of Rusanov and Ivan Ilyich are similar. Like Aviette, Ivan Ilyich's daughter was a 'handsome young woman ... determined and angry'.[7] And both families agreed in their dislike of the lower orders. The two officials are alike in their style of work. Of Ivan Ilyich Tolstoy wrote that 'he could ruin anybody he wished to ruin' and for him 'the thing was to exclude everything fresh and vital, which always disturbs the regular course of official business, and to admit only official relations with people...' When Ivan Ilyich consulted with his doctor the impression he received 'aroused in him a great feeling of pity for himself and bitterness towards the doctors' indifference to a matter of such importance'. Ironically, the treatment which both Ivan Ilyich and Rusanov imagine that they are accorded by the doctors is the same as they have often meted out to others. Tolstoy manipulates the bludgeon of pain and fear much more ruthlessly than Solzhenitsyn. Ivan Ilyich, carried to the point of death by his illness, finally sees the light, acknowledges that his life has been wrong and drops into the pit of death without fear. Rusanov, however, does not approach death. Solzhenitsyn refrains from showing the last moments of any of his cancer victims. Rusanov manages to climb out of the pit, bruised, but without seeing the light. The author releases him without allowing fear to wring the reappraisal of his past life which Ivan Ilyich achieves. Solzhenitsyn's reticence, which prevents him from exploiting the device of fatal illness to its ultimate limit, is perhaps a handicap. But he is a more ambiguous writer than Tolstoy. And his underlying purpose in writing *Cancer Ward* was quite different from Tolstoy's in *The Death of Ivan Ilyich*. Tolstoy wrote his story under the powerful influence of his own fear of death which tormented him all his life. Solzhenitsyn, on the other hand, has no fear of death, nor do his writings betray any interest in it as such. As he has said, *Cancer Ward* portrays life conquering death.

Over the years Rusanov has evolved a way of life which insulates him from physical contact with ordinary people whom he

7. Leo Tolstoy, *The Death of Ivan Ilych* (Oxford), 1971.

finds disagreeable. He travels by car in order to avoid meeting people in the street. Even his office is a secluded room with a mysterious dark little lobby which gives a caller the brief sensation of being in a prison cell. Rusanov has surrounded himself with a system of mental reflexes in order to secure himself against any threat of which he is able to conceive. He fortifies himself with Party bromides invoking Man with a capital 'M', the People with a capital 'P' and the virtue of optimism. When the patients discuss Tolstoy's question 'what do men live by?' Rusanov replies that men live by their ideological principles and by the interests of society. His own principles are the familiar slogans of the newspapers. The newspapers are his only contact with society.

On these comfortable foundations Rusanov has built his life. Everything seems so harmonious and well thought out. But within the space of two weeks all Rusanov's carefully contrived defences are knocked flat. Like Ivan Ilyich, Rusanov simply can't grasp the meaning of death. With his wife he avoids discussing it for they are totally unprepared for it and have no plans for coping with it. There is nothing in Rusanov's ideology to equip him to meet death. Childishly, he regards its onset as illegal and the bureaucrat in him can find no rules or directives to cover it. There are soon further misfortunes. The need to enter a public ward is almost as painful for Rusanov as the disease itself. There he is obliged to occupy a bed between two exiles, use communal facilities and suffer the foul language and insubordination of his neighbours to whom his former authority means nothing. To compound his misery the familiar world he has left and to which he hopes to return suddenly begins to slip away behind his back. The thought of what the nationwide changes about which he reads in the newspapers might mean strikes such fear into him that he begins to feel safer in hospital.

Unlike the other patients, Rusanov's long look at his past is induced as much by the fate which awaits him if he survives as by the fear of death itself. He reviews his life not in order to attain self-awareness, but for self-justification. In a long inner monologue he reflects on the social importance of his job and the harmony of his private life. And he reassures himself of the correctness of those of his actions which led to the arrest of the people whose return now so alarms him. Rusanov emerges from his self-analysis as a moral bankrupt dedicated to the pursuit of personal advantage. For every act of self-interest he can supply some spurious social vindication. Even now his first fear is not that he will be called upon to answer legally for what he has done. Rusanov is a physical coward as well as a bully. He was the first in the ward to be laid low by his relatively minor tumour. Rodichev and Guzun he fears most of all because they might decide to take matters into their own hands and do him physical violence.

Rusanov reaches his nadir when, under the influence of injections, he experiences a hallucinatory dream. Although also open to symbolic interpretation, Rusanov's dream is clearly an attempt by Solzhenitsyn to reveal the subconscious mind beneath its rigid exterior. Rusanov crawling along a narrow tunnel recalls Ivan Ilyich in his sack. The dream ends in a scene of Gogolian grotesque fantasy when Rusanov finds himself on an unnamed commission called to purge the intelligentsia. His first instinct is still to defend and justify himself. But there is now a hint of a feeling of guilt. Cancer, it seems, is prompting the first stirrings of conscience in Rusanov. Solzhenitsyn twice underlines the symbolic significance of Rusanov's injections against the ominous background of history on the move. As soon as he has read of the changes in the Supreme Court, Rusanov is confronted by Dr. Gangart, ironically a German, standing in front of him holding a hypodermic syringe. Two days later he learns that Malenkov has fallen and Rusanov feels his heart beating like the four famous Beethoven chords. As Dr. Gangart slips the symbolic syringe into Rusanov's vein, Kostoglotov runs out of the ward into the open air. For Kostoglotov too, the events are portentous. What brings the prospect of doom to Rusanov spells hope for Kostoglotov.

There is a providential justice in the nature of the cancerous tumours which afflict the patients in the cancer ward. The liar Podduyev and the old philosopher are stricken in the tongue, the promiscuous Asya in her breast, Rusanov in the neck. But there seems to be no rule which dictates who shall recover and who die. The forthright Vadim and the repentant Shulubin are doomed for sure. The only patients to leave hospital apparently cured and unmutilated are the two for whom justice demands the opposite— the camp guard Akhmadjan, who regards prisoners as sub-human, and Rusanov. As Rusanov's health improves, his anxieties remain, but his incipient conscience disappears again. As he receives Yuri, fresh from his official trip, the notion of clear conscience recovers its former meaning for Rusanov—social duty rigidly and uncompromisingly accomplished. And when he goes home, once more in the bosom of his family, all his old complacency and arrogance return. He has learned nothing from his experience in the cancer ward.

Rusanov's relationship with Vadim and Chaly is an effective example of Solzhenitsyn's use of personal foils. These two seem to have been put in the ward in order to show the discrepancy between the philosophy of life which Rusanov professes and the life he actually leads into sharper relief. Chaly is animated by the same motives as Rusanov. He is an opportunist, the artful dodger, for whom the pursuit of personal advantage is the object of his life and he sees no need to pretend otherwise. He tells Rusanov that we only live once, so why not live well? Rusanov cannot help recognising a kindred spirit and finds himself agreeing. Rusanov is shown up for the hypocrite he is when, on his departure from the hospital he endeavours to escape from Chaly. In the outside world it might not be advisable to be involved with such a person. But Chaly's offer to obtain black market tyres alters the position entirely. He quickly tears a page from his notebook and gives him his home and office telephone numbers.

In Vadim, the dedicated geologist, Rusanov imagines he has found his own kind. Vadim is a communist and speaks Rusanov's language. But while Chaly unashamedly admits his amoral attitude to life, Vadim tries to live honestly and sincerely according to his communist principles. In every way Vadim's behaviour is the opposite of Rusanov's. To the question 'what do men live by?' he answers that they live by their creative work, and his own aim is to accomplish something of lasting value for mankind before he dies. Rusanov's object is to get a good pension. Vadim hates the privilege and stringpulling by which Rusanov sustains himself and is genuinely humane. The 'principles' which Rusanov preaches to his son leave no room for Vadim's view that men should not be judged only by results and that it is more humane to take into consideration their intentions. Finally, instead of Rusanov's blind fear Vadim feels only anger that his life must be so short. Vadim's character and role in the novel are reminiscent of the traditional positive hero of socialist-realist novels. A new man, intelligent and resolute, as Rusanov foolishly considers himself to be, Vadim sets an example of courage and purpose to the younger patients and forcibly argues the Party line with heretics like Kostoglotov.

Vadim is certain that he will die, but refuses to give in. In an image from Lermontov whom to some extent Vadim resembles, Solzhenitsyn likens his cancer to a panther crouching beside him and with whom he has to struggle. Fortunately his whole life experience has prepared him for an eventuality such as this. All his life nothing has given him greater satisfaction than the feeling of time spent usefully and he determines to fill his last months with useful work. Vadim clenches his teeth and applies himself to the search for a new method of discovering ore deposits. In this way he hopes to compensate for his early death and die fulfilled.

After a month, during which the pain in his leg gets worse, Vadim begins to wilt. He reads less and the thought even occurs to him that it might after all be easier to give up the struggle and end it. He gradually uses his prized self-control and wants only to howl like a wild animal caught in a trap. Solzhenitsyn seems to be conducting a polemic against the classic of Soviet positive heroism, Ostrovsky's *How the Steel was Tempered*. Unlike Pavel Korchagin, Vadim is only human. Perhaps in the last resort he is no better equipped to cope with death than Rusanov. Solzhenitsyn does not finally answer the question. Vadim's last decline is not shown, for death itself is not Solzhenitsyn's theme.

The conclusion offered by Solzhenitsyn's examination of his patients' attitudes to their fatal disease is that social and materialist philosophies, however high principled, are an inadequate preparation for death. Adversity can be accepted and even welcomed only by those who have renounced worldly goods and aspirations and have discovered the spiritual dimension to their lives. When Nerzhin and his friends are returning to the camps 'they were as fearless as men who have lost everything they ever had—a fearlessness hard to attain but enduring once it is reached.' (p. 581) Kostoglotov and the Kadmins, who have no possessions they cherish and no position in society to defend, have no fear of death.

These people have managed to realise something of their spiritual wealth and are reconciled to whatever fate may have in store for them.

As in *The First Circle* the most important ideas which Solzhenitsyn wishes to convey in his novel are expressed in arguments between the main characters. Most of them involve Kostoglotov. Kostoglotov comes into conflict with Rusanov and with the doctors and he has a long discussion with Shulubin. The doctors themselves are divided over the problems which Kostoglotov raises for them.

Kostoglotov is Solzhenitsyn's most fully developed character. But he was at pains to point out that 'Kostoglotov is not the author. I tried my best to keep as far away from him as I could . . .'[8] There are many close similarities between Kostoglotov's experience and Solzhenitsyn's, and there are also important differences. Kostoglotov is not an educated man and has developed eccentricities which there is no reason to imagine Solzhenitsyn shares. But his self-reliance and his sceptical turn of mind link him with Nerzhin and with the author and it is feasible to consider him as a medium for Solzhenitsyn's own ideas.

Once he has got over the crisis of his disease the question of death no longer occupies Kostoglotov. He is concerned for the quality of the life he can now hope for, if only for a short time. He has been reading a medical book which he has borrowed from Nurse Zoya. From this he has learned about the risks involved in X-ray treatment. He tells Dr. Dontsova that twenty years ago they irradiated 'some old Kostoglotov' against his will, because they knew nothing about radiation sickness. Like Nerzhin, when he chooses to take his chance in the camps, Kostoglotov tells the doctors that he doesn't want to pay too high a price now for the sake of life sometime in the future. He prefers to rely on the defences of the organism. A little later he finds out about an even more unacceptable threat to his future—the effect on his sexual potency of hormone therapy. His will to resist treatment is redoubled. The doctors, on the other hand, are unable to conceive that their sacred duty to prolong life at any cost can be questioned. They are there to save life, no more and no less. Ludmila Afanasyevna is convinced that any damage to the body is justified if

8. Labedz, *op. cit.*, p. 62.

it saves life. Kostoglotov as a soldier and a prisoner has learned that the value of life is limited. Life which cannot offer a certain degree of happiness and fulfilment is not worth living. Kostoglotov's predicament symbolises the moral choice which the camps and, by analogy, Soviet society itself present to the individual. His letter to the Kadmins sums up the lesson which Solzhenitsyn's own life has taught him. It is the most important message his writings have to offer his fellow countrymen.

Kostoglotov's arguments with his doctors raise for them awkward questions of medical ethics which, being honest and self-critical, they find disturbing. At first Dontsova reacts indignantly to Kostoglotov's obstinacy. How dare he refuse his treatment? But Kostoglotov insists that he only wants to remind her of his right to dispose of his own life. Not even doctors have the right to dispose of another's life. He strikes a sensitive spot with Dontsova. Bad cases of radiation sickness have left her with a deep-rooted feeling of guilt. She is forced to ask herself whether the doctor's right to treat may indeed be questioned.

As so often in Chekhov's 'thesis' stories, the author's sympathy lies with both sides in the debate and the conclusion is ambiguous. Kostoglotov fails to live up to his own principles when he is unwilling to tell Proshka the real meaning of the Latin on his discharge certificate. But Dontsova is made to pay the ultimate price for saving patients' lives—her own. Nevertheless, when she submits to the diagnosis of her colleagues she sticks to her convictions. She refuses to be told the details of their conclusion.

It might be wrong to suggest that Solzhenitsyn intended Kostoglotov's conflict with the medical profession to be an allegory, although in the opening pages of his letter to the Kadmins he himself draws attention to the analogy between prison camps and the cancer ward. But the points Kostoglotov is trying to make do carry obvious implications extending beyond the patient–doctor relationship. From a writer so passionately opposed to the arbitrary use of draconian and untried methods in human affairs the idea of radiation sickness becomes a potent historical metaphor.

The image of the crippling effect of unnatural medical treatment is of course incomplete, even paradoxical. The learned and humane Dontsova or the skilful Lev Leonidovich are not the agents of Stalinism, but are themselves its victims, the so-called 'assassins in white coats'. But the late after-effects of Stalin's drastic and irresponsible measures were very much apparent in the Soviet psyche and upon the body politic by 1955.

Solzhenitsyn's chapters on the doctors are perhaps the best in the book. The little group of eight doctors meeting for one of their five-minute conferences does reflect a broader pattern in Soviet society. The two active surgeons and the radio therapists represent the forces of humanity and progress, while the rest, including the senior doctor, are 'dead wood'. The senior doctor himself, an Uzbek with the exotic name of Nizamutdin Bahramovich is an opportunist akin in his own sphere to Rusanov. He fills the hospital with staff unequal to their work, but impossible to get rid of. His own role is that of a pedant, in his element disciplining patients for petty infringements of the regulations. The real doctors under his administration are overworked and distracted by a feeling of oppression. Solzhenitsyn contrasts the senior doctor with the retired Dr. Oreshchenkov, a man who in half a century has raised himself no stone mansion. Speaking of general practice, Oreshchenkov makes a remarkable plea for private medicine to counter the depersonalized treatment offered by the free national health service. Oreshchenkov's theories are the only instance where Solzhenitsyn seems to be advocating a political doctrine which is overtly non-socialist.

Solzhenitsyn sums up the difficulties of the doctors when Lev Leonidovich recounts the trial of a colleague he has just attended. Fresh from two months in Moscow where he has doubtless imbibed something of the spirit which has so alarmed Rusanov, he speaks out insisting that only in an atmosphere of tolerance and trust can the doctor pursue his profession. And this, he significantly reminds his colleagues, is a problem which goes beyond medicine. It concerns the very nature of the whole society.

The mutual hostility between Kostoglotov and Rusanov flares up on the day Rusanov enters the hospital. Each immediately recognises in the other the sort of person he most despises. Even before he discovers Kostoglotov's independent way of thinking, Rusanov sees Kostoglotov as the type of representative of the People he hates and fears. For Kostoglotov in his turn, Rusanov is one of the parasites who have betrayed the Revolution, and are responsible for the persecution of such as himself. The arguments which regularly break out between them as they lie in adjacent beds reflect the current conflict between the liberal and dogmatist outlooks in the Soviet Union. In Kostoglotov's line of thought and the polemic tone with which he expresses it there is a strong echo of Solzhenitsyn's angry open letters to the leadership of the Union of Writers.

Rusanov, on the other hand, in the words of the Soviet writer V. Kaverin, is 'a powerful incarnation of the dead idol of Stalinism.'[9] In Rusanov's work the methods and spirit of Stalinism live on. His job in personal records administration is to co-ordinate all the little threads which radiate from every individual, threads which if they were to become visible would look like a spider's web across the whole sky. Like Stalin, Rusanov is the spider sitting in the middle of the web, bloated and suspicious. It is interesting that the generally favourable critics at the 1966 meeting at the Union of Writers were least satisfied with the character of Rusanov: 'the hatred he shows as a citizen is so great . . . that it has deprived Solzhenitsyn, the artist, of the use of nuances and the Tolstoyan methods by means of which Rusanov could have been made true to life and not just a journalistic figure, a caricature.' Solzhenitsyn accepted the criticism, but added, 'I tried to depict even Rusanov sympathetically, sometimes with all my resources—well, I suppose not with all of them . . . in Rusanov I attack the consequences, and I ought artistically to get down to the causes.'[10]

The elder children are another pair of foils to the character of their father. Notwithstanding the upbringing he must have had, Yuri has acquired a measure of humanity and tolerance which shocks Rusanov; all the more so since it leads him into 'mistakes' which will reflect on Rusanov's own reputation. In their relationship there is something of the fathers and sons conflict which developed in the Soviet Union in the 1950s and 1960s. Aviette, however, will never be a source of anxiety to her father. With her insufferable conceit and parrotlike command of official formulae, she is, if that is possible, a caricature of Rusanov. Solzhenitsyn makes her visit the occasion for yet another attack on the Soviet

9. *Ibid.*, p. 50.
10. *Ibid.*, p. 61.

literary establishment. To critics who complained that the chapter on Aviette is journalistic he replied:

> I agree. They say it is a farce—I agree. They say I
> broke away from my own style—I agree. But the
> journalism is not mine and the farce is not mine. I
> adopted here an impermissible device—there is not in
> the section about Aviette a single word of my own—
> she uses words spoken in the last fifteen years by our
> most important writers and literary critics.[11]

And Solzhenitsyn acknowledged the purely didactic purpose which led him to include this and other somewhat contrived passages generally ridiculing Soviet literature:

> From the point of view of eternity there is no need for
> that chapter. But after all, words like that were being
> spoken for such a long time from platforms higher
> than this one and to audiences bigger than this one.
> Is it right to forget this?[12]

The hospital ward provides conditions for an ideological debate which would be impossible in 'normal' Soviet life. For Rusanov the experience of hearing sacred truths contradicted and of himself being abused and sworn at is novel and disconcerting. Placed unexpectedly on equal terms with Kostoglotov, Rusanov can only counter the latter's passionate onslaught with his habitual trite phrases. Kostoglotov rudely brushes aside his plaintive cry of ideological sabotage, and he assails the hypocrisy behind the arguments put forward by Rusanov and Vadim. He dismisses their talk of bourgeois survival as sheer cant. It's nothing but human greed, he shouts. There'll be greedy people after the bourgeoisie just as there were greedy people before.

Kostoglotov's release from the cancer ward in a sense symbolises the release of all the other prisoners crowding the pages of Solzhenitsyn's works. The reader can imagine Ivan Denisovich, Nerzhin or even Solzhenitsyn himself stepping 'like a child (who) had

11. *Ibid.*
12. *Ibid.*, pp. 61–2.

only just been born' into the outside world. Kostoglotov's prospects are bright. His treatment has been successful. For the first time in fourteen years he is free to walk the streets of a Soviet city. He even has the choice of two attractive women with whom to spend the night. Kostoglotov's recovery and the changes in the country from which he will benefit are linked by the images of resurrection and spring which Solzhenitsyn invokes in the final chapters. The idea of life conquering death and the past being conquered by the future, the author has stated, is one of the main themes of the novel.[13]

Kostoglotov still has a painful readjustment to make before he can appreciate the true meaning of his release. At first he can find nothing in this newly made world of his that is uninteresting or ugly. He enjoys a *shashlyk*, a glass of wine, an ice cream, and he visits a chemist's shop. After fourteen years of war, the camps and exile, his vision of normal life has become distorted. There is a kind of Tolstoyan 'alienation' in his perception of things. His brain has become so warped that he can no longer see things as they are. The shadow of his past will always colour his view of the present. The crisis comes for Kostoglotov when he visits a department store, and Solzhenitsyn presses home his attack on the materialism inherent in the modern way of life. At the shirt counter Kostoglotov hears a man ask for a shirt, size fifty, collar size thirty-seven. He is thunderstruck. While men are slaving in labour camps and being herded around in crowded trains barely able to obtain a quilted jacket to keep out the arctic winter, here is a neat little man who can remember his collar size. Kostoglotov feels a spasm of revulsion for such a life and wonders whether refinements of this sort do not exclude something else, much more important.

The values which his life have instilled into him have nothing to do with the temple of materialism to which, following the idols of the market place, he has rushed so greedily. The dreams with which he set out, the rosy morning with its promise of a new life, the apricot tree, Vega, have dissolved and Kostoglotov wants only to escape, to lie down somewhere by a stream and be purified. He goes to the zoo.

The zoo proves to be no less depressing for Kostoglotov than

13. *Ibid.*, p. 97.

the department store. The latter symbolises the rapacious material world he despises, while the zoo reminds him of a grey spectre—the camps. He enters the zoo and sees meaningful examples of two opposite modes of existence. On one side stands a spiral-horned markhor, quite still, its slender legs identifying it_in Kostoglotov's mind with Vera. On the other there is a squirrel in a wheel running round endlessly. These two animals represent the alternatives which life offers—the graceful dignity of the markhor or the cruel obsessional treadmill chosen by the squirrel. And as Kostoglotov sees, the squirrel does have a choice. Attracted by the illusion of sham activity and movement it entered the wheel out of curiosity. By now it knows that however fast it runs it will not progress by a single step. Yet it does not climb out and into the tree spreading above. Kostoglotov reflects that nothing ever seems to change. There is nothing from without which can save the squirrel. Nothing can make it stop of its own accord. Its death is inevitable. This is a powerful image with much to say to Soviet readers.

As Kostoglotov walks round the zoo, he imagines each caged animal inhabiting some familiar region of Stalin's *univers concentra-tionnaire*. Then he comes to an empty cage with a notice that the occupant, a Macaque-Rhesus monkey has been blinded by tobacco, cruelly and senselessly thrown into its eyes by a visitor.

Kostoglotov is appalled. The man was not described as 'anti-humanist' or an 'agent of American imperialism', he was simply evil. For Solzhenitsyn man's attitude to animals is significant. Affection for them is an important virtue. For if people stop being kind to animals won't they also stop being kind to each other? The Kadmins love their dogs, so does Dr. Oreshchenkov. Even Rusanov has his Julibarse at home. But there are men who are cruel to animals. Zoya, dressed up as a monkey, is the victim of a cruel joke—her tail is cut off. The Kadmins' dog, Beetle, is shot and Kostoglotov asks, why? He puts the same rhetorical question about the Macaque-Rhesus—Why? It's senseless! Why?

Obsessed with the question 'Why?' Kostoglotov continues past the animals which are inherently evil, the reptiles and poisonous snakes, until he reaches the birds of prey. These he pictures as the camp gangsters, the trusties who eat up the food. Then he finds part of the answer to his question—Mr. Tiger with his whiskers, the most expressive part of his rapacious nature. At the Union of Writers' meeting in 1967 Solzhenitsyn denied that the 'evil person who throws tobacco in people's eyes' is meant to represent Stalin specifically.[14] Perhaps it was due to the pressures of the moment, but he was being less than frank. The tiger's eyes were yellow. In *Cancer Ward* he writes that Kostoglotov had come upon an old political prisoner who had been exiled to Turukhansk. He had spoken to Kostoglotov about the yellow eyes. Turukhansk was the place to which Stalin was exiled before the Revolution. In *The First Circle* Abakumov knew that Stalin 'never accused you; the only sign was a malignant gleam in his yellow, tigerish eyes and a slight puckering of his lower eyelids. (p. 105) Kostoglotov looks at the tiger with hatred and wonders again—why? The question haunts him to the last lines of the book. That in Stalin the evil which they see in men's natures all around them was intensified to a fearful degree, both Kostoglotov and Solzhenitsyn know. But what the ultimate source of evil itself is they are unable to say.

After his adventures in the town and the zoo Kostoglotov takes his place on the train. He has come to realise that poverty is no barrier to happiness. He has decided to live as the Kadmins lived, content with what they had. A wise man is content with little. Lying on the luggage rack, like Ivan Denisovich and Nerzhin just beneath the ceiling, Kostoglotov embraces the same concept of happiness as they—and as Solzhenitsyn himself.

In the chapter entitled 'Cancer of the birch tree' Solzhenitsyn shows symbolically that the resources to cure Russia of the disease of Stalinism are ready at hand, in the heart of Russia herself. Kostoglotov thinks of the camps explicitly as a tumour. If a man dies of cancer, how, he wonders can a country survive with labour camps and exile, which are also cancerous growths. Surgery or the haphazard application of little understood scientific treatments will not remove the growth. The cause of the disease is psychosomatic and it can only be cured in the mind of the patients. One day Kostoglotov reads to the cancer patients from Zoya's medical book about the link between tumours and the central nervous system. The reading of medical books is normally forbidden to patients, as books giving an objective view of their

14. *Ibid.*, p. 98.

condition are denied to Soviet citizens in general. Zoya's book suggests that the cure for cancer can under certain circumstances be self-induced. Kostoglotov then refers to an article he has read which offers the theory that the chemical processes dictating the formation or disappearance of a tumour depend upon a man's attitude of mind, on his conscience. The recovery of society, as Shulubin says in another context, is a matter of ethics.

A second pattern of imagery in the chapter centres on the belief that birch fungus, *chaga*, is a remedy for cancer. The birch tree is a Russian national emblem, growing in Russia, not in the desert conditions around Tashkent. A cure affected by means of the simple Russian folk remedy would emanate from the well-springs of the nation itself, through as Kostoglotov puts it, the natural defences of the organism. Significantly, Rusanov would like to bring his draconian methods to bear on the suppliers of *chaga*, whom he regards as speculators. Thus he would destroy the folk remedy with the dead hand of Stalinism before it can be brought to those who need it. The chapter on the cancer of the birch tree ends with Kostoglotov hearing from the park what he imagines to be Tchaikovsky's fourth symphony. He interprets the melody as the portrayal of a hero returning to life or maybe regaining his sight after being blind. The final movement of the symphony is based upon the Russian folk melody 'In the field a birch tree stood.'

The subject of sex and relations between men and women in general is much more prominent in *Cancer Ward* than in any of Solzhenitsyn's previous works. The earlier stories are either set in a man's world where women are only a distant memory, or, excepting *The Love-girl and the Innocent*, deal with situations where sexual relationships are not particularly relevant. In *Krechetovka Station* and *The First Circle* there is even an impression of typical Soviet reticence on sexual matters and the belief that sex should not be a major consideration in life, at any rate for men. In the hospital, however, men, some of whom are regaining or have not yet lost the capacity for a normal response to the opposite sex, are thrown into the daily company of attractive young women. Solzhenitsyn exploits the situation for a sensitive portrayal of sexual relationships unique in Soviet literature. Two of the patients in the male cancer ward become involved in love affairs.

Sixteen-year-old Dyoma is attracted to Asya, a girl a little older than himself from the women's ward. Their friendship does not develop until Asya discovers that her cancer will cause the removal of her breast and she turns to him for consolation. Kostoglotov becomes intimately involved with two of the hospital staff, Dr. Vera Gangart who is almost his own age, and Nurse Zoya who is ten years younger. Matters with these two reach a stage where both are ready to ask him home for the night. Kostoglotov's two love affairs, which he contrives to conduct simultaneously, with Vera during the day and with Zoya while she is on night duty, reflect his confused attitudes to women. With Zoya his affair begins as a flirtation and proceeds predictably as an almost entirely physical relationship. But his feeling for Vera is curiously spiritual. The matter is further complicated by Kostoglotov's hormone injections which gradually suppress his physical capacity for sex while leaving his attraction to women undiminished.

Kostoglotov's interest in sex revives with the improvement in his general condition. In fact he is more sensitive to women than are others because for six years he has hardly seen one and has almost forgotten what a woman's voice sounds like. He gets intense pleasure from talking to Zoya, admiring her figure and simply being with her. Zoya, who has had many casual love affairs, does not discourage his attentions and is quite ready to retire alone with him. Their relationship reaches a climax in the oxygen room where they kiss while an oxygen balloon is filling. The balloon symbolises the bubble of their friendship which is already filled to capacity and from that moment begins to go down.

Meanwhile Zoya has told Kostoglotov the real nature of the hormone injections. He is horrified and despairs for his future. As he blurts out to Vera, his first life was taken from him and now he is losing the right to perpetuate himself. He will be a cripple and the object only of pity or charity. Then, in a strangely oblique conversation with Vera in the transfusion room he recalls a book he read as a child and which shocked him no less than what Zoya has told him. The writer asserted that psychology is only of secondary importance in marriage and that physiology is all that counts. This for Kostoglotov is the negation of everything he values on earth and he dearly wants to persuade Vera to the same view. Vera does not require persuasion. Her own life has taught her to feel that spiritual values are more important than physical passion in love and can even replace it altogether. Her fiancé was killed at the beginning of the war and for fourteen years she has remained faithful to his memory. One of the millions of Russian women left alone by the destruction of Russian manhood, Vera devoted herself to her work and developed a theory of her own about men and women. Such creatures as Hemingway's supermen have not even attained human level. They do not provide what a woman really needs from a man—tenderness and a sense of security. Now, after many failures she has found a man who can confirm her theory for her, and all her years of faithfulness have found their justification.

Kostoglotov himself has yet to find the harmony of spirit which he has inspired in Vera. His attitudes to his possible future happiness and marriage remain ambiguous. After he has spoken to Vera he feels the urge to take her hand and to kiss it, even though it would contradict everything he has just said. He has made a bargain with Zoya that she will not give him the injections which will take away his sexual potency. Vera on the other hand knows she must persuade him by any means to accept them. Appropriately Vera's name means faith, her own and now his. Zoya's means life, the kind of life she can offer him.

The climax of the struggle between the two for Kostoglotov, who is only partially aware of what is happening, takes place during one of Vera's rounds. She observes that Kostoglotov is not responding to his treatment and guesses why not. Zoya denies complicity and wins the battle of personalities with Vera. But it is the end between her and Kostoglotov.

Vera's invitation to visit her delights and again confuses Kostoglotov. Several times during his day in Tashkent he changes his mind about whether to go. Alarmed, but encouraged by the reproachful gaze of the Nilgai Antelope, whose eyes so resemble Vera's, he goes to her flat only to find her out. He walks away defeated. His willpower is kindled once more by his visit to the registration office and the news that his exile may end. He boards the train but there his fate is finally decided. Pressed up beside a girl by the crush he experiences the blissful torture of feeling her body against his from knee to chin. But sexual desire is all he can experience, he has already lost the power to respond. Kostoglotov realises that living with Vera would be torture and deceit. He can neither keep their high minded spiritual agreement nor maintain an ordinary sexual relationship.

The denouement of the love affair between Dyoma and Asya brings a similar conclusion to that between Kostoglotov and Vera, only in a more exaggerated form. When the promiscuous Asya is told that her breast must be removed, she is probably the least equipped of all the patients to receive the blow. Her life has revolved round physical pleasures—games, dancing, boy friends— and all of these she supposes she will now lose. Her experience leads to only one conclusion, that she has nothing more to live for. Dyoma tries fumblingly to console her. People get married, he tells her, because they have similar opinions and similar characters. But such an idea is entirely alien to Asya and she asks angrily what sort of a fool would love a girl solely on account of her character, who would want a girl with only one breast, when she's seventeen?

Solzhenitsyn has no sympathy for the sexual profligacy of Asya or Podduyev. There is justice in the fate of both. His own ideal is the spirituality of Vera or the mutual affection of the Kadmins. Kostoglotov realises when living with the Kadmins that it is not material well being which brings happiness but the kinship between hearts, and a man's attitude to the world. Both of these attitudes lie within his grasp. If he chooses to be happy no one can stop him from doing so. Only the man who has prepared himself spiritually can meet death without fear; the relationship between men and women acquires true meaning when it has risen above the level of physical desire. Kostoglotov is not a superman. He aspires to Nerzhin's stoic ideal, but he hasn't yet achieved Sologdin's self-mastery. He accepts the principles which Solzhenitsyn proposes for him, but he cannot live up to them. In his final letter to Vera he tells her frankly that even when they were having the most intellectual conversations and he really believed everything he was saying, he wanted all the time to kiss her on the lips.

Direct political comment is sparse in *Cancer Ward*. Solzhenitsyn does not regard it as his duty to provide any, 'it is not the task of the writer to defend or criticise one or another mode of distributing the social product or to defend or criticise one or another form of government organisation.'[15] Is it possible to deduce anything about the politico-economic order which would carry his approval? A return to the ideals of Lenin would seem to be a step in the right direction. The old Bolshevik Shulubin speaks of the April Theses and Kostoglotov harks back to the 1920s as a time of real Marxism. In *The First Circle* the Leninist Rubin is the most sympathetically drawn of the professional communists. At the Makarygins' party the Yugoslav Dushan Radovic views their privileged mode of living objectively, and uses words similar to those with which Kostoglotov castigates Rusanov, 'we need a drastic cure for all this. We need to purge ourselves of this bourgeois corruption! Pyotr. Look at yourself! What have you become? . . . All I want is to get back to Lenin.' (p. 371) Shulubin, however, fires an oblique shaft even at Lenin when he criticises Lenin's widow for lacking the courage to raise her voice against Stalin. Radovic and Shulubin are adamant in their hatred of capitalism, although their ideas of the capitalist West betray little understanding of it. But when Shulubin asks Kostoglotov whether he has lost faith in socialism he has to reply that he is not sure. There are indeed certain things in capitalism which hold an attraction for him.

The philosophy which Solzhenitsyn puts forward through the lips of Shulubin is only in the broadest sense a political programme. He calls it socialism, but like the ideas with which Aleks counters the scientific materialism of Philippe in *A Candle in the Wind*, he believes that it will be better than socialism. Shulubin is concerned with the spiritual values and the ethical basis on which socialism will be built.

Seeing in Kostoglotov an honest and independent thinker, the only one in the ward, Shulubin explains to him that the high hopes that as soon as the revolution was accomplished man would change his nature were not realised. How could they be? It takes thousands of years for man to change fundamentally. Can there be socialism, wonders Kostoglotov, and Shulubin has to admit that it is an enigma. The concept of democratic socialism applies only to the structure of the state. It gives no guidance as to what

15. *Ibid.*, p. 97.

socialism will be built on. Shulubin rejects materialism as the basis for socialist society. Whether socialist or capitalist, material abundance only corrupts. Russia must show to the rest of the world that all relationships must be based upon ethics and upon ethics alone. This is the message of Solzhenitsyn's letter to the three students, written shortly after the completion of *Cancer Ward*.

Shulubin's ideas have a lot in common with those of some of the contemporary generation of political dissenters in the Soviet Union who have abandoned Marxism in favour of various brands of non-materialist thought. Unofficial groups have turned away from Western political models and have revived interest in the essentially Russian tradition of such nineteenth-century thinkers as Berdyayev, Solovyov, Kropotkin and even Dostoevsky. *Cancer Ward* is written in the same tradition. With the possible exception of *August 1914* it is the most Russian of Solzhenitsyn's novels. Echoes of Gogol, sympathy for the 'little man', Tolstoyan submission as preached by Aunt Styofa, and the perennial Russian love for truth-seeking are all intensely Russian features of the literary traditions to which Solzhenitsyn regards himself as heir. And his debt to Russian thinkers is quite specific. Shulubin talks about Russia with her repentances, confessions and revolts, her Dostoevsky, Tolstoy, and Kropotkin. A little later he mentions Solovyov who argued for a social order based on ethical premises, and Mikhailovsky, the populist socialist and believer in the doctrine of free will. Mikhailovsky, says Shulubin, was refuted and banned, but he omits to say that it was Lenin himself who attacked him in his first book. Indicative of the gulf separating Solzhenitsyn's social and moral thinking from official ideology is the fact that none of the philosophers whom he acknowledges as his intellectual forebears is seriously recognised in the Soviet Union. Even Tolstoy and Dostoevsky are accepted in a radically different way from that of Solzhenitsyn's understanding of them.

In all three of the areas of human behaviour which he examines in *Cancer Ward*—response to fatal disease, sexual relationships and the reconstruction of society—Solzhenitsyn dismisses material values and advocates instead spiritual principles and eternal moral truths. The Western reader may question the validity of this traditionally Russian and perhaps strangely old-fashioned approach. He may argue that Solzhenitsyn is lifting his character.

away from contact with social reality and placing before them goals which are impossibly idealistic. Solzhenitsyn, however, is not preaching in the dogmatic Tolstoyan manner. His novel is rather an illustration of his debate with himself. He makes no attempt to suppress his own uncertainties. His main characters fail to live up to his ideals. The only people to succeed continuously are the Kadmins and Vera. The Kadmins, charming though they are, leave an impression of caricature, a touch of Gogol's quaintly grotesque 'old world landowners.' And there is an air of unreality about Vera, especially in comparison with the worldly Zoya. Even the admirable Dontsova collapses when struck by cancer, confirming Dr. Oreshchenkov's opinion that modern man is helpless when confronted with death, that he has no weapon with which to meet it. The conversation between Shulubin and Kostoglotov in the hospital grounds embodies the conflict between the irrepressible idealism in Solzhenitsyn and his seasoned scepticism. When Shulubin insists that his doctrine of ethical socialism is entirely realistic, Kostoglotov objects that the idea is hardly possible, not at any rate for another 200 years. Shulubin offers no reply. And the novel ends on a note of questioning and bewilderment. Lying on his bunk in the train, Kostoglotov recalls with anguish the little Macaque-Rhesus and the evil man who threw tobacco in his eyes, for no reason at all.

7   *August 1914*

In the postscript to the first Russian edition of *August 1914*, published in Paris in 1971, Solzhenitsyn wrote that the idea of writing it first came to him in 1936 and that he had never ceased to regard it as the principal literary task of his life.

The débâcle of General Samsonov's Second Army in the opening campaign of the First World War was obviously a subject of fascination for Solzhenitsyn in itself. His essay written in 1937 was based upon such materials as he could find at the time in Rostov and was purely descriptive. As his knowledge of Russian history increased, however, Solzhenitsyn came to realise that the defeat of Samsonov was more than a disastrous episode in a long and disastrous war. It was a turning point, perhaps *the* turning point in modern Russian history. It was the moment when the hopeful social and political developments in Russia during the years prior to the war came to a halt, when a hole was opened in the bottom of the 'lake' of national life and the water of the lake began to drain away from it for ever.[1] Solzhenitsyn's literary conception expanded to embrace his broader interest in Russian society in 1914 and in the war which brought it decisively to an end.

Such an interpretation of Russian history conflicts sharply with the official view of Soviet historians that the October Revolution was the only real turning point and that the 'imperialist war' was a logical development from an imperialist Europe of which Russia was a part. Soviet literary and historical writing has focused on the events of 1917 and has tended to treat the earlier war years as part of the general circumstances which led up to them.

August 1914 is conceived as only the first part of a multivolume

1. Solzhenitsyn repeats the image of the lake as a symbol for Russia which he used in his prose poem *Lake Segden*.

work which Solzhenitsyn expects will take him as long as twenty years to complete and the plan of which is already quite clear in his mind.

The Germans call the defeat of Samsonov's army the battle of Tannenberg and regard it as their revenge for the rout of the Teutonic Knights at the same place by the Slavs in 1410. It was the first great battle of the war on the eastern front. In the German war plan the defeat of France was the first objective. It was estimated that six weeks would be sufficient and then the entire German army could be released to turn on Russia. The French, desperate to relieve the pressure, urged the Russians to invade as soon as possible. They did so with two armies, the First under Rennenkampf and the Second under Samsonov. The Grand Duke Nikolai Nikolaevich's strategy was for the German forces in Prussia to be engaged by Rennenkampf east of Konigsberg and for the Second Army to strike north-west to the Baltic and so cut them off. The road to Berlin would then lie open. The strategy began well, Rennenkampf inflicting a partial defeat on the Germans at Gumbinnen and driving them back. But conditions did not favour Samsonov. His advance was launched before the army was fully assembled. They were to march without a break for nearly two weeks through an area of sandy ground and pine forests without roads or railways. The men had insufficient food and transport and communications were rudimentary. Seeing the danger, Hindenberg and Ludendorf, who had taken command of the German forces after Gumbinnen, transferred their troops from the northern front to face Samsonov. Rennenkampf's fatal mistake in not pressing his attack made this move possible. Samsonov's exhausted army was met by a force equal in size to itself and vastly superior in artillery. Samsonov, without effective support from the Front headquarters under General Zhilinsky, was unable to get full control of his men, scattered over an area as large as Belgium. In spite of many individual instances of courage and initiative, the Russians, badly led and inadequately equipped and supplied, could not stand up to the hurricane artillery barrages of an enemy superior in almost every respect. Defeat turned into rout and the Russians were obliged to retreat to their own border leaving 20,000 dead and 70,000 encircled prisoners. These indisputable facts form the basis of Solzhenitsyn's narrative of the August campaign.

For all its ineptitude and needless sacrifice the Russian offensive achieved its object in French eyes. The invasion of Prussia demanded a change in the German strategy. Much-needed troops were sent from France to the East and the German onslaught on Paris was blunted. 'In a sense the Russian soldiers who died in the forests of East Prussia contributed as much to the Allied cause as the Frenchmen who died on the Marne.'[2] Tannenberg became a turning point in the history of Western Europe, as well as of Russia.

In 1967 Solzhenitsyn wrote that he had already written two books according to his polyphonic method and was getting ready to write another.[3] *August 1914* is indeed another carefully constructed series of episodes, with numerous characters, each one of whom becomes the hero when the narrative centres on him. The book consists of sixty-four chapters, three-quarters of which are devoted to a description of Tannenberg. The remaining sixteen contain episodes in Russia in the North Caucasus area, Rostov, Moscow and Petrograd. The war is observed mainly through the eyes and experiences of three people—the Army Commander General Samsonov, Kharitonov, a young lieutenant who leads a squad of men until, after being shellshocked and having his unit scattered, he manages to make his own way out of enemy encirclement, and Col. Vorotintsev, on a roving mission to the battle area from the Front headquarters. All three are mobile and from their different levels Solzhenitsyn is able to give a comprehensive view of the conflict. From the standpoint of one of the opposing generals, Herman von Francois, he also looks at the Russian military performance from the German side.

If Samsonov is the central figure in the book, Vorotintsev is the central hero. Impatient, intelligent and observant, Vorotintsev expresses Solzhenitsyn's own interpretation of the battle and the whole campaign. Although not of course autobiographical like the heroes of his earlier novels, Vorotintsev may be regarded as Solzhenitsyn's mouthpiece in *August 1914*, and when he reports to the meeting of officers at the Grand Duke's headquarters he is

2. Robert K. Massie, *Nicholas and Alexandra* (London), 1971, p. 278.
3. Licko, *op. cit.*, part of interview not included in translation in Labedz.

passing Solzhenitsyn's verdict on what has happened. In narration coming directly from the author Solzhenitsyn leaves no doubt as to where his sympathies lie—of whom he approves and whom he despises. When characters like each other, as Krymov and Vorotintsev like Samsonov and he them, it means that Solzhenitsyn favours them too. The reader's anger and contempt is directed in the same manner. Solzhenitsyn also expresses his personal judgements in the general survey chapters which, in addition to giving the facts about historical events, include his own direct comments. Finally he employs what may be thought the somewhat clumsy device of printing words or even sentences in large emphatic type. Solzhenitsyn feels the same anger at the fate of the Russian armies in 1914 as he does at the fate of his own generation and he does not allow ambiguity to disguise his meaning.

The first sixty-six pages of the book are set in the North Caucasus, in the area of Pyatigorsk close to where Solzhenitsyn was born, and in Rostov. In these chapters Solzhenitsyn introduces a range of characters who only reappear fleetingly in the rest of the book and some not at all. The three families, the Lazhenitsyns from the steppe, the prosperous capitalists the Tomchaks, and the Kharitonovs in Rostov will presumably become prominent in subsequent volumes. Isaaky Lazhenitsyn is possibly intended as a portrait of Solzhenitsyn's father. The choice of surname, his place of origin and his joining the artillery before he has finished his university course all coincide with the known facts about Isai Solzhenitsyn, who was killed in 1918. The books he is reported to have read at university, by Mikhailovsky, Kropotkin and Lavrov, formative writers for Solzhenitsyn's own thinking, suggest that he is destined to become a major character. The other brief episodes which occur in Russia itself may seem at first out of place in a book so obviously about a military campaign, but they are vital to the literary conception of *August 1914*. They consist of conversations and disputes in which, as in the arguments between important characters in his other books, Solzhenitsyn expounds the ideological substance of his work. Solzhenitsyn identifies two principal lines of development in pre-war Russia: the forces which formed themselves after the 1905 attempted revolution and which held out the promise of a peaceful and constructive future and those which led to the nation's destruction

—on the one hand the influence of the Court and its dependents, and on the other that of the revolutionary parties. In *August 1914* he shows that the defeat at Tannenberg was the consequence of the way of thinking and acting inspired by the Court, while the forces of intelligent progress, represented in Rostov by Arkhangorodsky and Obodovsky and in the army by Vorotintsev, were brushed aside. The revolutionaries were waiting in the wings.

It is not possible to offer final literary judgements of *August 1914* because it is an unfinished work. Any attempt to do so now would involve serious criticisms. The early chapters have little organic connection with what follows and consequently the work as a whole is unbalanced. The main body of the book is an attempt to give a historically accurate picture of the battle of Tannenberg using primary and where necessary secondary sources. Of the principal military figures only Vorotintsev, Blagodarev and Kharitonov are not real historical personages. But Solzhenitsyn makes liberal use of his literary imagination, particularly in recreating the character of Samsonov, and he does not systematise his data in the manner of a professional historian. He selects his material in order to bring out the flow and the essence of reality. He nevertheless stays much of the time close to the borderline between fiction and non-fiction. When seeking to establish that *War and Peace*, in spite of Tolstoy's own reservations, is indisputably a novel R. F. Christian wrote:

> ... there is no doubt that *War and Peace* has many of
> the characteristic features of earlier European novels.
> It has its love stories, happily crowned by marriage.
> It has many standard situations of entertainment and
> adventure: a girl's first ball, an attempted abduction, a
> wager, a duel, a gambling scene, a hero believed dead
> but in fact alive, a heroine who attempts suicide in a
> moment of despair. It has to do with basic human
> emotions and conflicts, passion, jealousy, courage, thirst
> for adventure. It has its fair share of journeys, meetings
> and partings. Coincidences play an important part in
> the development of its plots. This is not to imply that
> *War and Peace* is like any novel in particular, but that
> it has enough recognisable thematic and other points

of contact to establish it as belonging to that loose and ample genre.[4]

There are as yet very few of these or comparable elements in *August 1914*. The web of human relationships is still very fragile. If Solzhenitsyn's book is to be seen as part of the nineteenth-century novelistic tradition, as his previous books would lead the reader to expect, and not in some way related to the European 'new' novel, then an evaluation must be delayed until it can be viewed as only the opening chapters of the completed project.

Solzhenitsyn is himself sensitive to the question of genre. He does not call *August 1914* a novel. He has invented the term 'knot', and this is knot number one. Elsewhere he refers to it as a book and the first part, but never as a novel. In a sense all his other works are knots too, because they portray a crucial stage in the stories they take up.

Comparison between *August 1914*, even as incomplete work, and *War and Peace* is inevitable. Few Russian writers of historical novels have managed to ignore Tolstoy's intimidating shadow looming over them. Sholokhov began *The Quiet Don* in deliberate imitation of him and there are strong echoes of *War and Peace* even in such a dissimilar novel as *Doctor Zhivago*. The influence of Tolstoy on Solzhenitsyn's writing in general has already been referred to and it might be natural to expect this to intensify when he moved into a literary region which Tolstoy had made his own. There are similarities of circumstance relating *August 1914* to *War and Peace*. Tolstoy wrote his novel between 1863 and 1869, while *August 1914* was written in the late 1960's and was completed in 1970. Both writers took as their central subjects crucial wars which had engulfed Russia some fifty years before. And both interspersed their war sequences with scenes of peace. On the level of minor detail, there are portraits of Tolstoy in the Tomchaks' house striking his traditional poses—reaping and ploughing. Most interesting, perhaps, is the flashback when Isaaky Lazhenitsyn, who claims to be a Tolstoyan, goes to see Tolstoy at Yasnaya Polyana and the sage becomes a brief but palpable character in the book.

The meeting with Tolstoy in the second chapter, however,

4. R. F. Christian, *Tolstoy, A Critical Introduction* (Cambridge), 1969, p. 104.

does not seal Solzhenitsyn's identification with Tolstoy. It rather symbolises a break with him. The boy questions Tolstoy's emphasis on love as the only way of promoting good and creating the Kingdom of God on earth, by insisting that it is an impossible ideal. Tolstoy will not argue with him and repeats 'only love'. His Tolstoyan beliefs notwithstanding, Isaaky goes to war—as a volunteer.

As long ago as 1909 Merezhkovsky pointed out that the background to *War and Peace* was virtually Tolstoy's own and was barely distinguishable from that of *Anna Karenina* where the setting is contemporary. Later critics agree that there is little specifically period detail in *War and Peace*.[5] Tolstoy was concerned with the universals of human behaviour and the inscrutable laws of history. Eternal values are, of course, important to Solzhenitsyn. He has said that 'if a work is so actual that the author loses the point of view *sub specie aeternitatis* his work will soon perish'.[6] And his characters have some general thoughts about history. But he is also, perhaps primarily, interested in recreating a historical milieu in authentic detail. In *August 1914* there are *nouveau riche* capitalists (the Tomchaks), glimpses of the busy life of Rostov which Solzhenitsyn knew in his boyhood and youth, and a visit to the beer house sector of Moscow. His characters express most of the prominent political attitudes of the day. He has obviously researched pre-war Russia carefully, but is conscious that there may be mistakes. In the postscript he asks Russian readers abroad for criticism and for supplementary unpublished material on several Russian areas including the North Caucasus, Rostov, Moscow and Petrograd. Some Russian critics have already offered corrections. Roman Gul', for instance, who knew the student haunts in pre-war Moscow, has stated that well-known professors and army officers would not have been seen in a Moscow beer house such as Solzhenitsyn describes. Gul' also challenges some of the expressions which Solzhenitsyn puts into the mouths of his characters, pointing out that they were creations of a later era.[7]

5. *Ibid.*, pp. 121–2.
6. Licko, *op. cit.*
7. R. Gul', 'Chitaya avgust chetyrnadtsatogo', *Novy Zhurnal*, no. 104, 1971, pp. 72–3.

Fundamental to any comparison between *War and Peace* and another work of historical fiction is the question of Tolstoy's philosophy of history. Tolstoy's thesis turns on his belief that although there are laws of history, they are for the most part unknowable. Furthermore man is powerless to change the course of events, which is preordained. Neither Napoleon nor any other commander, by making a decision or issuing a command, could have made any difference to the outcome of the battles they thought they were directing. Kutusov's genius lay in his recognising this fact and relying on his untutored instinct to tell him when nothing could be done.

Solzhenitsyn did not write *August 1914* in order to demonstrate a dogmatically held philosophy of history. He does not believe in one comparable to Tolstoy's. His most explicit pronouncements on history, placed in the mouths of Varsonofiev and Andozerskaya, who have nothing to do with the battles of 1914, are not, as it happens, inconsistent with Tolstoy. Varsonofiev observes that history is irrational and is not directed by reason. He likens it to a river subject only to its own laws. When Isaaky asks where the laws regulating the stream may be found, Varsonofiev replies that it is a riddle which man may not be able to solve.

But within the broad currents of history man has a capacity to influence his own destiny and those of others, even on a national scale. Solzhenitsyn's interpretation of the battle squarely contradicts Tolstoy. He believes that individuals not only can but must be responsible for what happens. The Russians lost at Tannenberg precisely because they were badly led or not led at all and the Germans won because they had superb leadership. Had Zhilinsky done his job of co-ordinating the two Russian armies, had the corps commanders with the exception of General Martos not been incompetent or cowards the brave and willing soldiers would have been able to do themselves justice. Samsonov was helpless to direct the battle, not as Tolstoy maintains in the cases of with Napoleon or Kutuzov because it was beyond the control of a single man, but because he was not put in a position by his bungling superiors to direct it. When they were well led the Russians fought effectively. Martos' men did all that could have been asked of them. The Dorogoburzhsky regiment achieved feats of desperate heroism under the inspired Col. Kabanov and

Solzhenitsyn says that had some of the other regiments been led by Kabanov, in spite of Tolstoy's ideas, their performance would have been different. On several other occasions Solzhenitsyn openly contradicts Tolstoy. General Blagoveshchensky who is portrayed as an ineffectual coward and is more than once the butt for Solzhenitsyn's sarcastic mockery, has read Tolstoy and tries to model himself on Tolstoy's Kutuzov.

Another point at which Solzhenitsyn challenges Tolstoy is the latter's vehement denial that insignificant accidents such as Napoleon's cold can have an appreciable influence on events. Samsonov was not appointed in Spring 1914 to the post of Governor General in Warsaw and Commander of the army, on account of his poor knowledge of French. Thus he was not able to gain a thorough knowledge of the military plans before the war. And so, says Solzhenitsyn, the fate of the north-western front finally depended on the French language. Somewhat later Solzhenitsyn observes that the fate of battalions or even regiments may depend on such apparently trivial circumstances as the lighting or a blunt pencil.

The theme of personal responsibility is central to *August 1914*. In the 'Russia' scenes the characters of whom Solzhenitsyn indicates his approval—Arkhangorodsky and Obodovsky—accept responsibility for Russia's future. So does Isaaky Lazhenitsyn. On a theoretical level Professor Andozersky tells her students that everyone must accept responsibility for what he does and what others do in his presence. In the thick of the battle the feeling uppermost in Col. Vorotintsev is one of responsibility for what is happening even though he has no official position of authority. He does his best to play a role wherever the situation demands—as when he organises the defence of Neidenburg, instilling in turn a feeling of responsibility into the demoralised Estland regiment, and when he leads the little group of men out of encirclement. He concludes his report to the army headquarters by telling the assembled generals that as officers of the Russian army, they are all answerable for Russian history.

There is reason to believe that Solzhenitsyn in assembling source material for *August 1914*, is quite as industrious as was Tolstoy and, as he has stated, he began as early as 1936. But by comparison with Tolstoy he has laboured under severe handicaps.

In recent years he has been denied access to libraries. In his post-script he said: 'in my own country collections of historical material which are available to others are closed to me', and in his inter-view with American journalists: 'I am writing about Russia, but it is as hard for me to gather material as it would be if I were writing about Polynesia.'[8] Archives are entirely closed to him and elderly survivors of the war are afraid to talk to him.

In the absence of definite information as to what books he was able to use, it is nevertheless possible to make certain deductions from *August 1914* itself. One important advantage he enjoyed was that his own military career was much more intensive than Tolstoy's brief exploits in the Crimea. At the end of his four years' service he fought in East Prussia in 1945 close to the scene of the Samsonov disaster. In the 1960s he was able to revisit the area, now part of Poland. His special interest in and knowledge of artillery is evident. It is likely that the Russian soldiers in the Second World War were as full of admiration for the neat little German towns as they were in the First.

Solzhenitsyn quotes few actual documents in *August 1914* and only those which he would have been able to find in books, but he had access to contemporary newspapers and uses them to compose impressionistic collages of extracts and headlines to invoke the atmosphere in Russia at the time. There was, as Vorotintsev demanded, an inquiry into the defeat of the Second Army, but it was printed in a very limited edition and is now available in the Soviet Union only to specialists. Solzhenitsyn has probably not seen it. Many reliable studies and eyewitness accounts were published in the years following the battle and there are few historical facts which Solzhenitsyn could not have obtained from reading a selection of these. One which he un-doubtedly used was by General Nicholas N. Golovin, published in 1926.[9] Golovin's book is cited as a reference in one of the general survey passages together with an indication that Solzhenitsyn had also read the memoirs of General Ludendorf, and there are nearly verbatim quotations from Golovin on the same page. Somewhat earlier in the book Solzhenitsyn says that

8. *New York Times,* 3 April 1972.
9. Nicholas N. Golovin, *Nachalo voiny 1914g. i operatsii v Vostochnoi Prussii* (Prague), 1926.

Vorotintsev was associated with Golovin at the General Staff Academy where he had imbibed the latter's ideas. Vorotintsev's attitudes are close to Golovin's, especially in his emphasis on the incompetence of the Russian war preparations and her folly in taking the offensive before she was ready. Although Golovin did not himself fight at Tannenberg, he possibly served partly as a model for the character of Vorotintsev. It may be significant that Solzhenitsyn has a fortune teller predict that Vorotintsev will die a military death in 1945 at the age of 69. Golovin died during the Second World War aged 69.

Among foreign sources which Solzhenitsyn used were the memoirs of General Herman von Francois, the only German general who appears in *August 1914*. Solzhenitsyn refers, at times somewhat ironically, to von Francois' being accompanied by his son to take notes for the future book. All Solzhenitsyn's background information about von Francois and his military career is taken from this book, although there are details and comments which are not found there.[10] There is no incident upon which could be based the meeting with Vorotintsev in von Francois' book. Solzhenitsyn invented the episode in order to create a brief personal contact between the two sides. The capture of General Martos is taken from von Francois as is his meeting with the Commandant of Neidenburg, although there is no mention of the latter's name. The coincidence of their both being of French emigré origin is a creation of Solzhenitsyn's. The toy lion which the Vyborg Regiment has found and which later appears as a talisman on von Francois' car is a historical fact. In his diary for 27 August [11] von Francois records visiting the trenches abandoned by the Russians and finding the lion there. He gave it to his chauffeur and it became famous in the German army as von Francois' mascot, being accorded a military rank which was raised after every victory. Solzhenitsyn mentions the lion's being awarded the rank of N.C.O. by the Germans.

10. See Gleb Struve, 'Ob odnom istochnike avgusta chetyrnadtsatogo', *Novoe Russkoe Slovo* (New York), 3 October 1971.

11. Solzhenitsyn gives the dates in *August 1914* according to the Julian calendar (old style) in use in Russia until 1918. Old style dates were two weeks behind the Western Gregorian calendar.

Another foreign officer who appears as a character in *August 1914* is the British military attaché General Knox. Samsonov is irritated by Knox's presence at his headquarters, but Knox gave him a sympathetic portrayal in his book published after the war.[21] Solzhenitsyn's descriptions of Knox's movements and meetings with Samsonov generally agree with Knox's own accounts, although the timings do not coincide entirely. One almost verbatim borrowing, however, shows that Solzhenitsyn has read Knox's book. His final parting with Samsonov is described by Knox as follows:

> I prepared to go off too, but he beckoned me and took me aside. He said that he considered it his duty to tell me that the situation was critical. His place and duty was with the army, but he advised me to return while there was time.[13]

Solzhenitsyn's description of Samsonov's last journey through the forest with his staff also tallies closely with Knox's version. Knox of course got his facts from others, but he got them on the spot and at the time.

> All the night of the 29th and 30th they stumbled through the woods that fringe the north of the railway from Neidenburg to Willenberg, moving hand in hand to avoid losing each other in the darkness. Samsonov said repeatedly that the disgrace of such a defeat was more than he could bear. 'The Emperor trusted me. How can I face him after such a disaster?' He went aside and his staff heard a shot.[14]

Emigré critics have questioned whether the Russian generals at Tannenberg were really as inept and cowardly as Solzhenitsyn makes them appear. The evidence provided by this and other sources suggests that they were. Indeed he chose not to use one

12. Major-General Sir Alfred Knox, *With the Russian Army 1914–1917*, Vol. 1, (London), 1921.
13. *Ibid.*, p. 73.
14. *Ibid.*, p. 82.

very damning passage from von Francois' memoirs. After the Germans had occupied the Neidenburg–Mlava highway a car passed by containing three elderly officers in German uniforms who saluted. Before the Germans could act on their suspicions the car was gone. Von Francois surmises that this was General Kondratovich making his invidious escape.

The Russian generals could not take refuge in the excuse that they were less experienced than their German counterparts. On the contrary, most of them had served in the Japanese war of 1904–5 and some in the earlier Turkish wars. On the German side, only Hindenberg had seen active service, over forty years before in the Franco-Prussian campaign of 1870. After Tannenberg most of the surviving Russian generals were dismissed including Zhilinsky, Blagoveshchensky, Kondratovich and Artamonov. The court of inquiry acquitted Artamonov, but he was never again in command of troops in the field.

General Samsonov's fate symbolises the meaning of Tannenberg for Russia. He is the victim of the jealousies and incompetence of the army command from the feckless Minister of War, Sukhomlinov, down to the corps commanders who served under him. Zhilinsky, the man in Solzhenitsyn's view most responsible for the disaster, tries to thrust the entire blame on to Samsonov. Solzhenitsyn sets out to absolve him. A man of simple faith in God, and almost naïve loyalty to the Tsar, Samsonov made operational errors, but from the beginning he was never given a chance. He was driven towards an impossible objective by directives and taunts from the Front headquarters. He was particularly wounded by Zhilinsky's accusation that it was cowardice which prevented him from advancing more rapidly. Unprepared and unsupported, Samsonov and the Second Army were sacrificed upon the altar of the Entente. Braced by his victory against the Austrians in Galicia, the Grand Duke remarked of Tannenberg, 'we are happy to make such a sacrifice for our allies.'

From the first chapter in which he appears Samsonov carries the mark of doom. As he learns of the first blow to his army, the cutting off of the left hand, the statue of Bismarck looms over him and shortly afterwards he has a premonition of his own death in a bedroom dominated by a picture of Frederick the Great and his generals. At his last meeting with Samsonov Vorotintsev notices an impression of his having been doomed from birth written all over Samsonov's face. Solzhenitsyn again uses the Tolstoyan device of making a physical feature a leitmotif reflecting his character's inner condition. With Samsonov it is his forehead. To begin with Samsonov's forehead is rounded and calm, smooth and furrowless, but as his fortunes inexorably decline his spiritual state is shown upon his brow as if it were a screen. It becomes at different stages defenceless like a target, bare and puzzled. Finally, in a strange anticipation of Samsonov's suicide Lenartovich observes that a good blow on the forehead awaits him.

During the four days of the battle Samsonov, like his army, gradually disintegrates. Solzhenitsyn imaginatively reconstructs the processes of his mind and spirit as he sustains setback after setback. Betrayed by his commanders and still smarting from Zhilinski's taunt, Samsonov cannot blame them, he blames himself. After berating his fleeing soldiers he silently agrees with them. When his last despairing attempt to save his army has failed and he realises that Christ, and the Virgin, his country's traditional protector, have deserted Russia he loses all sense of his responsibilities. He thanks and bids farewell to the army a broken man, burned by the feeling that he has given the Tsar bad service. Solzhenitsyn's description of his last moments is a moving passage.

Samsonov, like Solzhenitsyn's earlier heroes, is an intensely Russian figure. His whole appearance, with his characteristically Russian face, thick black beard, broad ears and nose and his slow 'prepetrine' gait, is reminiscent of a medieval *bogatyr*. A former hetman of the Don Cossacks, devoted to his Church, the Tsar and his country, Samsonov is an incarnation of the timeless rural Russia. He commands the affection of his officers and when he bids farewell to the army he has led to defeat no one curses him, and there were no expressions of hatred. Samsonov and his men were sent to die *in vain* by the liars and the deceivers, the selfish and inept people with whom, he sees, the Tsar has surrounded himself. As Vorotintsev observes at the end of the book, pointing to Zhilinski, when Russia committed herself to rendering assistance, she did not promise to commit suicide. Solzhenitsyn believes that the death of Samsonov at Tannenberg symbolised the suicide of Russia herself.

During the years between the failure of the 1905 Revolution and Tannenberg, despite the continuing suffocating influence of the autocracy and the threat of revolutionary violence, Solzhenitsyn is convinced that there were real signs of a national renaissance in Russia. The former revolutionary, Obodovsky, echoing Stolypin[15] says that ten years of peaceful development would bring unbelievable changes, and he puts before Russia two equal tasks— the development of industry and the development of socially profitable employment. Both he and Ilya Arkhangorodsky are engineers who place creativeness at the head of the list of social necessities. They see the future not in the hands of the Union of the Russian People[16] but in the Union of Russian Engineers. Obodovsky prophesies that the centre of national gravity will shift from the south-west to the north-west, to Siberia, from the Pechora to Kamchatka.

The 36-year-old Obodovsky has a counterpart in the army two years older than himself—Vorotintsev. Vorotintsev, one of the group of young Turks (Solzhenitsyn asks whether they might even be thought of as Decembrists) who emerged after the Japanese war, like Obodovsky despises the autocracy and the revolutionaries alike. In a long inner monologue Vorotintsev analyses the prevailing mentality of the army with its frivolous emphasis on seniority and influence and its contempt for merit. He loathes the Baltic barons, with names more appropriate to the German army than the Russian, the courtiers and the generals with their rows of meaningless medals. The Germans themselves he has to admire as a professional and he has made a careful study of their military methods. The present war Vorotintsev also thinks will be crucial. It will either bring about a Russian renaissance or signal the end of Russia for ever.

The outlook of Vorotintsev, a genuine patriot anxious to make a beneficial impact on the history of his country, in some ways resembles that of Pavel Milyukov, the leader of the Constitutional Democrat Party. The revolutionary parties proper are comprehensively dismissed in *August 1914* by all serious thinkers. The most outspoken attack comes from Ilya Arkhangorodsky who, after

15. P. A. Stolypin, Prime Minister of Russia until his assassination in 1911 by a Socialist Revolutionary terrorist.
16. An extreme right-wing organization encouraging anti-semitism.

accusing his young Socialist Revolutionary guests of being no less exploiters than those whom they seek to overthrow, tells them that revolutions do not bring renewal to a country but only senseless destruction. And the more bloody and prolonged the revolution the greater the likelihood of its being called Great. The would-be young Bolshevik Lenartovich is not so much unattractive as ineffectual. He is bewildered by the unresponsiveness of the peasant soldiers to his attempts at propaganda and is uncertain how best to follow his revolutionary calling—by retreating or by giving himself up to the enemy and emigrating. Solzhenitsyn subtly condemns him by having him speak the same words—'it is a pity that Napoleon did not beat us in 1812, there would at least soon have been freedom'—as the repulsive Smerdyakov uses in *The Brothers Karamazov*.

Some of the more idealistic trends in current Russian thought fare no better in *August 1914* than the revolutionaries. Tolstoyanism, as already noted, was by that time losing its appeal; so too were antiquated populist notions. Varsonofiev quickly disillusions his young listeners about the practical possibilities of loving and helping the 'people'. Kharitonov, at first delighted to find that he has real Russian peasants in his section, discovers the animal side which Chekhov knew when they go looting in Hohenstein. Solzhenitsyn maintains his own belief in simple people and particularly rural people, but there is no mystery about them. There were no Karataevs at Tannenberg. Arseny Blagodarev possesses the same instinctive common sense as Spiridon, the same self-reliance and sense of personal worth as Ivan Denisovich. Solzhenitsyn shows a new facet of the essential Russianness of his peasant characters in one of the most moving scenes in all Russian literature, when it is discovered that Blagodarev was in the Church back at home in the Tambov province and is thus able to sing the entire Orthodox burial service at the simple funeral they give Col. Kabanov in the woods of East Prussia. There are many scenes depicting the stoic courage and loyalty of the Russian peasant soldier, but none more powerful than that of the resistance of the Dorogoburzhsky regiment, who faced the deadly German guns armed with fixed bayonets alone.

Beyond that of constructive work and courage, the philosophy which Solzhenitsyn recommends should have been embraced in

1914 is difficult to define precisely. Varsonofiev ends his conversation with the two students, like Shulubin and Kostoglotov, asking questions and posing riddles. He cannot prove what he believes, he only feels it. One of the students suggests justice and Varsonofiev readily agrees. But his idea of justice is not something which man himself has evolved. It is an entirely independent force which existed before man, and the nature of which man can only guess at. Varsonofiev's ideas are close to the philosophy of 'personalism' which emerged in Russia in the early twentieth century inspired by the Slavophiles and Dostoevsky, among others. Like other facets of Solzhenitsyn's thought, they link them with Berdyaev and hence find an echo in some of the things expressed by Yuri Zhivago. Less to be expected perhaps, in view of the hitherto exclusively Russian cast of Solzhenitsyn's mind, is the informal lecture which Professor Andozersky gives to the students. Andozersky reiterates Solzhenitsyn's familiar anti-political and in this context anti-revolutionary standpoint. She maintains that history is not politics, is not views, but sources. But her tracing of the source of European spiritual life to the Western middle ages, where it transcended material life in a manner which man did not know before or after, is a new departure for Solzhenitsyn's pen.

One of the Soviet critics of *Cancer Ward* declared, rightly, that the end of the story leads to the conclusion that 'a different road should have been taken'.[17] He means, of course, after 1917. The impression that a different road should have been taken is even stronger in *August 1914*. It was the engineers and the young Turks who were pointing to the right road, according to Solzhenitsyn. But their message was swamped in the inevitable catastrophe of the war. Sickened by the callousness of the Russian military leaders and sacrificing his own prospects of advancement, Vorotintsev tries to persuade the Grand Duke and his staff to face the lessons of Tannenberg lest the disaster be repeated again and again. The reaction to the telegram which arrives on the last page of the book as he leaves the meeting reveals that his efforts are in vain. The authorities have learned nothing. Samsonov is already forgotten as they hail a colossal victory and hasten to inform the newspapers.

Solzhenitsyn has given little indication of how his multivolume

17. Labedz, *op. cit.*, p. 93.

novel will develop. In addition to asking for unpublished material on Rostov, Moscow and Petrograd in his postscript he also mentions Tambov, Blagodarev's home region. He probably intends to restore the balance of his work by concentrating more on life in Russia. Meanwhile, he has completed the next knot, which is to be called *October 1916*, and is working on the third, *March 1917*. These two, he has said, will be published together. They will 'incorporate extensive treatment of the social and spiritual current in Imperial Russia on the eve of the Bolshevik Revolution'—as with a swirl and a roar the water drained away for ever from the lake.

8 *The Gulag Archipelago*

Shortly after his arrest in 1945 Solzhenitsyn was being led up an escalator in the Moscow Metro. Why, he asks, did I keep silent? Why did I not try to enlighten the crowd during my last minutes out in the open? Because, he answers, the listeners were too few. 'Here my cry would be heard by 200 or twice 200, but what about the 200 million? Vaguely, unclearly, I had a vision that someday I would cry out to the 200 million.' (p. 18) Solzhenitsyn's novels are indeed an anguished cry to his fellow-countrymen and many have heard him. But even his big novels provided insufficient scope for all he needed to say. So, alongside them he compiled *The Gulag Archipelago*.

Written between 1958 and 1968, *The Gulag Archipelago* parallels almost exactly Solzhenitsyn's fictional writings based on contemporary themes and can to some extent be regarded as the novelist's raw material. There are many points of similarity in both style and thinking. A comparison between certain chapters in the novels and the corresponding sections in *The Gulag Archipelago* helps to illuminate Solzhenitsyn's creative process. Innokenty Volodin's arrest and his experiences in the Lubyanka in *The First Circle* is a good example. But as he observes in part three of *The Gulag Archipelago*, Solzhenitsyn had no expectation of ever seeing it printed and consequently he can have felt no need even of the degree of personal restraint he exercised in *The First Circle*. In *The Gulag Archipelago* Solzhenitsyn surpasses the towering indignation of Dostoevsky and as he piles up the details in all their horror he constantly asks the basic questions: Why? Who was to blame?

Solzhenitsyn wrote *The Gulag Archipelago* for several reasons. In his Nobel lecture he spoke of his sense of duty toward those who died and he dedicates *The Gulag Archipelago* 'to all those who did not live to tell it . . .' Justice demanded that they be given a memorial and Solzhenitsyn determined to provide that memorial. He was determined, too, that the record of the Soviet terror should not be lost, even if all the documents were destroyed. Unable to consult the archives, he augmented his own recollections with the testimony of 227 survivors whose reports, memoirs, and letters he collected to produce a veritable encyclopaedia of Soviet forced labour and the injustices which condemned millions to endure it.

The main thrust of *The Gulag Archipelago,* however, is toward the future. In his reinterpretation of Soviet history, obscured and falsified as it has been by the requirements of the Party, Solzhenitsyn traces the terror back to Lenin and the camp system to 1918. He insists that the injustice and persecutions under Soviet rule far exceed those under the Tsars or even Nazi Germany. The future can only be secured by a full acknowledgement of this terrible past. By 1966, 86,000 Nazi criminals had been convicted in West Germany, but in the Soviet Union a mere handful.

> A country which has condemned evil 86,000 times from the rostrum of a court has irrevocably condemned it in literature and among its young people, year by year, step by step, is purged of it. . . . We have to condemn publicly the very idea that some people have the right to repress others. . . . In keeping silent about evil, in burying it so deep within us so that no sign of it appears on the surface, we are *implanting* it, and it will rise up a thousandfold in the future. . . . Young people are acquiring the conviction that foul deeds are never punished on earth, that they always bring prosperity. It is going to be uncomfortable, horrible to live in such a country! (pp. 176–78)

Finally, *The Gulag Archipelago* is Solzhenitsyn's personal statement, an act of contrition for himself and his generation. They all submitted weakly to evil or stood idly by. And hundreds of thousands actually participated in it. Solzhenitsyn looks back with shame on his behaviour as an officer and wonders how easily he too might have ended up on the other side. As in *August 1914,* Solzhenitsyn acknowledges collective responsibility. Those who did not resist are the guilty, including himself.

Solzhenitsyn calls *The Gulag Archipelago* 'an experiment in literary investigation' and the genre is indeed difficult to define. On the one hand it is a historical work, an attempt to bring together all the facts available to the author on every aspect of judicial abuse and on every facet of the Soviet penal system in so far as they involved political prisoners. All that he has written, he believes is true. On the other hand, Solzhenitsyn's approach is not that of a dispassionate historian. He evaluates his material from a very personal moral point of view. And he expresses his attitude to it using every device in the polemic arsenal. His intention is not only to record the facts and inform the reader, but also to recreate the atmosphere and infect him with his own feeling of horror at what he is describing. The author's manner is thus often that of the novelist employing the techniques, the language, and the eloquence to be found in the novels, particularly in *The First Circle.* Both as a whole and in its separate parts, that proportion of *The Gulag Archipelago* published so far is a considerable work of art, different but inseparable from the novels.

As with his historical novels, Solzhenitsyn was handicapped in his work on *The Gulag Archipelago* by very limited access to written source materials. Apart from his experiences and those of his 227 witnesses, he had to rely mainly on Soviet printed sources, which bore only obliquely on the subject. Thus for the early trials he used N. K. Krylenkoe's *Za pyat lat*

(1918–22) and M. I. Latsis's *Dva goda borby na vnytrennom fronte* (1920). On the labour camps in part three he frequently refers to a collection entitled *Ot tyurem k vospitatelnym uchrezhdeniam* (1934) and I. L. Averbakh's *Ot prestuplenia k trudu* (1936). For his description of work on the White Sea Canal he makes ironical use of *Belomorsko-Baltiiskii Kanal imeni Stalina* (1934) edited by Gorky and contributed to by such writers as Viktor Shklovsky, Vsevolod Ivanov, Vera Inber, and Aleksei Tolstoy, a book which omits to mention that the workers were slave labourers. Elsewhere Solzhenitsyn writes approvingly and cites Evgenia Ginsberg's *Krutoi marshrut,* Varlam Shalamov's *Kolymskie rasskasy,* and General Gorbatov's memoirs. With Western sources Solzhenitsyn exhibits virtually no acquaintance at all. It is significant that of all the numerous references quoted by Robert Conquest in *The Great Terror,* a book covering much of the same ground and written at the same time, Solzhenitsyn mentions only *Forced Labour in the Soviet Union* by David Dallin and B. I. Nicolaevsky (1949). Solzhenitsyn's heavy dependence on oral testimony and the need to conceal the identity of his witnesses inevitably detract in some measure from *The Gulag Archipelago* as a source of historical information. But his honesty of purpose and the fact that his descriptions broadly agree with those of Conquest and others nevertheless encourage confidence that *The Gulag Archipelago* is essentially an accurate record.

To date (August 1974) only the first four parts of *The Gulag Archipelago* have been published and thus it is not possible to analyse the broad structure of the work. It is already clear, however, that Solzhenitsyn has succeeded in ordering logically the vast mass of material, generally organizing it by theme rather than strict chronology. In part one after an opening chapter describing the act of arrest in all its subtle variety, Solzhenitsyn presents an outline history of successive political repressions before returning to the subjects of interrogation and the security police and to descriptions of life in Moscow prisons where he was himself held. He then devotes three chapters to the development of Soviet law and its abuse and the long sequence of political trials of the 1920s and 1930s. Part one concludes with chapters dealing with the death penalty and special prisons. Part two is devoted to the various methods of transferring sentenced prisoners to the labour camps. Part three traces the spread of the camp system from its beginnings in 1918 on the Solovetsky Islands, across Siberia and Central Asia, and then discusses the many facets of camp life. Finally, in the short part four Solzhenitsyn discusses the spiritual and mental effects of camp life upon prisoners and on Soviet life in general.

A professional historian might have chosen just such a layout for his study, but Solzhenitsyn employs also the imaginative approach of a novelist by structuring his book in a pattern of images as in *The First Circle* and *Cancer Ward*. The central image, evoked by the title of the book, is that of a vast system of islands ranging from a tiny detention cell to the wastes of Siberia, which, though widely scattered is 'fused into a continent—an almost invisible, almost imperceptible country inhabited by the *zek* people.'

> And this Archipelago crisscrossed and patterned that other country within which it was located, like a gigantic patchwork, cutting into its cities, hovering over its streets. Yet there were many who did not even guess at its presence and many, many others who had heard something vague. And only those who had been there knew the whole truth. (p. x)

Within this far-flung empire are a few legendary 'paradise islands,' the special technical prisons or *sharashki* on one of which, Marvino, Solzhenitsyn was himself washed ashore.

Solzhenitsyn uses a knot of subsidiary images to describe the endless process of repression and shipment to the Archipelago—the ideas of underground sewage pipes and of waves and rivers of those arrested. The trains feeding the camps with prisoners are likened to ships and the transit prisons are the ports of the Archipelago. All this water imagery creates the impression of the Soviet Union as in a state of constant flux with every citizen living in fear that a wave or unseen current will sweep him off from his family to one of the distant islands. Solzhenitsyn also employs the metaphor of the cancerous tumour as in *Cancer Ward*. In part two of *The Gulag Archipelago* (p. 582, note 6) it stands for the secretiveness which smothers Soviet life. In parts three and four, however, the labour camps are referred to specifically as a cancer. In the words of the title of part three, 'The Archipelag throws out Metastases.' In chapter four Solzhenitsyn observes that 'during the war the entire cancerous tumour of the Archipelag seemed to be an important and necessary organ of the Russian body—apparently it was also working for the war effort, on it also victory depended.' Finally, in part four, chapter three Solzhenitsyn compares the poisonous influence of the Archipelago on the life of the nation as a whole with the effect the cancer in his own stomach had upon his life.

The Gulag Archipelago is a heterogeneous work, the variety of the material reflecting the disparate sources on which the author has drawn. The pace and narrative manner change frequently. When recounting his own experience, as he does in several chapters of parts one and two, the narrative is that of the novelist and recalls *The First Circle*. In contrast, Solzhenitsyn sometimes tabulates his material formally, for instance, the methods of interrogation and the contamination of Soviet life by the presence of the Archipelago, or he may simply give a list such as that of enterprises undertaken with forced labour with which he concludes part three. The book is interspersed by short biographies of individuals, included to illustrate the general theme after the manner of Spiridon's story in *The First Circle*. From time to time the author pauses to indulge in philosophical speculation or to draw the moral from what he has been relating as, for example, pages 175–78 of part one. And there are lyrical passages, chapter four of part two contains several such, and chapters where the material is arranged impressionistically (Chapter two of part one, 'The Supreme Measure.') In chapter two of part two he uses the device of eavesdropping with the reader to describe life in a transit prison.

The organizing principle which assembles the material into a coherent statement is the strong oral quality of much of the writing. The author's voice can be clearly heard venting his anger, contempt, grief, and personal rancour. His tone is constantly rhetorical and passionate. Sometimes it is strident. He often addresses the reader directly in the second person, asks rhetorical questions, and intrudes remarks. Solzhenitsyn's favourite method of conveying his own attitude is sarcasm. As in *The First Circle,* he employs it in bitter comments and asides, drawing attention to the ironies in situations. In *The Gulag Archipelago,* however, the sarcasm is sustained to the extent that it becomes the dominant narrative mode. He recounts the trial of the SRs almost entirely in this manner. The effect is sometimes humourous, more usually it conveys the sheer absurdity of the behaviour of the terrorist organizations. In Solzhenitsyn's presentation absurdity and ludicrousness are as much characteristics of Stalinism as its cruelty and inhumanity.

In *The First Circle* and *Cancer Ward* the source of all evil was Stalin. In *The Gulag Archipelago* the villain is Lenin. Following Khrushchev, the Soviet leaders have maintained that the murder of Kirov in 1934 marked the departure from 'socialist legality' and launched the purges, that Stalinism was merely an aberration which deflected the Leninist ship of state from its true and just course. Solzhenitsyn is at pains to trace all the major political evils he identifies in the Soviet system back to the Revolution. The terror, the security police, the death penalty, contempt for law, political trials, and the camps are all laid at Lenin's door. The notorious purges of the 1930s and 1940s were merely crests in an endless succession of waves beginning in 1918. Stalin did not pervert Lenin's designs so much as perfect them.

> In my preprison and prison years I, too, had long ago come to the conclusion that Stalin had set the course of the Soviet state in a fateful direction. But then Stalin died quietly—and did the ship of state change course very noticeably? The personal, individual imprint he left on events consisted of dismal stupidity, petty tyranny, self-glorification. And in all the rest he followed the beaten path exactly as it has been signposted, step by step. (p. 613, note 4)

Solzhenitsyn hammers home the point of Lenin's guilt throughout the book until it becomes a refrain. There are other similarly repeated refrains. While in no way condoning the Tzarist autocracy, Solzhenitsyn purports to show how all too often prerevolutionary practices were preferable to the *The Gulag Archipelago*. Executions were minimal compared with those of the Cheka and its successors. Interrogation and prison conditions were infinitely more humane. Even the serfs were not obliged to endure the conditions of Soviet zeks. They were not slaves. Even less flattering to the Soviet order are Solzhenitsyn's comparisons with Nazi Germany.

> There is no way of sidestepping this comparison. . . .
> The Gestapo accused him [Divnich] of Communist activities among Russian workers in Germany, and the MGB charged him with having ties to the international bourgeoisie. Divnich's verdict was unfavourable to the MGB. He was tortured by both, but the Gestapo was nonetheless trying to get at the truth, and when

> the accusation did not hold up, Divnich was released.
> The MGB wasn't interested in the truth and had
> no intention of letting anyone out of its grip once he
> was arrested. (p. 145, note 1)

When Stalin deported the kulaks he destroyed more peasants
than Hitler did Jews. The Soviets were using concentration
camps twenty years before the Nazis did; Solzhenitsyn delights
in pointing out that the head of the first such camp was
named Eichmans.

Solzhenitsyn's hatred for the oppressors is matched only
by his contempt for the Old Bolsheviks who in their turn
became their victims.

> One misunderstanding in particular results from the
> image of these men as old revolutionaries who had
> not trembled in Tsarist dungeons—seasoned, tried
> and true, hardened, etc., fighters. But there is a plain
> and simple mistake here. These defendants were not
> those old revolutionaries. They had acquired that
> glory by inheritance from the association with the
> Narodniks, the SRs, and the Anarchists. They were
> the ones, the bombthrowers and the conspirators,
> who had known hard-labour imprisonment and real
> prison terms—but even they have never in their lives
> experienced a genuinely merciless interrogation
> (because such a thing did not exist at all in Tsarist
> Russia). (p. 409)

Solzhenitsyn is unfair to Bukharin and his account of
Bukharin's trial is an occasion when he presses his didactic
purpose at the expense of historical accuracy. It is clear
from *August 1914* that Solzhenitsyn has little sympathy for
any of the revolutionary parties, the best hope for Russia's
future lay with the engineers. In *The Gulag Archipelago*
he comes close to idealising them:

An engineer? I had grown up among engineers, and I could remember the engineers of the twenties very well indeed: their open shining intellects, their free and gentle humor, their agility and breadth of thought, the ease with which they shifted from one engineering field to another, and for that matter, from technology to social concerns and art. Then, too, they personified good manners and delicacy of taste; well-bred speech that flowed evenly and was free of uncultured words; one of them might play a musical instrument, another dabble in painting; and their faces always bore a spiritual imprint. (p. 197)

Solzhenitsyn's purpose is to show how the Revolution placed the worst elements in authority over the best, how the engineers together with the main progressive force in the countryside, the kulaks, were systematically eliminated—Homo sapiens the victim of Homo rapiens.

In *The First Circle* and the stories, the most shocking affront to Solzhenitsyn's sense of justice was Stalin's conduct of the war and his treatment of the returning Soviet prisoners. He elaborates on the theme in *The Gulag Archipelago* at great length. The deportation of kulaks was callous and inhumane, the campaign against wreckers simply absurd, but the fate of the POWs was a tragedy. He learned about it in Butyrki prison:

I felt that the story of these several million Russian prisoners had got me in its grip, like a pin through a specimen beetle. . . . I came to understand that it was my duty to take upon my shoulders and share of their common burden—and to bear it to the last man until it crushed us. (p. 239)

It was claimed that the POWs had betrayed the motherland but:

> It was not they, the unfortunates, who had betrayed
> the Motherland, but their calculating Motherland who
> had betrayed them, and not just once but thrice.
> The first time she betrayed them was on the battle-
> field, through ineptitude . . .
> The second time they were heartlessly betrayed by the
> Motherland was when she abandoned them to die in
> captivity.
> And the third time they were unscrupulously betrayed
> was when, with motherly love, she coaxed them to
> return home . . . and snared them the moment they
> reached the frontiers. (p. 240)

How, Solzhenitsyn asks, could this have happened?

> How many wars Russia has been involved in! Had
> anyone observed that treason had become deeply rooted
> in the hearts of Russian soldiers? Then under the
> most just social system in the world came the most
> just war of all—and out of nowhere millions of tractors
> appeared, from among the simplest lowliest elements
> of the population. How is this to be explained?
> It is frightening to open one's trap about this, but
> might the heart of the matter not be in the political
> system? (p. 242)

Solzhenitsyn concludes that 'they imprisoned all of them
to keep them from telling their fellow villagers about
Europe. What the eye doesn't see, the heart doesn't grieve
for.' (p. 243)

The Soviet press in its reaction to *The Gulag Archipelago*
called Solzhenitsyn a literary Vlasovite and accused him of
siding with the Vlasov men themselves. This is untrue, but
he is moved to sympathise with them. Betrayed by their
Motherland what alternative did they have?

> I would like to issue a reminder, through these pages,
> that this was a phenomenon totally unheard of in all

> world history: that several hundred thousand young
> men, aged twenty to thirty, took up arms against their
> Fatherland as allies of its most evil enemy. Perhaps
> there is something to ponder here: Who was more to
> blame, those youths or the gray Fatherland? (pp. 261–62)

Solzhenitsyn is aware of the futility of attempting to under-
pin his narrative with precise figures. Even in the Lubyanka
archives there are probably no accurate records. On the few
occasions when he allows himself to speculate his figures
are not less likely to be correct than the estimates of others.
Thus his figure of 1 to 1.7 million for those executed in
1937–38 compares with Conquest's 0.8 million, an N.K.V.D.
estimate of 2 million and a Jugoslav estimate of 3 million, but
the latter two seem high. The same, however, must be said
of Solzhenitsyn's own estimate of 15 million kulaks deported
to Siberia (Stalin told Churchill 10 million) and it seems
unlikely that as many as a quarter of the population of
Leningrad was 'cleaned out' in 1934–35. Nicolas Bethell has
pointed out that Solzhenitsyn's assertion that the handing
over by the Western Allies of thousands of unwilling former
Soviet soldiers has been hushed-up in the West is untrue.[1]
The relevant documents have been available in London for
some time. They show Solzhenitsyn's figure of 90,000 cossacks
handed over by the British to be incorrect. There were fewer
than half that number. Nor was the British action as
perfidious as Solzhenitsyn makes out. He omits to mention
that Stalin was threatening to withhold large numbers of
Western ex-POWs liberated by the Russians should the Allies
fail to return all Russians. But with his limited access to
sources Solzhenitsyn was perhaps unaware of this.

For readers of Solzhenitsyn's novels *The Gulag Archipelago*
is most of all valuable for the further consideration it contains of the moral problems to be found at the centre of his

1. *The Times* (London), 6 January 1974.

fiction, the question of personal responsibility, freedom, and good and evil. Solzhenitsyn elaborates in several places on the concept of freedom so defiantly expressed by Bobynin in front of Abakumov in *The First Circle*. The camps confer a unique freedom on the prisoner including ironically, political freedom. 'Freedom of the mind—is not that the advantage of life in the Archipelago?' asks Solzhenitsyn in part four. 'And,' he says, 'there is one more freedom: they can't deprive you of your family and property—you have already lost them.' What you haven't got, not even God can take away. That is a fundamental freedom! The only way to retain your moral ascendency over the interrogator is to put your past behind you and say that 'from today on, my body is useless and alien to me. Only my spirit and my conscience remain precious and important to me. Confronted by such a prisoner the interrogation will tremble. Only the man who has renounced everything can win that victory.' (p. 130) Solzhenitsyn's advice to those who wish to survive morally in the camps confirms the close identification of the author with his hero Nerzhin:

> Own nothing! Possess nothing! Buddha and Christ
> taught us this, and the Stoics and the Cynics. Greedy
> though we are, why can't we seem to grasp that simple
> teaching? Can't we understand that with property
> we destroy our soul? . . .
>   Own only what you can always carry with you: know
> languages, know countries, know people. Let your
> memory be your travel bag. Use your memory! Use
> your memory! It is those bitter seeds alone which
> might sprout and grow someday. (p. 516)

When compiling his voluminous catalogue of inhumanity and crime, Solzhenitsyn is often troubled by the question of the source of evil—the question he left unanswered at the end of *Cancer Ward*. And as a loyal and proud Russian he

wonders 'where did this wolf-tribe appear from among our
own people? Does it really stem from our own roots? Our
own blood?' And he is impelled to the conclusion: 'It is our
own.' In *The Gulag Archipelago* Solzhenitsyn still does not
attempt to identify the source of evil absolutely, but he
formulates his ideas on the forces of good and evil in man
which he embodied in the characters of his novels. Pages
160–78 of part one are the key passage. The dividing line
between good and evil cuts through the heart of every
human being, Solzhenitsyn believes:

> During the life of any heart this line keeps changing
> place; sometimes it is squeezed one way by exuberant
> evil and sometimes it shifts to allow enough space for
> good to flourish. One and the same human being is,
> at various ages, under various circumstances, a totally
> different human being. At times he is close to being
> devil, at times to sainthood. But his name doesn't
> change, and to that name we ascribe the whole lot,
> good and evil. (p. 168)

Hence it was possible for almost anyone to be dragged into
the evil system and corrupted by it:

> Confronted by the pit into which we are about to toss
> those who have done us harm, we halt, stricken dumb:
> it is after all only because of the way things worked
> out that they were the executioners and we weren't.
> (p. 168)

The great writers of the past, Solzhenitsyn believed, de-
picted evildoers clumsily and inaccurately. Their villains
recognised themselves as evildoers:

> But no; that's not the way it is! To do evil a human
> being must first of all believe that what he's doing
> is good, or else that it's a well-considered act in con-

formity with natural law. Fortunately, it is in the
nature of the human being to seek a *justification* for
his actions. (p. 173)

That justification Solzhenitsyn identifies as ideology:

Ideology—that is what gives evildoing its long-sought
justification and gives the evildoer the necessary
steadfastness and determination. That is the social
theory which helps to make his acts seem good instead
of bad in his own and others' eyes, so that he won't
hear reproaches and curses but will receive praise and
honors. (p. 174)

Although he has clearly not always been sure about it,
Solzhenitsyn implies that the converse is also true. Man is
inspired to resist evil by religion: 'I understood the truth
of all the world's religions,' he writes in part four, 'they
combat evil in man (in every man). Evil cannot be entirely
banished from the world, but in every man it can be
suppressed.' Ideology drives an ordinary man to that level
of evil where he becomes a willing accomplice in the
Archipelago.

A human being hesitates and bobs back and forth
between good and evil all his life. He slips, falls
back, clambers up, repents, things begin to darken
again. But just so long as the threshold of evildoing
is not crossed, the possibility of returning remains,
and he himself is still within reach of our hope. But
when, through the density of evil actions, the result
either of their own extreme degree or of the absoluteness
of his power, he suddenly crosses that threshold, he
has left humanity behind, and without perhaps, the
possibility of return. (p. 175)

Stalin himself perhaps, and some of the bureaucrats in
Solzhenitsyn's novels—Rusanov, Knorozov, and the Mavrino

officials—illustrate this idea. They have passed beyond the point of return. Innokenty Volodin has not. But psychologists will point, no doubt, to other characteristics of man's make-up which impel him to commit evil. Solzhenitsyn himself suggests in the same chapter of *The Gulag Archipelago*, 'The Bluecaps,' that members of the security police were responding to different motives. Some compelled themselves simply not to think, others were intoxicated by their powers, still others were plainly sadistic, and yet others rapacious. The *blatnye* so thoroughly described in *The Gulag Archipelago*, the prisoners in *The Love-Girl and the Innocent*, and the degrading influence of the camps detailed in part four, chapter two are all further examples of the manner in which the evil side of the human heart may respond to circumstances without reference to any ideology. Although providing ample material for investigating the subject, Solzhenitsyn has not resolved the problem of evil.

Beyond the similarities in philosophy, attitude, and interpretation, and the numerous instances already referred to, the student of Solzhenitsyn's fiction will find other rich veins of source material in *The Gulag Archipelago*. The gulf separating the real soldiers from those who remained behind —Shchagov in *The First Circle* (p. 615), and the wives of prisoners are treated at length. Solzhenitsyn's liking for proverbs, awareness of the significance of names (p. 154), and even familiar images such as the squirrel on the treadmill (p. 70) are all here apparent. The similes, sparingly used, have the aptness of those noted in the stories—pride in the human heart likened to lard on a pig (p. 163), politicians to a boil on the neck of society (p. 391), prisoners to shoals of herrings (p. 237) or crabs in a basket (p. 578), the author to an interstellar wanderer. (p. 595)

Western students of the Soviet Union will probably find few facts and figures in *The Gulag Archipelago* which have not been available in the West for many years. Westerners writing about forced labour in the Soviet Union have had at their disposal the testimony of many more than the 227 who aided Solzhenitsyn. Nevertheless Solzhenitsyn's is the only work which endeavours to span and interpret the whole process from the beginning. And no other writer has asked the leading questions quite so bluntly. It would be a shattering revelation if freely available to the younger generations in the Soviet Union—those for whom it was written. Solzhenitsyn's emphases and his apparent desire to denigrate the entire Soviet experiment from the beginning will not command the agreement of all those who are broadly in sympathy with him. Roy Medvedev, for instance, has tempered his admiration with criticism. In any event, no assessment of the strengths and shortcomings of *The Gulag Archipelago* either as history or as a work by Solzhenitsyn is feasible until it is published in its entirety. In particular as Solzhenitsyn has himself emphasised, it ought to be considered alongside his multivolume novelistic history of the Revolution when it eventually appears. Many admirers of Solzhenitsyn's fiction may feel that he is at his best and most effective even as a propagandist when he has his high moral indignation and predilection for sarcasm firmly under control as in the earlier stories. They may even begin to find the sheer volume of his writings burdensome. But Solzhenitsyn is driven by a strong sense of destiny and *The Gulag Archipelago* is an essential part of its fulfillment. In his Nobel lecture he acknowledged, 'This is a duty that was laid upon us many years ago, and we understood it. In the words of Vladimir Solovyov:

> Although in chains, we must ourselves complete
> That circle chosen for us by the gods.

Bibliography

The most comprehensive and up to date bibliography of works by and about Solzhenitsyn is:

Alexander Solzhenitsyn: An International Bibliography of Writings by and about them, 1962–1973. Compiled by Donald M. Fiene. Ann Arbor: Ardis 1973 XVIII + 150 pp.

1   Literary works by Solzhenitsyn

Odin den' Ivana Denisovicha, Moscow, 1962. Novella. Tr. as *One Day in the Life of Ivan Denisovich*, Max Hayward and Ronald Hingley, New York (Praeger), 1963; Ralph Parker, London (Gollancz), 1963 and New York (Dutton), 1963.

Sluchai na stantsii Krechetovka, Moscow, 1963. Story. Tr. as *An Incident at Krechetovka Station*, Paul W. Blackstock, Columbia (Univ. of South Carolina Press), 1963; Andrew R. MacAndrew, New York (Bantam Books), 1969; Michael Glenny, London (The Bodley Head), 1971 and New York (Farrar, Straus and Giroux), 1972.

Matryonin dvor, Moscow, 1963. Story. Tr. as *Matryona's House*, Paul W. Blackstock, Columbia (Univ. of South Carolina Press), 1963; Michael Glenny, London (The Bodley Head), 1971 and New York (Farrar, Straus and Giroux), 1972.

Dlya pol'zy dela, Moscow 1963. Story. Tr. as *For the Good of the Cause*, David Floyd and Max Hayward, New York (Praeger), 1964; Michael Glenny, London (The Bodley Head), 1971 and New York (Farrar, Straus and Giroux), 1972.

Etudy i krokhotnye rasskazy, Frankfurt, 1964. Prose fragments. Tr. as *Prose Etudes and Short Stories,* H. T. Willetts, *Encounter,* London, 1965 and *New Leader,* New York, January 18, 1965; Michael Glenny, London (The Bodley Head), 1971 and New York (Farrar, Straus and Giroux), 1972.

Zakhar-Kalita, Moscow, 1966. Story. Tr. as *Zakhar the Pouch,* Michael Glenny, London (The Bodley Head), 1971 and New York (Farrar, Straus and Giroux), 1972.

Rakovy korpus, Milan, London, Paris, 1968. Novel. Tr. as *Cancer Ward,* Rebecca Frank, New York (Dial Press), 1968; Nicholas Bethel and David Burg, London (The Bodley Head), 1968.

V pervom krugu, Belgrade, London, New York, 1968. Novel. Tr. as *The First Circle,* Thomas P. Whitney, New York (Harper and Row), 1968; Michael Guybon, London (Harvill), 1968.

Pravaya kist', Frankfurt, 1968. Story. Tr. as *The Right Hand,* Michael Glenny, London (The Bodley Head), 1971 and New York (Farrar, Straus and Giroux), 1972.

Paskhal'ny krestny khod, Frankfurt, 1968. Story. Tr. as *The Easter Procession,* Michael Glenny, London (The Bodley Head), 1971 and New York (Farrar, Straus and Giroux), 1972.

Olen' i shalashovka, Frankfurt, 1969. Play. Tr. as *The Love-Girl and the Innocent,* Nicholas Bethel and David Burg, London (The Bodley Head), 1969 and New York (Farrar, Straus and Giroux), 1969.

Svecha na vetru, Frankfurt, 1969. Play. Tr. *Candle in the Wind,* Keith Armes and Arthur G. Hudgins, Minneapolis (Univ. of Minnesota Press), 1973.

Avgust chetyrnadtsatogo, Paris, 1971. Novel. Tr. *August 1914,* Michael Glenny, London (The Bodley Head), 1972 and New York (Farrar, Straus and Giroux), 1972.

Archipelag gulag, Paris, 1973. (Parts I and II). Tr. *The Gulag Archipelago,* Thomas P. Whitney, New York (Harper and Row), 1974; (Parts III and IV). Tr. *Gulag Archipelago,* Thomas P. Whitney, New York (Harper & Row), 1975.

2   Criticism

An immense amount has been written about Solzhenitsyn and his work, much of it of a political and ephemeral character. But the following contain some of the more enduringly valuable comments.

Atkinson, D. and Pashin, N., 'August 1914: Art and History,' *The Russian Review*, Vol. 31, no. 1, 1972, pp. 1–10.

Avgust Chetyrnadtsatogo Chitayut na rodine. Sbornik statei i otzyvov, Paris, 1973.

Brown, Edward J., 'Solzhenitsyn's Cast of Characters,' *The Slavic and East European Journal*, Vol. 15, no. 2, 1971, pp. 153–66.

Burg, David and Feifer, George, 'Solzhenitsyn. A Biography,' London, 1972. *Canadian Slavonic Papers*, Vol. XIII, nos. 2 and 3, 1971. Ten essays by different hands.

Clive, Geoffrey, 'The Broken Icon. Intuitive Existensialism in Russian Fiction,' New York, 1972.

Dunlop, John B., Haugh, Richard and Klimoff, Alexis, eds., 'Alexander Solzhenitsyn: Critical Essays and Documentary Materials,' Belmont, Mass., 1974.

Feuer, Kathryn B., 'Solzhenitsyn and the Legacy of Tolstoy,' *California Slavonic Studies*, no. 5, 1971, pp. 113–28.

Kern, Gary, 'Solzhenitsyn's Portrait of Stalin,' *The Slavic Review*, Vol. 33, no. 1, 1974, pp. 1–22.

Koehler, Ludmila, 'Alexander Solzhenitsyn and Russian Literary Tradition,' *The Russian Review*, Vol. 26, no. 2, 1967, pp. 176–84.

Koehler, Ludmila, 'Eternal Themes in Solzhenitsyn's "Cancer Ward,"' *The Russian Review*, Vol. 28, no. 1, 1969, pp. 53–65.

Kovaly, P., 'Problems of Antihumanism and Humanism in the Life and Work of Alexander Solzhenitsyn,' *Studies in Soviet Thought*, Dordrecht, no. 11, 1971, pp. 1–18.

Lakshin, V., 'Ivan Denisovich, ego drugi i nedrugi,' *Novy Mir*, no. 1, 1964. Tr. (in part) in Priscilla Johnson, *Khrushchev and the Arts*, Mass, 1965, pp. 275–88.

Lukacs, Georg, *Solzhenitsyn,* tr. William David Graf, London, 1970.

Medvedev, Zhores A., *Ten Years After Ivan Denisovich,* London, 1973.

Mikhailov, Mikhailo, 'Dostoevsky's and Solzhenitsyn's House of the Dead,' *Bulletin of the Institute for Study of the USSR,* Frankfurt, 1965, pp. 3–18; and no. 10, 1965, pp. 13–25.

Muchnic, Helen, 'Solzhenitsyn's "The First Circle," ' *The Russian Review,* Vol. 29. no. 2, 1970, pp. 154–66.

Pletnyov, R., *A. I. Solzhenitsyn,* Munich, 1970.

Rothberg, Abraham, *Alexander Solzhenitsyn: The Major Novels,* Cornell, 1971.

Rzhevsky, L., *Tvorets i podvig: ocherki po tvorchestvy Aleksandra Solzhenitsyna,* Frankfurt, 1972.

Shilyaev, G., 'Lagerny yazyk po proizvedeniam A. I. Solzhenitsyna,' *Novy Zhurnal,* no. 95, 1969, pp. 232–47.

Vinokur, T. G., 'O yazyke i stile povesti A. I. Solzhenitsyna "Odin den' Ivana Denisovicha," ' *Voprosy Kul'tury rechi,* no. 6, 1965, pp. 16–32.

Zavalishin, V., 'Solzhenitsyn, Dostoevsky and Leshenkov-Klychkov,' *Bulletin of the Institute for the Study of the USSR,* no. 10, 1963, pp. 40–48.